Leading English in the Primary School

Leading English in the Primary School is a comprehensive guide for both aspiring and experienced leaders of primary English. It supports you in navigating your way through the role and offers practical guidance to help you develop a clear understanding of how to improve the teaching of English in your school.

Written by experts with extensive experience of both leadership and the primary classroom, it explores skills required for effective subject leadership while continually considering the specific implications for English. With action and reflection points throughout the book, it offers a detailed introduction to:

- the role of the English subject leader
- implementing strategy and vision
- adapting to new educational policy
- methods for leading teaching and learning
- how and why leaders evaluate and monitor progress
- contemporary changes to the curriculum.

Rich case studies reveal how schools lead English in practice, and provide real-life examples of English subject leaders' decision-making processes and actions. Grounding the subject leader role in the current curriculum, *Leading English in the Primary School* is a source of advice, support and inspiration for all professionals embracing the complex, challenging, yet fulfilling role of Primary English Leader.

Lisa Baldwin is Senior Lecturer in Education at the University of Winchester, UK. She completed her NQT year in a Dorset school before becoming a senior teacher in a school in the London Borough of Brent. In 2007 she became a school improvement adviser for the London Borough of Hillingdon, delivering training and providing school support for English and school leadership. Her research interests are in all aspects of English, but particularly early reading.

Leading English in the Primary School

A Subject Leader's Guide

*Lisa Baldwin with
Liz Chamberlain, Mary Scanlan,
Sandy Stockwell and Neil Suggett*

Routledge
Taylor & Francis Group

LONDON AND NEW YORK

First published 2019
by Routledge
2 Park Square, Milton Park, Abingdon, Oxon OX14 4RN

and by Routledge
711 Third Avenue, New York, NY 10017

Routledge is an imprint of the Taylor & Francis Group, an informa business

British Library Cataloguing-in-Publication Data
A catalogue record for this book is available from the British Library

Library of Congress Cataloging-in-Publication Data
Names: Baldwin, Lisa, 1971- Congratulations you're the subject leader. |
Chamberlain, Liz. Pedagogical choices in primary English. |
Scanlan, Mary, 1960- Working with families to support literacy development.
Title: Leading English in the primary school / Lisa Baldwin with Liz Chamberlain, Mary Scanlan, Sandy Stockwel and Neil Suggett.
Description: Abingdon, Oxon ; New York, NY : Routledge, 2019. |
Includes bibliographical references.
Identifiers: LCCN 2018027235| ISBN 9781138304918 (hbk) |
ISBN 9781138304925 (pbk) | ISBN 9780203731444 (ebk)
Subjects: LCSH: English language--Study and teaching (Primary)--Great Britain. |
Language arts (Primary)--Great Britain. | Educational leadership--Great Britain.
Classification: LCC LB1529.G7 L43 2019 | DDC 372.6--dc23LC record available at
HYPERLINK "https://protect-us.mimecast.com/s/UHMKC4xk97tBG3D7zsW59DS?
domain=lccn.loc.gov" https://lccn.loc.gov/2018027235

ISBN: 978-1-138-30491-8 (hbk)
ISBN: 978-1-138-30492-5 (pbk)
ISBN: 978-0-203-73144-4 (ebk)

Typeset in Optima
by Integra Software Services Pvt. Ltd.

This book is dedicated to Mr Philip Copson, my A-level English teacher who, many years ago, ignited a life-long love for literature through his sheer enthusiasm for the books we studied.

Thanks, too, to my lovely Joe, who serves as a daily reminder of why primary education is so important to young lives.

Contents

Figures and tables

Figures

Tables

Acknowledgements

This book draws on the work of two colleagues, Dr Liz Chamberlain (Senior Lecturer in Education, Open University) and Dr Naomi Flynn (Associate Professor, Reading University), who devised and created the original module for undergraduate English subject specialists at the University of Winchester. Their expertise and knowledge laid firm foundations for me to build on, and I am thankful for the continued guidance and encouragement that Liz has offered during the writing process as well as her contributory chapter on classroom pedagogy.

Teaching the English subject specialist module on the undergraduate degree led to the realisation that there was a significant gap in literature for the English subject leader. Whilst quality literature existed about leadership and primary English teaching they were usually discussed as discrete topics. This book aims to follow in the footsteps of Tony Martin and Mick Waters' excellent book *Coordinating English at Key Stage 2*, which brought the two important elements of English and leadership together. I am delighted that Tony Martin was able to write the foreword to this book.

My previous role as an advisory teacher in London encompassed the delivery of training and support for schools. The school improvement agendas I supported focused on English (in particular the National Strategy Literacy training), the Workforce Remodelling agenda and school leadership. It has been both fruitful and interesting to reflect on how each of these roles has provided practical experience and knowledge of factors that impact on today's English subject leader.

Throughout my career I have had the pleasure to work alongside some of the most innovative and knowledgeable school leaders and teachers. This has enabled the book to offer practical insight and expertise in each chapter. I'd particularly like to thank Dr Neil Suggett, the truly inspirational (now retired) head teacher of Hayes Park Primary School, and my fellow Leadership Advisor in the London Borough of Hillingdon. Neil taught me (almost) everything there is to know about headship, effective leadership and coaching, and he makes a valuable contribution to the book with his chapter on managing effective change.

I would like to thank my friends and colleagues at the University of Winchester. Thanks to Sandy Stockwell and Dr Mary Scanlan, both of whom contribute their own areas of expertise to the book. Their respective chapters on digital learning and home–school partnership strengthen the reach and depth of the book. Thanks, too, to Dr Bridget Egan and Richard Cole for their time reading and critiquing chapters.

Particular thanks must go to those schools whose good practice provides the case studies in the book. Thanks to Richard Charlesworth (English subject leader) and David Jones (head teacher) at Grove Park Primary School, West London for their contributions to Chapter 6 on pedagogic knowledge and decision making. Thanks to Hannah Shin (English subject leader) and Evelyn Chua (head teacher) of Hampden Gurney Church of England Primary School for their contribution to Chapters 1, 2 and 4. Hannah, a previous student on the English specialist subject route, took on the English subject leader post in the second year of her teaching career, and to document her journey in the role provided great insight into the complexity and enormity of the post.

Thanks go to Chris Brooks-Martin, the head teacher of Otterbourne Primary School (previously Hurstbourne Tarrant Primary School), for wading through the data with me and sharing planning documentation and expertise that contribute to Chapter 5. And lastly, thanks go to Lyndsey Whettingsteele (English subject leader) and Anne Moir (head teacher) at South Baddesley Church of England Primary School, for sharing good practice in English teaching over the years and fostering our joint working relationship that enabled Chapter 9 to be written. All of these school leaders embody the philosophy that creative and inspirational English subject leadership underpins effective teaching and excellent outcomes for primary pupils.

Finally, thanks extend to the students I teach, who constantly serve to inspire and challenge my thinking. Each graduating English subject specialist cohort provides constant hope and optimism that good quality English teaching will endure.

Contributors

Lisa Baldwin is a Senior Lecturer in Education (Primary English) at the University of Winchester. Lisa's previous school roles include subject coordinator and senior leader. She has been an advisory teacher for English, Workforce Remodelling and school leadership. Lisa is currently responsible for leading Early Reading across both undergraduate and post-graduate programmes and delivers the English subject specialist module on leadership to undergraduate trainees. Lisa's areas of interest and expertise are in early reading, government policy and leadership.

Liz Chamberlain, EdD, is a Senior Lecturer in Education at The Open University and is currently the Programme Leader for the Education Studies (Primary) degree. Her previous roles include Leading Literacy Teacher and Assistant Head Teacher. Liz is recognised internationally for her research on what it means for children to be writers. She was the strategic consultant for the *Everybody Writes* national writing project and is author of the recently acclaimed book *Inspiring Writing*.

Mary Scanlan, PhD, is a Senior Lecturer in Education at the University of Winchester. She is currently the programme lead for Early Years and also teaches on the English team. Mary's PhD research, undertaken at Bristol University, explored how parents and teachers working together can support children's literacy learning. Mary's main areas of expertise are in Early Years education, child development, literacy and qualitative research with young children, and she is the author of many publications in these research areas.

Sandy Stockwell is a Senior Lecturer in Education (Primary English) at the University of Winchester. She is a former English subject coordinator, senior teacher and primary literacy consultant. Sandy currently leads the English Team and is module leader for a range of undergraduate and post-graduate programmes. Her main areas of expertise are digital literacies, children's writing, film and assessment.

Neil Suggett, PhD, is an authority on coaching and leadership development. He has worked as a teacher, Head Teacher, school inspector and leadership coach. Neil has been a researcher at the National College, a visiting fellow at the Institute of Education and a visiting lecturer at Loughborough University and Brunel University. As one of the first National Leaders of Education, he has worked extensively in people development and school improvement. In 2010 Neil was awarded the CBE in recognition of his services to education at home and abroad. In 2017 he published his book *Living a Coaching Lifestyle*.

Foreword

In 1999 Mick Waters and I wrote a book titled *Coordinating English at Key Stage 2* as part of a series called 'The Subject Leader's Handbooks'. In the years since our book, the pressures on primary schools in terms of 'accountability' have increased dramatically and English is where a lot of that accountability is felt. Add to that the changing nature of English (or should that be literacy?) in our digital world and we really do have a high stakes, complex 'subject' being taught in primary school classrooms. This means that being the subject leader for English in a primary school is certainly challenging!

The need for an accessible book which draws together the different elements of the role will be welcomed by English subject leaders faced with the challenges every working day. The chapter headings in Lisa Baldwin's book encompass such diverse areas as a 'Shared vision for English' to 'Documentation' and from 'Literacy in the 21st century' to 'Working with families to support literacy development'. In some cases, such as the elements of an effective English lesson, I am reminded of the saying 'the more things change, the more they stay the same', while in others, because of the way society and literacy are changing or because of government-led initiatives, things are certainly very different.

If you are reading this, the likelihood is that you are either already leading English in a primary school or are considering such a role for your future. You may be confident in some aspects but less so in others. Perhaps your strength is your subject knowledge of English and literacy, although given the scope, which ranges from trying to instil a love of poetry in your pupils to teaching grammar, it is likely that you are more confident in some aspects than others. Perhaps you know you are good at engaging and leading your colleagues but less confident in general with your subject knowledge. Each chapter in this book provides background knowledge and ideas as well as case studies of teachers, subject leaders and (in Chapter 9) a school, all designed to build your knowledge of the different aspects of the role and enable you to reflect on your school and how you might lead the teaching of English in it.

Teaching and learning – how to teach in order that children learn – are and always will be complex. It seems obvious that if we want children to learn something, we have to teach it. Part of the complexity (but also the richness) of 'English' is that what appears to be obvious might not in fact be the case. One powerful example is the link between reading and writing. It might appear that if we want children to improve as writers we can 'teach' all of the writing skills and knowledge they will need. However, it is now clear that our teaching is unlikely to be successful unless children are also doing something else. They need to be reading and reading and reading for different purposes, including just the pleasure of it, absorbing writing knowledge as they do so. When successful authors are asked for advice about writing, they nearly always respond with the need for writers to read. Leading English in the primary school often means convincing colleagues of the importance of such subtle subject knowledge. Yes it can be a challenge, but if the subject leader succeeds, the impact on children can be huge.

I have really enjoyed reading Lisa Baldwin's book, revisiting areas and issues which Mick Waters and I grappled with nearly twenty years ago but which have been brought up to date for today's English subject leaders.

Tony Martin
Past President, United Kingdom Literacy Association

Introduction

Welcome

Welcome to the book *Leading English in the Primary School: A Subject Leader's Guide*. This book aims to inspire and guide the leadership of primary English. It is intended for an audience of relative newcomers to the role, but current coordinators looking to refresh their practice will also find the chapters helpful.

You may be embarking on the role with good English subject knowledge, gained from your educational background or teacher training experience, but equally among the audience may be readers who do not perceive themselves to be an English specialist and who have limited training and experience in the subject. Either way I hope that you are an enthusiast for the subject if nothing else and that this book guides you to cultivate a clear understanding of how to improve and develop the teaching of English in your school.

The book will focus on supporting you, the subject leader, in navigating your way through the role and its inherent requirements. Each chapter intends to help you to clarify objectives, determine practical ways forward and ultimately achieve success within your school context. The book endeavours to discuss a range of key themes that are essential to both leadership and English: addressing the skills required for effective subject leadership whilst at the same time continually considering the specific implications for English.

You'll notice that some of the supporting literature in this book is relatively old. Whilst it is still relevant, its date reflects the fact that primary subject leadership has been missing from the agenda for some while. This book brings together current research on English pedagogy, the requirements of the new National Curriculum and generic school leadership theory. This and first-hand experience from case study schools combine to make sense of the role of today's primary English subject leader.

Organisation and structure

The book is organised into three areas:

1. the English subject leader;
2. strategy, vision and policy;
3. leading teaching and learning.

Chapters 1, 2 and 3focus on the English subject leader's role. Consideration is given to how the post has evolved over time, mapping the evolution of subject leadership to the current day. Thought is given to the changing requirements of the English curriculum and how this shapes the focus of the subject leader's role and primary English practice. The book reflects on what is meant by the terms 'literacy' and 'English' and considers how this might shape your own philosophy of English teaching.

Chapters 4, 5, 6 and 7 focus on strategy, vision and policy. The qualities of good leadership and management are unpicked, and support is provided to help you reflect on your own strengths and areas for development as you progress into English subject leadership. Chapter 5 examines the range of documentation used to shape whole-school actions and set priorities for English. Chapter 6 gives wider consideration to how effective subject leaders decide on the pedagogic approaches appropriate to their school's needs. Chapter 7 considers how to adapt your curriculum to incorporate new technology and digital literacies.

Chapters 8, 10 and 11 consider how to lead teaching and learning and how to work with colleagues effectively to support their development. How to manage change and support team working is also explored and practical support is given on conducting lesson observations and other monitoring practices. Chapter 9 provides a case study example of one school's journey to improve writing in their school, providing a model for action research and whole-school development. Chapter 12 considers the importance of working with the wider school community to include parents and carers in English education. And finally, Chapter 13 discusses the 'hot topic' of grammar and writing, mapping the impact of the new National Curriculum (DfE, 2013) focus on grammar, punctuation and spelling. This final chapter serves to illustrate the constant shifts in education priorities and how important it is to be true to the principles of high-quality English teaching in the face of policy change.

Guides and prompts

The book contains checklists and audits that provide a starting point for your own reflection. Each chapter will provide prompts to spur you to consider how things might work best in your own unique school. Permeating the book are guides that support you to understand effective processes and case studies that illustrate successful practice. Thoughts and actions of outstanding English subject leaders offer additional insight into effective curriculum leadership and help shape your own decisions and actions.

Each chapter will contain the following elements to aid your thinking:

 ## *Reflection point*

Reflection points aim to provide useful tasks and prompts to guide your thinking on key points. You might also find them useful for whole-school staff purposes, aiding discussion during staff meetings or training events.

 ## *What do good subject leaders think?*

Contemplation prompts provide insight into the thought processes of good subject leaders as they make decisions, judgements and choices about English leadership.

 ## *What do good subject leaders do?*

Action prompts provide insight into the actions, behaviours and processes of good subject leaders in order to lead and manage English effectively.

Case studies

Case studies document how individual schools lead English in practice and provide real-life examples of English subject leaders' decision-making processes and actions.

✓ **Learning points** from the case study summarise key ideas and ways of working.

The role of the English subject leader is wide and challenging. I hope that this book will both inspire and support you in achieving great things for all the children in your school. Good luck.

 ## Reference

Department for Education (DfE) (2013) 'English programmes of study: Key Stages 1 and 2 National Curriculum in England.' Available at: https://assets.publishing.service. gov.uk/government/uploads/system/uploads/attachment_data/file/335186/PRI MARY_national_curriculum_-_English_220714.pdf [accessed 3 July 2018].

Congratulations, you're the English subject leader!

Lisa Baldwin and Liz Chamberlain

This introductory chapter will consider the personal and professional qualities required to be an effective English subject leader. There will be an outline of the many roles and responsibilities of the subject leader and the chapter will begin to explore the terms 'leadership' and 'management'. Different models of leadership and descriptors of leadership styles will be discussed. There will be guidance and practical steps to support you in the early stages of English leadership, including keeping an English file and knowing where to go for advice. We will begin to raise the question – how do English subject leaders know where to start?

The role of the English subject leader

Leading English and taking charge of this subject are of crucial importance to primary education and improving literacy outcomes for children in your school. There is no doubt that leading this subject brings great responsibility, but with it comes the knowledge that you have chosen to lead a subject that offers opportunities for creativity and access to new worlds of knowledge. The acquisition of English skills is crucial to every child's success across the curriculum. Ultimately, success in English ensures each individual pupil has access to life-long learning opportunities that reach far beyond their school life. In short, you will be leading a subject that is the very life-blood of learning.

In the current education world the stakes are high with regards to pupil performance and the stakes are highest in the most tested areas of the curriculum: namely, English and mathematics (Alexander, 2009; Moss, 2017). The current PISA (DfE, 2016; OECD, 2015) rankings dominate discourse around what it means to be successful in English (reading), and the success (or otherwise) of the reading test attainment of 15 year olds influences the direction of policy and in turn the practice seen in school. Your leadership role is therefore crucial to wider school success.

The role itself is likely to encompass a range of responsibilities. Your key duty will be to ensure English subject teaching is constantly developing to meet the needs of the pupils. Whatever the context and incumbent duties of your particular English subject leader post it is unlikely to be a role that stands in isolation. You will probably be a class teacher, you may have phase (or Key Stage) leadership responsibilities, you may be a senior leader and you may even be the head teacher. This chapter acknowledges that you are likely to be juggling subject leadership with a number of different roles and aims to ensure clarity about your responsibilities.

Duties and responsibilities

It is important to clarify what the role of English subject leader entails and the responsibilities you hold. You have to be passionate about your subject but you are not expected to know everything about English. You will need to be a hub of information but you are not required to write everyone's plans, scrutinise their books or mark their tests. You are expected to know the targets and why they may not have been reached but you are not responsible for the Key Stage 1 or Key Stage 2 English SATs results.

There has long been debate about how to determine what it is that subject leaders should 'do', and at the end of the last century Waters and Martin (1999) drew on the Teacher Training Agency (TTA, 1998) standards for subject leaders to define the subject leader's responsibilities:

- securing the high standards of teaching and learning;
- raising standards and achievement;
- supporting, guiding and motivating teachers and other adults;
- monitoring and setting targets for English;
- contributing to policy development within the subject and across the school.

(Waters and Martin, 1999: 14)

The list covers duties that can be broken down into four key areas:

- strategic responsibility;
- teaching and learning;
- leadership and management of the whole-school staff;
- organisational management.

(Adapted from TTA, 1998)

The *strategic* element of the role encompasses policy and practice development. Understanding pupil progress and teacher confidence in English will ensure you know how to improve outcomes across the school. It also encompasses target setting, monitoring, curriculum design and long-term planning across the school.

The responsibility for *teaching and learning* encompasses the need to secure high-quality teaching and learning outcomes for all pupils. This involves evaluating English planning and teaching to ensure teachers deliver high-quality learning. The subject leader has to understand pupil progression in English across the school, identifying areas for development. It also involves partnership working with the wider school community.

The *organisational management* of the subject encompasses the resourcing and management of the learning environment for English. This might include the development of new resources and the maintenance of existing ones. The whole-school library, book corners, reading, spelling and phonics schemes, intervention programmes, deployment of support staff and display are just some of the aspects that contribute to this area. It is important to understand that whilst these contribute to the physical learning space they also impact on the wider culture of English in the school.

The *leadership and management of staff* requires effective working relationships that offer support and guidance. The subject leader must lead by example, motivating staff to commit to subject development aims, adopt new practices and deliver high-quality teaching of English.

 Consider the list of responsibilities in relation to your own role and job description.

- Is there a balance of strategic, organisational, teaching and learning, and leadership and management duties?
- Are there additional aspects to the role, unique to the school you are working in?
- The TTA standards were developed in 1999. Do you think they still have bearing on the tasks you're required to do twenty years on?

However different the above list is to your own responsibilities, busy school environments often offer little time for planning, reflection or sharing good practice, so this book aims to support you in doing the role well and making the best, most efficient use of time to cover the range of duties. So let's begin by thinking about both the professional and personal qualities that you will need to embody in order to be a successful leader of English.

What do we mean by leadership?

Effective 'leadership acts as a catalyst for unleashing the potential capacities that already exist in the organisation' (Leithwood *et al.*, 2006: 15). The key is to understand that you cannot do well alone. You cannot find success in the role purely by the measure of your own teaching ability and expertise in English. The important resonance in the quotation is that you have to enable others. In order to become an effective leader it is important to unpick the qualities and attributes that underpin good leaders. Then you can begin to model these characteristics in your new role as English subject leader.

 Consider a school leader whom you have worked with during your time in school, albeit as a trainee teacher or as a recent member of teaching staff. Reflect on the type of leader they embody by considering the following questions:

- What do you observe them doing or saying?
- What actions do they undertake?
- What procedures do they follow?
- How would you describe their personal qualities?
- What behaviours do they exhibit?

The answers to your questions will usually divide into two distinct attributes: actions in the form of organisation and procedural skills, and the individual's personal qualities and behaviours. Let's consider these two areas further.

Leadership: Organisation and procedural skills

When you listed the qualities of the effective leader you had worked with, you would have considered the actions and activities they undertook. Management of the subject requires different qualities and skills from the personal and behavioural requirements, but they are just as integral to effective subject leadership.

Although leadership and management are different, to try to separate leadership from management is to separate the means through which your goals will be achieved. Managing a subject requires (amongst other things) organisation, planning, target setting and resourcing. The task of management is often described as more procedural and serves to ensure that *how* English is taught in your school continually evolves to meet the needs of the pupils.

Leadership: Personal qualities and behaviours

Subject leadership of English requires you to define a vision for the subject in your school. This vision will serve to illustrate the desired goals for English. It will articulate how learning should be happening, and how the subject should be viewed by children, parents and staff. It should also define the desired outcomes for pupils, communicating what the school wishes them to achieve and defining the skills they should acquire.

Leadership requires knowledge of how to motivate staff to achieve the vision. This may involve the motivation of staff to teach a subject that they do not enjoy or may not feel confident in and this will require your encouragement, assistance and support. As the leader of English it is your role to support the whole-school staff to embrace change, try new teaching strategies and provide children with exciting opportunities in their English lessons. To do this you will need to guide, cajole, support and challenge your colleagues. Kaplan and Owings (2013) state, 'Schools are complicated places—multifaceted organisms as well as part of larger systems' (2013: 4). This is reflected in the nature of the relationships that occur with these complex systems. Acting as a role model is a powerful and effective way to communicate the vision for English to your colleagues. To lead is to embody your vision of English.

You as leader

So are you ready to lead and manage staff? Commencing a leadership role is a daunting prospect for new leaders and understanding how to approach the role is important. To be an effective English subject leader you will need to develop strong procedural and personal qualities. It is important to consider where your own strengths and areas for development lie, as this will affect how well you are able to carry out your responsibilities. A SWOT (Strengths, Weaknesses, Opportunities and Threats) analysis can be a helpful way for you to assess your own starting point to becoming an effective English subject leader.

 Consider the following questions to assess your own starting point to becoming an effective English subject leader:

Table 1.1 SWOT (Strengths, Weaknesses, Opportunities and Threats) analysis for the English subject leader

Strengths	Weaknesses
• What are the best things about my English teaching?	• What are my areas of weakness in English knowledge and understanding?
• What experiences and expertise am I beginning to build?	• What aspects of leadership and management do I need to develop?
• What leadership and management strengths do I already have?	

(Continued)

Table 1.1 (Cont).

Opportunities	Threats
• What opportunities can I capitalise on to develop my English teaching, knowledge and understanding?	• What threats are there to my beliefs in English subject knowledge and pedagogical understanding?
• What opportunities can I capitalise on to develop my leadership and management skills?	• What threats are there to my leadership and management of English?

When completing each quadrant it is important to consider the subject of English as well as your leadership and management skills. The following checklist will help:

Strengths

- What aspect of English are you confident you teach well?
- Is there a particular age-phase that you are more experienced or competent in teaching?
- In terms of leadership and management skills, what can you already do effectively? Are there any personal attributes that you embody that you feel will support your leadership role?
- Are your relationships with the staff team positive?
- What procedural skills do you already do well?

Weaknesses

- What aspects of the taught English curriculum are you less secure about?
- Do you have limited subject knowledge of any aspects of English?
- Do you need to develop your understanding of any age-appropriate pedagogy due to limitations in your own teaching experience?
- Which aspects of leadership and management of staff are you less comfortable with?
- Are there any procedures that you do not understand or have had limited experience of?

Opportunities

- What actions or opportunities could support you in developing the skills and knowledge you need?
- Could peer support, in-house training, reading, membership to an association or school networks help you to develop your understanding of English teaching?

- Is there an opportunity for shadowing, or cross-school working, to enable you to learn leadership and management traits from other, more experienced staff members?

Threats

- What are the potential threats to your success in the role?
- Are there outside pressures, out of your control, that will impact on your leadership of the subject? These might include restrictions on time, money or resources, government pressures and other tensions that can affect a school.

If you are in the early stages of your career it is important to understand that it takes time and experience to develop true leadership skills. The SWOT analysis will help you to identify your strengths and the foundations on which you can build your knowledge and expertise.

Personal qualities of effective leaders

The personal qualities required to motivate staff to achieve your vision for English will only be realised if you can embody certain personal qualities that enable you to lead them to success.

- They are cheerful and optimistic about English;
- They are welcoming and enthusiastic to enquiries about the subject, requests for help or exchange of ideas;
- They listen carefully to their colleagues and give time and pay attention to what is being communicated;
- They are a good role model and are considered by others to be an effective user of time;
- When things are successful they celebrate others' achievements; when things go wrong they will blame themselves or reflect on what they could have done better;
- They manage change effectively;
- They have a clear philosophy about the school's approach to the teaching of English and they set a personal example.

(Adapted from Brighouse and Tomlinson's seven qualities of effective leadership, 1991)

People who embody the attributes listed above are often defined as **social orientated** (or people-orientated) leaders. They keep the human side of the school team going strong and are attuned to the emotional responses of their colleagues. Social orientated leaders embody personal attributes that mean they will get the best from others. They enable others to both achieve and *want* to achieve. The real value of this approach comes from making the group produce better results than would come from the sum of its parts alone.

Theory of leadership management

Next we will begin to explore some key definitions and theoretical terms applied to different leadership styles. Goleman's (2000) seminal work on leadership style underpins the definitions below:

Autocratic, commanding or authoritative leadership styles give low consideration to social orientated factors (Goleman, 2000). Autocratic leaders make decisions autonomously, often without consultation, or with limited consultation. This leadership style can be required of leaders if time is an issue and decisions need to be made quickly; however, this way of working can often alienate staff.

Transactional leaders work on the assumption of hierarchy and the power that leadership brings. The transaction will often involve reward, or punishment systems, that ensure employees' work meets a certain standard. This style of leadership is unlikely to be an approach that a relatively new member of staff would engage in, as a level of seniority is required, but it is a useful leadership style in some school situations. When there is a question about the competence of a member of staff, capability issues need to be clearly linked to performance. This leadership approach will ensure that the roles and responsibilities are made clear.

Transformational, coaching leadership styles invest in their staff, enabling them to develop performance over a period of time (Burrows, 2004). Transformational leaders are inspirational to those they work with. They are passionate and concerned in supporting individuals within the staff team to succeed and achieve the vision.

An **affiliative** leadership style will serve to create strong, positive relationships with staff teams. This style will motivate staff but will place lower emphasis on getting things done. This approach can be very helpful to staff during times of stress or challenge.

Democratic leaders try to get things done by consensus. They will seek advice from colleagues and court opinion but will make any overall, final decisions.

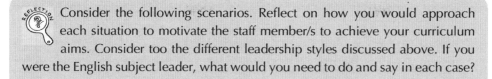

Consider the following scenarios. Reflect on how you would approach each situation to motivate the staff member/s to achieve your curriculum aims. Consider too the different leadership styles discussed above. If you were the English subject leader, what would you need to do and say in each case?

1. The Year 5 teacher refuses to stay behind for an English working party meeting.
2. You'd like your school to take part in an Everybody Writes Day just after half term.
3. A newly appointed Year 1 teacher has never used Letters and Sounds to plan phonics, as his previous school used Jolly Phonics.

Flexing your leadership style

How did you decide to deal with each situation? Let's consider each scenario in turn. Arguably, the first situation requires a strong *authoritative* leadership style: telling the teacher what is and isn't negotiable. However, many other factors need to be considered too. Would you have the seniority to exert authority over this member of staff? Relatively new members of staff are unlikely to be in a position to deal with this teacher in a *commanding, authoritative* way. Reporting obstructive behaviour to another, senior member of staff is the best way forward. Alternatively, you might have considered that there could be a possible reason for this refusal. If this behaviour were unusual for this individual, then there would be mileage in exploring the reason for the refusal to attend the working party. The need to understanding the context for the behaviour might well rule out an *authoritative* approach in the first instance.

In the second situation you might well argue that it would be best to gain consensus from the staff and build support for the project through a *democratic* leadership approach. The risk with this approach is that time spent gathering staff views and listening to the general consensus would impact on how quickly the project could get up and running. A *democratic* leadership approach might also meet some negativity, but if more staff were in agreement this would give valuable leverage to the English subject leader to forge ahead with the event. The *democratic* leader would need to ensure that unilateral decisions were clearly communicated so that no one had any doubt that the event will happen and they will have a role to play. Equally, you might have considered just 'telling' people what will happen on the day and communicating the importance of the event and your expectations of staff. This *authoritative, commanding* leadership approach would mobilise staff to follow your lead with planning and contributing to the event, but you may well find some individuals are reluctant participants.

In the third, and final, example it appears that the member of staff needs support to enable him to plan in a new way: to *transform* his practice. A *coaching* approach might well be the best way forward. But what if, after weeks of support, he remains at a loss to plan effectively and he starts to insist that he needs the structure of a scheme? A *coaching* approach assumes that the teacher is competent. If the situation evolves in this way, then the situation will demand a different approach to ensure he provides quality phonics teaching. When competency begins to become an issue, then the scenario rapidly begins to require a more *commanding, authoritative* approach.

For each of the three situations there is a range of possible approaches required from the subject leader. As events and contexts are explored the required approach can alter. What this exercise illustrates is that you will have to use a range of approaches to meet the needs of varying situations and personalities.

The relationship between social orientation/task orientation and leadership styles

As already stated, **social orientated** (or people-orientated) leaders are responsive to their colleagues' emotions and work well with people to get the best from others, but leaders also need to focus on the task in hand. Leaders that have a high focus on **task-orientated** aspects of leadership are excellent at getting things done. They rely on strong procedural organisation to manage the mechanics of what they want to achieve. Their ability to get things done is of great value to a school team, provided they employ good communication skills when they interact with staff.

Figure 1.1 serves to illustrate the relationship between leadership styles and the centrality of people or task to individual leaders' modes of operation (Coleman and Earley, 2005). Terms relating to different leadership styles are placed within one of

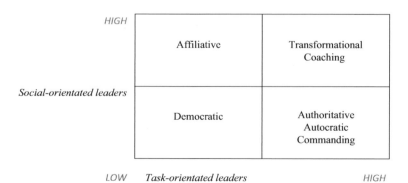

Figure 1.1 Leadership styles and social modes of operation

four quadrants in the diagram, depending on the amount of influence that social orientation or task orientation has on a leadership approach.

There are many terms associated with leadership style. This chapter serves only to provide a rough guide to the most common leadership traits appropriate to school settings. Any one leader can, and arguably should, fluctuate between the styles. Knowing *which* style is the best approach in the circumstances is key to effective leadership.

The early stages of English leadership

We will now move on to focus on the practical steps you might initially undertake in the role. One of the initial tasks is to locate and update an English subject file. In some instances you may need to put together a file from scratch. The file should contain most of the following documentation, although obviously the file will vary from school to school.

Main documents

* English subject leader job description
* English policy
* The School Development Plan (highlight points that relate to English)
* Curriculum overview (scheme of work, any long-term planning, any document that maps the English curriculum coverage and depth across the school, including cross-curricular opportunities)
* Excerpts from the latest Ofsted report relevant to English

Audits and development plans

* Any monitoring schedules or evaluation reports for English
* English action plan (yearly targets and actions for English)
* A record of the budget (if applicable)
* Professional development activities (include copies of materials and any impact evaluations)

The wider learning environment

* Events and activities that support the culture of enjoyment for English (displays, author visits, World Book Day, cross-curricular, creative opportunities for English, competitions, clubs, etc.)
* Resources (details of any reading schemes, whole class texts, Big Books, etc.)

- Intervention programmes (details of any reading, phonics, spelling, handwriting or writing resources for specific pupil support)

Evaluation and standards

- Pupil outcomes (data records, any useful assessment documentation)
- English planning examples
- Evaluation and assessments of pupil work (results of book scrutiny or samples from across the school)
- Classroom observations/monitoring (schedule and format of approach, overall findings but not information about individual teachers)
- Pupils' voice (pupil conferencing information or interviews)
- Staff and other stakeholder questionnaires/interviews

Once you have located relevant documentation, you should begin to familiarise yourself with the School Development Plan (SDP) and identify aspects that relate to English and any specific English actions. Begin to clarify the school's existing priorities for English, the targets you need to achieve and the timescales within which to achieve them. This information will detail the focus of your role and the aims you are trying to achieve. It can also be useful to confirm your budget allocation and establish if any finances are already committed.

Case study: Hannah – Congratulations, you're the English subject leader!

Hannah had just finished her first year of teaching when she accepted responsibility for English at Hampden Gurney Church of England Primary School. The school is a one-form entry primary in Central London with an ethnically diverse pupil demographic. For many pupils English is not their first language. The school is deemed 'outstanding' by Ofsted and is highly successful in achieving excellent outcomes for pupils in reading and writing.

Hannah's teacher training route enabled her to specialise in English and she was very keen to take on the subject leader role. With strong subject knowledge Hannah already had her own ideas and views on the direction of English teaching but as a new teacher she was also very aware of the things that she was still learning. She therefore valued the support and guidance of the staff. She also wanted to listen to and learn from her colleagues, drawing on their experience and expertise. She also wanted to be an inspiration to the school and promote exciting approaches to English.

How do English subject leaders know where to start?

Once you are familiar with the school targets for English the next step is for you to consider the most effective way you can support the school to meet them. These steps to success may already be defined in the English action plan, but it is still worth revisiting these and ensuring that you think this approach will be effective. In order for any strategy to be effective you need to find out the underlying reasons for the improvement target. This knowledge cannot be gained through remote working or through reading documentation in isolation. Acquiring a clear understanding of the causes of pupil under performance or the need for further school development of an aspect of English requires exploration of the views of staff and pupils. This exploration should happen before deciding on your own actions to remedy the situation.

Case study: Hannah's understanding of English in the school

There was so much that Hannah already knew about English in the school, gained during her first year of teaching. Her understanding of factors that might feature on the English action plan felt broad and it was easy to feel overwhelmed at the scale of the role. It was key for Hannah to acknowledge everything she knew and understood about English first, before trying to plan how and when the things that needed doing should happen. Firstly, Hannah needed to consider what she knew about English in her school and the reason why she felt certain issues needed to be considered in the English action plan.

The standard of reading and writing was high, and expectations in English already good. In order to continue to develop pupil attainment Hannah felt that she had to consider how to continue to challenge pupils, particularly those in the upper year groups, who were already achieving 'above expected outcomes' for reading and writing. The school was currently meeting pupils' needs well through differentiation by outcome, but Hannah was keen to explore other options too.

The inherited English action plan included a focus on guided reading. Reading comprehension was something the head teacher had also said she wanted Hannah to review. Hannah understood that there were different approaches to the teaching of guided reading across the school. Hannah thought these differences were to do with classroom management of the lessons and difference in texts and activities. Staff also made use of a range of assessment tools and approaches to assess pupils' reading comprehension skills. The head teacher had told Hannah she was keen for staff to make use of

---

more consistent approaches that best suited the needs of the pupils and staff. The head teacher had passed PIRA reading assessment tools to Hannah for her to consider as a support to reading comprehension. The school already made use of Bloom's taxonomy to support a range of planning and Hannah felt that there might be room to explore the potential for this approach to underpin the guided reading planning. The school also used 'Reading Cloud' to support children's home–school reading, but this was not being used regularly.

Hannah also knew that she wanted to revise the curriculum overview for English so she could capture the texts taught and the writing foci across the school. She wanted to be able to support staff in teaching new and exciting texts and using this overview to offer support and provide guidance on texts that might support the teaching of particular genres and themes in English.

Part of her vision for English was to get an author to visit the school to inspire some writing. In her particular context she felt it was important to try to invite a male writer. She wanted Adam Horowitz.

What did Hannah decide to do next?

- Seek opinions from staff about guided reading. Hannah wanted to ask staff to clarify their approach to the teaching of reading comprehension and guided reading.

- Trial the PIRA reading comprehension tools. Hannah was keen to try out the papers suggested by the head teacher. She planned to try them with her class and see how useful she found them in supporting the teaching of reading comprehension.

- Find out if there were any outside services the school could draw on. Hannah wanted to be supportive and helpful to her colleagues and find and suggest texts to support all curriculum learning. She did not know if the school bought into the library service.

- Seek pupil views. Hannah mentioned that a child had articulated their difficulty in transferring known grammatical information and applying it to the test paper conditions. Hannah was keen to know what else the pupils thought would help them with their English.

- Develop her understanding of pupil progress and assessment. Hannah wanted to develop her understanding of English across the school in terms of pupil progress, assessment and coverage. She felt that a learning walk would help and that this would also give her the opportunity to talk to her colleagues and ascertain their views on the successes and areas for development required.

Case study learning points

✓ **Find out as much information about English teaching in the school as you can.** Find out what is working and what requires improvement before devising and implementing an improvement plan.

✓ **Ask the views of everyone with a stake in English learning.** This will facilitate your understanding and will serve to ensure that your plans are based on evidence.

✓ **A fact-finding approach is particularly relevant to relatively new post-holders** who will need to seek higher levels of consultation with senior staff in order to make decisions.

✓ **A collegiate approach** enables relatively new post-holders to build relationships and gain consensus for change.

Establishing your knowledge and understanding of the school context

You may consider using the questions below as a basis for your own fact-finding discussions. It can be helpful to focus questioning on key aspects of English already identified as a target in existing plans – for example, reading comprehension or writing – but you might not want to limit your discussion.

- What do the teachers think about their English teaching?
- What aspects of English teaching do they think they do well?
- Is their confidence level high for each aspect of the English curriculum?
- Is their subject knowledge secure?
- Can they define areas for personal improvement?
- What do they think the pupils do well in English and how do they know?
- What do they think pupils need to develop further in the subject and how do they know?

Once the subject leader has an array of responses to these questions it is time to consider where areas of consensus within staff feedback exist. The next step is to consider how this might be acted on.

Joining up staff and pupil perceptions

It can be fruitful to ask similar questions of the pupils. Given the opportunity to articulate their own experience in English the children's opinions can provide new insights into the areas of English learning that need development. Sometimes there are areas of consensus between pupils and staff. What pupils say needs to change in order to support them better in English hopefully relates to teachers' own perceptions of where they need to better support the learning. There are also other stakeholders that you might want to include such as parents, governors, support staff, volunteers and community members. Similar questions might be useful in framing your fact finding. Armed with your newly gained information, the next step is for the English subject leader to consider how to move forward.

Hannah's approach illustrates how she sought to canvass the whole staff. The conversations and meetings enabled them to support her in the role, arming her with information to take forward. Sometimes expertise and support are also available beyond the school. Find out if the school already works with other schools and make contact with the English subject leader. It can also be helpful to find out if the school works with any other external agencies, such as local authority advisers or external consultants, who might hold English subject leader events. Through consultation with colleagues and pupils, and scrutiny of documentation, you will have a stronger understanding of the task in hand.

Hopefully, you are beginning to feel more confident and aware of your own emerging identity as an English subject leader. Armed with increased knowledge of both yourself and the school's needs you are ready to begin to consider how to tackle the changes that need to be made.

References

Alexander, R. J. (ed.) (2009) *Children, their World, their Education: Final report and recommendations of the Cambridge Primary review*. London: Routledge.

Brighouse, T. and Tomlinson, J. (1991) *Successful Schools*. London: Institute of Public Policy Research.

Burrows, D. (2004) *Tidying the Cupboard? The role of subject leaders in primary schools*. Nottingham: NCSL.

Coleman, P. and Earley, M. (2005) *Leadership & Management in Education: Cultures, Change, and Context*. Oxford: Oxford University Press.

Department for Education (DfE) (2016) *Achievement of 15-Year-Olds in England: PISA 2015 National Report*. Available at: https://assets.publishing.service.gov.uk/government/uploads/system/uploads/attachment_data/file/574925/PISA-2015_England_Report.pdf [accessed 3 July 2018].

Goleman, D. (2000) 'Leadership that gets results.' In: *Harvard Business Review*. March–April, 82–3. Available at: www.powerelectronics.ac.uk/documents/leadership-that-gets-results.pdf [accessed 3 July 2018].

Kaplan, L. and Owings, W. (2013) 'School culture and change as learning.' In: Scheukman, L., Kaplan, L. and Owings, W. (eds), *Culture Re-Boot: Reinvigorating school culture to improve student outcomes*. London: Sage.

Leithwood, K., Day, C., Sammons, P., Harris, A. and Hopkins, D. (2006) *Successful School Leadership: What it is and how it influences pupil learning*. Nottingham University: DfE Publications.

Moss, G. (2017) 'Assessment, accountability and the literacy curriculum: Reimagining the future in the light of the past.' *Literacy*, 51 (2), 56–64.

The Organisation for Economic Co-operation and Development (OECD) (2015) 'Country Note: Results from Programme for International Student Assessment (PISA) 2015 United Kingdom.' Available at: www.oecd.org/pisa/PISA-2015-United-Kingdom.pdf [accessed 3 July 2018].

Teacher Training Agency (TTA) (1998) *National Standards for Subject Leaders*. London: HMSO.

Waters, M. and Martin, T. (1999) *Coordinating English at Key Stage 2: The subject leader's handbook*. London: Falmer Press.

What's in a name?

Lisa Baldwin

This chapter will explore the nature of the role of the subject leader and how it has developed. There will be a discussion that outlines the many name changes the role has had in the last twenty years and how these different names led to different notions about priorities for the role. Research into the role of the subject leader will be used to highlight what subject leaders think they do and what they actually do. The chapter will further explore what specific personal and professional qualities are required to effectively lead a core subject in a primary school.

The changing nature of the role

Currently, there are many different titles and names for the role of the English subject leader. A quick survey of forty-five primary schools generated eleven different titles, which included: subject leader for English; English leader; subject coordinator of English; English manager; primary teacher with literacy expertise; core subject leader; class teacher with teaching and learning responsibility for English; specialist teacher of English; leader of learning in English; phase leader with core responsibility for English; and leading practitioner in English. Over the last twenty years there has been a significant shift in role titles and the inherent duties undertaken by the post-holder. The current diversity of titles reflects the range of responsibility, organisational placement of the role in the school and the expectations of tasks commensurate with the post.

There has long been the need for head teachers of primary schools to devolve some level of responsibility for English, and other subject areas, to teachers on the general teaching staff. Bell and Ritchie (1999) link this as far back in educational history as 1905, but the idea of the post entitled 'curriculum coordinator' was first referred to in the Bullock report in 1975 (DES, 1975).

The advent of the National Curriculum in 1989 set out distinct expectations for individual subject teaching in primary schools. Indeed there was a time in the 1990s when it was a requirement for all post-graduate trainee teachers to possess a degree subject that related to one of the primary curriculum areas (Burton and Brundrett, 2005). In many schools a nominated teacher with responsibility for English already existed, but the introduction of the National Curriculum increased the need for each curriculum area to have a member of staff as the allocated coordinator. This member of staff would usually be responsible for interpreting the curriculum orders and putting them into practice in their school (Hammersley-Fletcher, 2002). In small schools this often meant teachers adopting responsibility for multiple roles. Coordinator duties usually involved tasks such as the organisation of resources, the ordering, cataloguing and maintaining of resources, the purchase of schemes and other teaching materials, the running of In-Service Training days (INSET days) for staff and the design of long-term curriculum plans.

It is important to note that the allocation of responsibility for English was not uniform across all primary schools. The coordination of English might have been assigned to a teacher for any number of different reasons. It may have been because a teacher had a particular interest in (or flair for) the subject, it might have occurred because the member of staff had management responsibilities commensurate with the role of English subject leader, but equally it might have occurred just because there was no one else, either available or willing, to take on the responsibility at the time of delegation. Because of the variety of means through which teachers found themselves in the role, not every English subject leader had (or indeed has today) specialist training or expertise in the teaching of English.

In the early 1990s it was common for the primary English coordinator to be mainly responsible for the organisation of documents and resources necessary for the efficient teaching of the National Curriculum content. Any influence the post-holder had on the teaching and learning of English was usually limited to providing advice when colleagues sought it and meeting resource requirements. In 1998 the Teacher Training Agency (TTA) published a set of subject leader standards that shifted the focus of the role towards the provision of strategic leadership. The TTA made the clear distinction between subject coordination as a reactive role, and subject leadership as proactive. The shift arose from emerging report evidence that espoused links between the effective leadership of subject areas and improvement in the quality of teaching and pupil learning.

As the definition of the English subject leader post became more focused on leadership, the role began to shift into new territory. Spillane (2005) defines leadership as activity designed, or intended, to influence the motivation, knowledge, and practice of other members of the school organisation. Affecting and influencing practice required a very different approach, and required post-holders to develop their role beyond the previous remit.

Taking responsibility for the instigation of whole-school change in English practice was a significant shift in role, and one fraught with challenge. The level of challenge for the primary English subject leader is made apparent when compared to subject leaders in secondary schools. Secondary English leaders often have the organisational hierarchy to support them in adopting a leadership role over their department. Secondary English leaders usually work almost exclusively with teaching staff that have significant subject knowledge and expertise exclusively in English (Busher and Harris, 2000). Primary subject leaders usually have neither the hierarchical status to instruct other teachers how to teach, nor the ease of working with teachers who are equally knowledgeable, or enthused, about the teaching of English (Busher and Harris, 2000). The new expectations of primary English subject leaders impacted on existing working relationships and forced change to embedded ways of working. Many teachers experiencing this shift found the evolution of the subject leader to be an uncomfortable and challenging process.

Hammersley-Fletcher's research in 2002 focused on revealing the extent to which the TTA standards reflected the actuality of the subject leader's role in school. Her research was based on diary records and interviews with twenty subject leaders. During the interviews subject leaders defined their role as inclusive of policy review, curriculum planning, developing schemes of work, action planning and other paper-based tasks relating to their subject. The activities they highlighted in discussion covered the following broad headings:

What did the subject leaders think they did?

- **Resource the subject.** Purchase materials, organise equipment and associated administrative tasks;
- **Documentation.** Write plans, develop and review policies, and write schemes of work;
- **Monitor.** Oversee assessment procedures and subject displays, check pupils' work and the appropriateness of subject materials, and conduct lesson observation;
- **Liaise.** Communicate with parents, teachers, pupils, senior staff, visitors and governors;
- **Personal professional development.** Attend courses, read literature to stay up to date, talk to other subject leaders and advisory teachers, and attend relevant groups or meetings;

- **Influence practice.** Teach classes across the school, advise colleagues on lesson planning and content, demonstrate good practice, deliver staff training and organise external providers.

(Based on Hammersley-Fletcher, 2002)

Hammersley-Fletcher (2002) noted that during interview teachers articulated a view of effective subject leadership that was in direct accord with the TTA standards (TTA, 1998). Subject leaders spoke of their role and purpose in relation to activities such as monitoring and developing practice, supporting colleagues and implementing change. Interestingly, the traits and activities articulated as being the most effective at interview, were not evident in the diary entries that recorded what they *actually* spent their time doing.

 ## What did the subject leaders actually do?

- Organise, purchase and maintain resources
- Motivate staff
- Discuss with advisor
- Record keeping
- Develop policies and schemes of work and put them in place
- Put up subject displays
- Keep subject knowledge up to date
- Monitor planning documents and children's work

Where there was a correlation between the subject leaders' views of an activity being useful (articulated during interview) and being something that they actually performed (evidenced in the diary), it was frequently the case that the task was unobtrusive to their colleagues. Whilst the subject leaders acknowledged that it was insightful to be in a class with another teacher, watching a lesson and interacting with children during their learning, monitoring was less likely to happen through first-hand experience.

Hammersley-Fletcher's research (2002) illustrates the shift in staff perception of the role as it moved from the 'coordinator' of the early 1990s to 'leader' in the late 1990s. What hadn't entirely changed, at the time of her research, was *what* the subject leader actually *did*. So whilst there was a shift in the subject leader's mind-set, by way of what they understood made the role effective, the reality of their day-to-day activity was far removed from their discourse about the role. This is likely to be due to the fact that enacting TTA standards required subject leaders to go beyond helping colleagues. There is a huge difference between supporting colleagues with subject delivery, and leading English. Subject leadership requires issues to be confronted, ways forward defined and practice monitored (Waters and Martin, 1999).

It is useful for subject leaders to spend their time on activities that impact on the teaching and learning of English. Over the course of a week keep a diary of your activity. Keep a list of tasks undertaken as part of your English subject leader role. At the end of the week match the activities you undertook against the following four themes:

- influencing classroom practice;
- planning, documentation and paper-based tasks;
- monitoring and evaluation;
- resources.

Use this information to reflect on whether you spent your time effectively. Were you conducting activities that were purposeful and impactful? How much of your time was spent influencing colleagues' English practice?

A focus on effectiveness

Faced with studies by the School Teachers' Review Body (Vineall, 2001) and the PricewaterhouseCoopers' Teacher Workload Study (2001), it became apparent to the Labour administration that heavy workload threatened a crisis in teacher recruitment and retention. In response to teacher recruitment issues the New Labour government formed an alliance with some teaching unions to agree new statutory recommendations. The statutes aimed to relieve bureaucratic burdens on teaching staff and focus on school effectiveness. As a consequence a National Agreement between government, employers and school workforce unions was reached in January 2003 (with the notable exception of the National Union of Teachers). It was known as the 'Workforce Remodelling' agenda: a complex reform, implemented over the duration of three years, or phases, with significant changes to conditions of teachers' service.

In Phase one, introduced in September 2003, administrative and clerical tasks were removed from teachers with the intention of improving their work–life balance. In addition, a time allowance was introduced for all teachers with management responsibilities. Phase two, a year later, limited the time a teacher could be asked to cover classes for absent colleagues. Phase three, in September 2005, brought regular, timetabled Planning, Preparation and Assessment time (PPA) for all teaching staff. The invigilation of exams was removed from teachers' duties and dedicated headship time was introduced. It was intended that education would improve by enhancing teachers' professional development and providing focused, timetabled opportunity for reflection on teaching and learning.

The Workforce Remodelling agenda

In 2003 the implementation of Phase one focused on the removal, or redistribution, of administrative tasks away from teachers. The '21 tasks' included:

* bulk photocopying;
* typing or making Word-processed versions of manuscript material and producing revisions of such versions;
* keeping and filing records, including records based on data supplied by teachers;
* preparing, setting up and taking down classroom displays in accordance with decisions taken by teachers;
* ordering, setting up and maintaining ICT equipment/software;
* ordering supplies and equipment;
* cataloguing, preparing, issuing and maintaining materials and equipment and stocktaking the same;
* transferring manual data about pupils not covered by the above into computerised school management systems;
* managing the data in school management systems.

The list of '21 things teachers should not be asked to do' is by no means the definitive sum of Phase one implementation, but it provides an insightful glimpse into the types of task schools were forced to remove from teachers' duties. Hammersley-Fletcher's research (2002) evidenced that subject leaders carried out a number of the '21 tasks' in relation to their role. The statutory order forced them to cease doing these tasks and ensured they focused on more effective leadership tasks.

The result was that schools needed to either allocate the task to another member of non-teaching staff or review the need for the task to be carried out at all. The introduction of statutory changes meant schools had little choice but to transform their working practices and the roles that accompanied them. Work tasks were examined and redeployed accordingly, and in many cases new non-teaching positions (such as the Higher Level Teaching Assistant) evolved to undertake these duties and provide the dedicated PPA time made statutory for all teachers to receive.

Workload today

Once again, workload is impacting on the teaching profession. Recent government surveys and reports acknowledge the significant pressure on the school workforce at the current time (DfE, 2015; Higton *et al.*, 2016). It might therefore be timely for subject leaders to revisit the list of '21 tasks' and consider how many they regularly undertake today. If tasks undertaken today do not impact on teaching and learning, then it is worth considering the value of subject leader time being spent on such activity. It is important to question whether the task could be carried out in a more efficient way, or even abandoned completely.

Consider the '21 tasks' removed from teachers in 2003.

- How does the statutory change affect your role today?
- How many of the '21 tasks' do you carry out as part of the English subject leadership role?
- How many of the above tasks are you regularly doing?
- How many of the tasks are no longer required in schools today?
- How many of the '21 tasks' are conducted by a member of non-teaching staff in your school?

The role today

Workforce Reform required schools to implement changes that ensured statutory compliance. Organisational and structural changes to staff roles began to distinguish between teaching and learning, and administrative duties. Today school staffing structures are often organised around teaching and learning foci, with leadership posts and support staff roles complementing these structures. Increasingly complex staff organisation exists today due to partnerships that evolved with the emergence of federated leadership and academy chains. However, it is equally important to recognise that many primary schools still comprise a small staff workforce, with multiple roles assumed by one teacher.

Whatever the scale and complexity of the staffing structure, where it places the English subject leader determines the leader's position within a school hierarchy. This in turn influences the leadership routines the post-holder is likely to engage in, the level of involvement of administrative staff in offering support to the post-holder and the level of finances devolved to fund training and subject resources. When the subject leader's post sits outside the Senior Leadership Team (SLT) it is important that channels of communication enable them to access information about English (Burrows, 2004). It can be helpful to consider how such a communication process works in practice for recently qualified subject leaders.

Case study: Communication between senior leaders and a newly appointed English subject leader

Hampden Gurney Church of England Primary School, Central London

Hannah is a newly appointed English subject leader. It is her first year in the post after having successfully completed her Newly Qualified Teacher (NQT) year. She is not a member of the senior leadership team and relies on having good communication with the SLT to gain knowledge of the monitoring and evaluation processes at whole-school level. Data analysis and lesson observation information, relevant to the subject, is regularly communicated to Hannah. This serves to shape and guide her next steps and ensures the full support of senior members of staff.

When Hannah took on the role, the head teacher informed her that reading comprehension required development. The head teacher shared some possible development indicators. She shared information about the performance of pupil groups in the school and insights from her own lesson observation about varying approaches to delivering and assessing reading comprehension. After this initial discussion she left Hannah to explore the teaching of reading comprehension for herself.

Hannah began the task of investigating current practice in reading comprehension. She wanted to fully understand what needed to change. Once she had gathered more knowledge she began to make informed decisions about the way in which the school could move forward.

In order to ensure she had the head teacher's backing, Hannah regularly updated her on her findings, thoughts and considered ways forward. Hannah was given the right balance between direction from the head teacher and being able to make autonomous decisions about how to progress the subject. She was able to receive guidance about the focus priorities for English, seek counsel from more experienced, senior staff and gain SLT endorsement of her proposed changes before moving forward. This is a healthy and productive way of working.

Case study learning points

✓ **Ensure communication.** A newly appointed English subject leader must establish a way of working that facilitates good communication with the SLT.
✓ **Explore received information.** Hannah was told which aspect of English to develop, based on the head teacher's school evaluation processes. The

subject leader then took this information and investigated further in order to find out exactly what needed to change.

✓ **Keep communicating.** Hannah kept talking to staff to feed her ideas on how to progress, and she regularly fed-back her thoughts and findings to the head teacher.

✓ **Gain support.** Hannah had the full backing of the SLT before making changes. She had also paved the way to change with her colleagues.

Some schools will link the responsibility of English to generic leadership teams, focused on leading effective change across a range of subjects, which rotate as priorities are defined through the school's development processes. As a core subject English is unlikely to ever be absent from the remit of teaching and learning development, unlike some wider curriculum areas, which might not require development *every* year. English covers a large range of skills and the specific English focus will shift depending on the school's self-defined areas for improvement. The position of the role in the staffing structure will impact on how the English subject leader can access the school self-evaluation and development information. It will also influence the amount of release received to carry out English leadership duties.

Spillane's (2005) research cited subject leaders' views that reading and mathematics were key priorities for school leadership, and today English and mathematics still dominate the taught curriculum. The prevailing focus on English and mathematics is in response to external pressures on schools to achieve required targets in mathematics, reading and writing. The pressure to meet targets, combined with statutory changes to teachers' pay, has resulted in school-wide accountability for pupil outcomes in these subjects. In today's schools all class teachers, from Newly Qualified Teachers (NQTs) to experienced senior staff, are accountable for pupil achievement in English and mathematics.

The spread of accountability has given rise to increased pressure and scrutiny, but at the same time it has resulted in a culture of devolved responsibility for English. Today's English subject leader is arguably working in a different culture to the English coordinator of the 1990s. The shift in responsibility may go some way to overcome the tension that subject coordinators felt when trying to offer advice to staff who had not requested it (Hammersley-Fletcher, 2002; Waters and Martin, 1999). Whilst increased shared accountability might support the subject leader to carry out school improvement activity, it is important to note that the increased focus on standards and targets has also impacted negatively on teaching and the curriculum (Alexander, 2009; Moss, 2017). As the English subject leader it is imperative that your vision for English is not just shaped by targets and pupil progress, but also by the realisation that a love of reading and writing is important beyond school life.

The required personal and professional qualities to lead primary English

In order to define effective subject leadership of primary English, it is essential to combine research about successful English teaching and pedagogy, with leadership theory. Burton and Brundrett (2005) consider the following five aspects as essential knowledge for a general subject leader:

- organisational knowledge;
- subject knowledge;
- curriculum knowledge;
- pedagogic knowledge;
- pupil knowledge.

This chapter will explore both the personal and the professional qualities that the effective subject leader needs to develop. Time will now be given to explore where your current strengths lie and where you need to develop skills in leadership and management, English subject knowledge and effective pedagogy.

Leadership and management skills

Over the years various studies have contributed to knowledge of what constitutes effective leadership and management in schools. This has enabled the identification of certain practices and actions that support improvement in children's educational achievement. The strategic aims of the subject leader are as follows:

> **Define the school's mission.** *Frame and then communicate the school's goals.*
> **Manage the teaching programme.** *Supervise and evaluate teaching, coordinate the curriculum and monitor pupil progress.*
> **Promote a positive learning climate.** *Promote professional development, maintain high visibility, provide incentives for teachers and provide incentives for learning.*
>
> *(Based on Leithwood et al., 2006)*

The key thing to understand is how to achieve these strategic goals and which practices, behaviours and actions support effective leadership. As the subject leader you will be an ambassador and role model for English teaching. It will be highly important for you to exude good practice. A teacher's enthusiasm for English and their ability to encourage children to find pleasure in spoken language, reading and writing make a significant difference to children's attitudes to English. Consider yourself as a role model for English teaching. Do you enthuse about the subject? How do you communicate this enthusiasm to the children you teach? Do you have any particular activities or pieces of work that are an excellent model of how to teach English? How can you showcase this to your colleagues?

- Inspire pupils and colleagues by modelling and suggesting creative and exciting approaches to English;
- Invite colleagues into their lessons and lead by example;
- Talk to colleagues about their teaching and planning, offering advice and suggestions, e.g. recommending books;
- Routinely celebrate and share good practice in English;
- Keep abreast of developments in the subject nationally. Post news and email updates, and provide information about English on the staff noticeboard;
- Celebrate children's success in English, both across and beyond the school;
- Shape the school's English curriculum to promote and sustain a thirst for knowledge and a love of learning;
- Run book clubs after school, or during lunch-time;
- Engage with parents and carers to the benefit of pupils;
- Focus continuously on improving teaching and learning, and provide focused professional development for all staff;
- Regularly scrutinise pupils' English work and understand school assessment data across the school;
- Organise displays in communal school areas to promote English and showcase pupils' work;
- Organise enjoyable, off-timetable events in school that raise the profile of English.

 Consider which of the above actions support the strategic aims of the English subject leader:

- Which of the above tasks support and motivate staff?
- Which of the above tasks aims to raise standards and achievement?
- Which of the above tasks monitor English teaching?
- Which of the above tasks support policy development?

* How many of the above points do you carry out on a regular basis?
* Which aspects could you do more of ... and how?

(Based on Leithwood *et al.*, 2006)

English subject knowledge

As well as certain personal qualities, strong subject knowledge and understanding of English is an essential requirement for the role. Success in the role will 'hinge' on knowing what defines quality English teaching (Waters and Martin, 1999: 12). It is therefore extremely important to reflect on the strength of your understanding of *all* aspects of English. Your knowledge should include a comprehensive understanding of phonics, reading comprehension, writing composition, writing transcription and secretarial skills: knowledge beyond curriculum requirements. You should have a secure understanding of child development in both reading and writing, and recognise the important role speaking and listening plays in underpinning all aspects of literacy learning.

You may have undertaken English as a specialist subject during initial teacher training, and your first degree may be in English or a related subject. Equally, you may just have a personal interest in the subject that has grown whilst you have been in school. Either way it is unlikely, in the early stages of your career, that you will have a broad knowledge of all aspects of English throughout the primary age-range. Let's consider early reading as an example. This is a hugely complex subject matter, with many component parts. Early reading has a very high profile in primary schools, linked to the phonics screening check, which focuses solely on a child's ability to decode lists of decontextualised words (some real words and some 'alien' nonsense words) using synthetic phonics. All the evidence suggests that reading requires much more than phonics instruction alone (Dombey, 2016). As the English subject leader you must understand what experiences ensure a child's success in reading. You should have good knowledge of the importance of phonological building blocks as a prerequisite to phonics instruction. You should clearly understand the link between phonics and reading and spelling, and the importance of combining a phonics approach to spelling with morphological and etymological strategies. You should have an evidence-based knowledge of reading development, as well as an understanding of the National Curriculum age-related expectations. You should understand the importance of children acquiring a range of cueing strategies to support the development of their fluency in reading. You should also have knowledge of how motivation, reading for pleasure and children's perceptions of themselves as readers impact on reading attainment.

If you are not secure in your understanding of the subject, then it will be difficult for you to comment effectively on the planning, learning and teaching of English in your school. In turn it will be difficult for you to identify where your school needs to develop practice in order to improve pupil achievement. It is therefore imperative you reflect on the extent of your own personal subject knowledge in English. By considering each of the audit questions below you will begin to identify areas where you need to secure your own understanding. Knowing your personal areas for development will pave the way for you to develop your English subject knowledge.

Knowing what you don't know

Consider the questions below in order to gauge your own English subject knowledge. There is a full audit questionnaire in Appendix 1, but this will give you a flavour of where your subject development areas lie.

 Consider the questions below to measure your knowledge and understanding of different aspects of English:

Spoken language and standard English

- Do you understand how standard English is different to dialect and accent?
- Do you understand the importance of sound discernment and phonological development?
- Can you define the different types of sentence there are? (Exclamatory, simple and complex, commands, and statements)

Reading and spelling

- Do you understand technical terms associated with phonics, such as grapheme, decode, encode and phoneme?
- Can you segment words by phoneme?
- Do you understand terminology such as morpheme (bound and unbound), root, suffix and prefix?

Grammar

- Can you explain the difference between a simple, compound and complex sentence?

- Can you identify components of sentences – phrases, clauses – and define a main clause, a subordinate clause and an adverbial phrase?
- Can you explain the difference between an active and a passive sentence?

Punctuation

- Can you identify common errors such as the comma splice and suggest alternatives?
- Can you explain how to use an apostrophe to show possession and omission?
- Are you aware of the conventions of punctuating dialogue as direct and indirect speech?

Texts

- Do you know how to identify a high-quality text?
- Do you have a working knowledge of texts suitable for use in the classroom?
- Do you understand features of poetry such as onomatopoeia, assonance, alliteration, personification, metaphor, simile and rhythm?

Reading comprehension

- Do you know how attitudes to reading affect attainment?
- Do you have a knowledge of books that means you could recommend texts to pupils and staff alike?
- Do you understand the importance of dialogic talk in developing reading comprehension?

Writing

- Do you understand the distinction between transcription and composition?
- Do you understand the writing process?
- Do you understand how drama supports the provision of meaningful contexts for writing?

Pedagogic knowledge

Effective pedagogy underpins successful English teaching and learning. It is therefore important that you are well informed of effective teaching approaches, proven to impact on children's learning. A good understanding of effective English pedagogy will equip you in determining *what* and *how* your school needs to develop, how staff should be supported to develop their practice and where pupils' experiences and opportunities in the classroom should be expanded.

Good English teaching will nearly always include teacher demonstration or modelling. It is always much more effective to learn by being shown a good example, than being told what to do. Modelling enables the child to understand new concepts, as the teacher's demonstration explicitly reveals the techniques and skills that good writers and readers use.

Let's consider how modelling supports the development of reading comprehension. When teaching comprehension skills it is vital that the teacher demonstrates and verbalises the thoughts and processes a good reader employs when reading a text. It is important that the teacher models the meaning-making processes, thinking aloud, puzzling over the plot and events, posing questions, considering the motivation of characters, re-reading sentences for sense or skimming passages to search for information and check for meaning. The demonstration of these, and other skills, helps reveal to children, processes that otherwise remain unseen.

Of course effective teacher modelling manifests itself in many other forms too: from being a role model who enjoys a good book, to being someone who can demonstrate how close regard for the punctuation in a book is knowledge to be interpreted for meaning, intonation and expression. Knowing the many ways in which effective modelling can support pupil learning is essential to the delivery of high-quality English teaching.

Other key pedagogic approaches include scaffolded learning, effective questioning, planned opportunities for dialogic and exploratory talk, and the use of drama to support reading comprehension and writing composition. Further guidance and advice are given on these areas in Chapters 6 and 8. In order to build and develop your understanding of effective teaching approaches it is important to keep up to date with new research and guidance. Belonging to a good English association is a valuable and inspirational way to keep up to date with current teaching approaches. Among the best of these English organisations is the UKLA (United Kingdom Literacy Association). Their journal *Literacy* will ensure that you are up to date with the latest research and critical thought, and the magazine *English 4–11*, also available through their membership, provides illustrated case studies of practical, innovative approaches to teaching English in the classroom.

The National Literacy Trust, Booktrust, Poetry Society and Centre for Literacy in Primary Education (CLPE) are also among some of the best hubs of good-quality information, guidance and resources for English teaching, with many of the resources being available free of charge. A full list of helpful website sources is listed below:

www.literacytrust.org.uk – a hub of all things literacy, latest news, policies and special projects www.booktrust.org.uk – a charity promoting a love of reading, free resources, recommended reads and organisers of National Children's Book Week

www.worldbookday.com – resources and information about March's World Book Day

www.poetrysociety.org.uk – organisers of National Poetry Day

www.clpe.co.uk – everything teachers need to know about language, literature, literacy and learning

www.readingagency.co.uk – organisers of the annual library event, Summer Reading Challenge

www.justimagine.co.uk – excellent suggested texts and resources for reading

www.researchrichpedagogies.org/research/reading-for-pleasure – Open University website dedicated to effective reading pedagogies and practice

References

Alexander, R. J. (ed.) (2009) *Children, their world, their Education: Final report and recommendations of the Cambridge Primary Review*. London: Routledge.

Bell, D. and Ritchie, R. (1999) *Towards Effective Subject Leadership in the Primary School*. Buckingham: Open University Press.

Burrows, D. (2004) *Tidying the Cupboard?: The role of subject leaders in primary schools*. National College for School Leadership. Available at: https://core.ac.uk/download/pdf/4155074.pdf [accessed 15 March 2018].

Burton, N. and Brundrett, M. (2005) *Leading the Curriculum in the Primary School*. London: Sage.

Busher, H. and Harris, A. (2000) *Subject Leadership and School Improvement*. London: Sage.

Department of Education and Science (DES) (1975) *Report of the Committee of Enquiry appointed by the Secretary of State for Education and Science under the chairman of Sir Allan Bullock (A Language for Life)*. London: HMSO.

Department for Education (DfE) (2015) 'Government response to workload challenge.' London: DfE Publications. Available at: https://assets.publishing.service.gov.uk/government/uploads/system/uploads/attachment_data/file/415874/Government_Response_to_the_Workload_Challenge.pdf [accessed 3 July 2018].

Dombey, H. (2016) *Teaching Reading: What the evidence says*. Leicester: UKLA.

Hammersley-Fletcher, L. (2002) 'Becoming a subject leader: What's in a name? Subject leadership in English primary schools.' *School Leadership and Management*, 22 (4), 407–20.

Higton, J., Leonardi, S., Richards, N., Choudhoury, A., Sofroniou, N. and Owen, D. (2016) *Teacher Workload Survey 2016 Technical Report*. Nottingham University: DfE Publications.

Leithwood, K., Day, C., Sammons, P., Harris, A. and Hopkins, D. (2006) *Successful School Leadership: What it is and how it influences pupil learning*. Nottingham University: DfE Publications.

Moss, G. (2017) 'Assessment, accountability and the literacy curriculum: Reimagining the future in the light of the past.' *Literacy*, 51 (2), 56–64.

PricewaterhouseCoopers (2001) *Teacher Workload Study*. London: DfES.

Spillane, J. P. (2005) 'Primary school leadership practice: How the subject matters.' *School Leadership and Management*, 25 (4), 383–97.

Teacher Training Agency (1998) *National Standards for Subject Leaders*. London: TTA.

Vineall, T. (2001) 'School Teachers' Review Body Tenth Report.' DfEE: The Stationery Office. Available at: www.gov.uk/government/uploads/system/uploads/attachment_data/file/265726/4990.pdf [accessed 11 October 2017].

Waters, M. and Martin, T. (1999) *Coordinating English at Key Stage 2: The subject leader's handbook*. London: Falmer Press.

3 | Leading the English curriculum

Lisa Baldwin

In this chapter we will reflect on our principles and beliefs about the teaching of English. We will begin to consider what we mean by literacy, and what experiences of literacy children need to ensure success in English. A historical perspective of the development of the English curriculum in the last forty years will be covered with a view to answering the question: 'Where are we now and how did we get here?' The wider role of subject associations will be discussed and how belonging to a network of like-minded practitioners can be beneficial.

Beliefs about English

English is complex and encompasses a broad array of knowledge, skills and understanding. There is widespread agreement that it is a difficult subject to define. Holbrook describes two aspects of English: the practical aspect of functional language use, and the broader knowledge and appreciation of the subject in a cultural and aesthetic sense (Holbrook, 1961; Laugharne, 2007). These two definitions illustrate the divide between the notions of literacy and English. Until the mid-18th century literature and literacy meant almost the same thing (Meek, 1991), but today there is a distinction between the terms. Literacy denotes knowledge and skills that are useful in society: knowledge separate from the literary text. Views and opinions differ about where the emphasis between functional literacy skills and the appreciation of text on an aesthetic level should lie in an English curriculum. These views are often politically driven, and shift over time as different ideologies come into play (Beverton, 2001; Cambridge Assessment Review, 2013).

Effective English subject leadership will require you to think about definitions of language use and their place in English teaching (Beverton, 2001). It is therefore important to unpick the differences between definitions of English and literacy, not least so that you, as the subject leader, can consider which term would be the best for you to use in your vision, policy and school documentation relating to the subject.

English and literacy: What is the difference?

There is no fixed definition of literacy, but it is a term that is often used in place of 'English' within the context of primary English (Limbrick and Aikman, 2005). Definitions of literacy tend to refer to a 'tangible set of skills' (UNESCO, 2006: 149) that support reading, or to reading and writing (Gee, 2000). Gee (2000) defines the degree to which a child acquires competency in reading and writing as the measure of how literate they are. However, this measure is not universal in standard and is open to debate (Lawton and Gordon, 1996). Children who leave secondary school unable to read independently would not be deemed to be literate, adults who struggle to undertake the English tests expected of an 11 year old would not be deemed to be literate, and these types of markers are often levels of 'functional literacy' (Cambridge Assessment Review, 2013; Deeqa and Dugdale, 2012).

Arguably, literacy is much more than this. This view limits literacy to the decoding and encoding skills required to read or write words on the page. Other explanations of the term literacy go beyond this narrow definition of skill acquisition and encompass broader literacy skills that serve to socially empower the individual (Gee, 2000). Wider definitions of literacy include terms such as 'critical literacy', 'cultural literacy' and 'digital literacy'. Brief definitions of these terms are as follows:

- **Critical literacy** enables an individual to respond to, challenge and critique language (arguably essential skills in today's world of fake news);
- **Cultural literacy** enables understanding of a common heritage of knowledge that aims to ensure all of society can access the same cultural capital;
- **Digital literacy** encompasses the understanding, knowledge and skills to enable the effective use of digital devices and digital texts in society (Becta, 2010).

The United Nations Educational Scientific and Cultural Organization (UNESCO) definition of literacy has evolved from the 1950s' definition of literacy as the ability to 'read and write, with understanding' to today's definition of literacy as the ability to 'identify, understand, interpret, create, communicate and compute using printed and written materials' in 'varied contexts' (UNESCO, 2015: 137). Today's wider definition of literacy is more likely to include skills that enable the individual to participate and engage fully in society (UNESCO, 2015).

Consider each of the four definitions of literacy (functional, critical, cultural and digital). How is each definition essential to your day-to-day life? Consider the emails you have written, media articles you have read, scribbled notes and memos, books or magazines you have read, online browsing and searching, and professional documentation you have read or written.

- What activities did you undertake this week that relate to each of the four definitions of literacy?
- What would be the consequence of not having skills in each of the four definitions of literacy?
- How do the four definitions of literacy relate to the children in school?

Literacy as social practice denotes language skills as useful for functioning within society; however, in the context of schools, the term literacy has its own definition. The National Curriculum (DfE, 2013) offers its own meanings and shapes practices that are '"ideological": rooted in a particular world-view and in a desire for that view of literacy to dominate' (Street, 2003: 77). Policy compels teachers to ensure pupils master literacies required by the curriculum, but it is important to remember that these definitions are fluid. As political ideology changes, so too does the influence on national guidance and the literacy learning requirements within the school context (schooled literacy). There is a strong argument that the definition of literacy has to evolve and adapt in order to equip each generation with the skills necessary to navigate and participate in an ever-changing society, but often the curriculum is slow to adapt to meet societal change. The question is, do you, as the English subject leader, want to incorporate wider aspects of literacy learning into your school curriculum?

English knowledge

In most schools, what constitutes English knowledge for the pupils we teach is a matter determined at government level through political policy (Alexander, 2009). This state of prescription has arisen through successive governments as they impose their definition of English and literacy through a curriculum shaped by their own philosophical viewpoints. In order to be an effective subject leader of English it is important to understand the context within which subject leaders have to operate: a context that will invariably influence much of your role, and determine the measure of your school's success in teaching the subject.

Debate continues today between those who view English as a functional 'means to an end', and those who view the subject as a means of developing 'personal response' and knowledge of language, based on literacy experiences (Beverton, 2001: 129). Where the current curriculum sits in this debate is worthy of further discussion. The DfE expresses a commitment to a 'high-quality education in English ... [that will enable pupils to] ... communicate their ideas and emotions to others ... [and] develop culturally, emotionally, intellectually, socially and spiritually' (2013: 13). However, the curriculum also contains weighty, technical appendices that focus on the functional aspects of writing. The current assessment of primary English also focuses on knowledge about English over effective English use, and it is this fact that sustains the idea that greater value is placed on functional English.

Debate about the curriculum, voiced by the political world, the teaching profession and academics, highlights this tension. The reality is that a polarised view is unhelpful, as both definitions of literacy are of value, but it is important for subject leaders to recognise that beliefs about the purpose of English undoubtedly lead to certain classroom practices, not all of them desirable. Whilst the government's literacy goals are important (and inescapable) to deliver, it is also essential to provide English teaching that promotes lively opportunities for the application of skills: opportunities founded on well-researched, sound pedagogy. The key to good leadership of English is to balance a need to meet government-defined goals with providing imaginative and engaging approaches that are pedagogically effective and meet the needs of pupils (Bearne, 2017).

Determining the correct balance between government-defined outcomes, your own philosophical beliefs and research-led practice is given consideration throughout this book. Ultimately, how you determine this balance will influence the practices and approaches of English teaching in your school.

The development of the English curriculum

In order to better understand the context of English and literacy teaching today, we need to consider how we got here. The English curriculum has evolved, shaped by political context, and driven the direction of teaching in primary schools through government policy and guidance.

The introduction of the National Curriculum in 1989 (DES, 1989) focused on separating individual subjects to be taught in primary school. As schools took on board the new curriculum and worked to ensure coverage of all nine subjects, concern was raised that the broadening of the subject curriculum was detrimental to the so-called 'basics' of literacy (Goodwyn and Fuller, 2011: 3).

As teachers attempted to find time for nine separate subjects they began to hold the view that they were focusing less on the teaching of English (Goodwyn and

Fuller, 2011). This opinion was supported by the Dearing Review (1994), which testified to the need for a reduction in the volume of taught material. The Review stated the importance of continuing to deliver all National Curriculum subjects, but with a call to redefine the curriculum into a statutory core with emphasis on the 'prime importance of literacy, oracy, numeracy and ... information technology' (Dearing, 1994: 8).

In 1991 the annual testing for 7 and 11 year olds began, underpinned by the introduction of published league tables. Testing determined whether schools were seen as successful in teaching English. This new public accountability placed pressure on all schools in an unprecedented way (Beard, 2011).

School standards and English

In 1994 the Dearing Review reported that (in comparison to many other countries) standards in reading had plateaued, revealing a tail of underachievement (Beard, 2011). The Review, combined with the growing need to demonstrate improving standards in English, set the stage for the National Literacy Strategy (NLS), and in 1998 the Framework was produced. The NLS Framework comprised a folder that provided curriculum objectives linked to the National Curriculum structure. The Framework endorsed approaches such as guided and shared reading and writing. It also included the 'literacy hour' with its distinctive clock-face of prescribed time allocations for specific literacy instruction.

The NLS was a significant attempt to unify the teaching of English and signified the first real move by government to demand *what* and *how* English should be taught (Goodwyn and Fuller, 2011). Whilst the NLS Framework was not statutory it was underpinned by a plethora of NLS training for teachers and subject leaders. The rollout of the Framework approach was widespread and fast, accompanied by significant professional development training for schools and English subject leaders. National and regional literacy advisors were employed to support implementation and it was very rare for a school not to adopt the NLS Framework, particularly in schools where improvement in English was deemed necessary. Schools required to improve would come under increasing scrutiny to adopt the recommended NLS content and approach in order to raise standards.

There are differing views about the success of the NLS Framework in raising standards of literacy, but there was one definite outcome: that the Framework defined *how* English should be taught to such an extent that it negated the need for teachers to utilise their own understanding of teaching approaches (Beverton, 2001). Teaching approaches became uniform and the texts used to teach became less variable (Beverton, 2001). English subject knowledge was not required to shape the school curriculum when delivering such prescribed units of work.

Units of work became onerous to deliver and learning was increasingly focused on the quantity of genres covered. Over the course of time schools took some ownership over the content and the Framework became less rigid in delivery. The structure of the literacy hour had largely been abandoned before the coalition government came in, but schools were still largely delivering a genre-focused English curriculum. However, teachers were still less likely to deliver learning using their own choice of literature, and the children less likely to practise skills of extended writing and self-expression.

 Terms such as units of work, text-type, genre, literacy hour and language features were all indicative of language from the NLS Framework.

- Do you still hear teachers use language that relates to the NLS Framework?
- To what extent have schools abandoned the NLS Framework?
- Do you still see evidence of 'units' of English planning that refers to the NLS Framework content?

The English curriculum today

The coalition government, elected in 2010, appointed Michael Gove as the Minister for Education and, like most of his predecessors, he took the view that education was in crisis and only significant reform from his government would enable standards to improve. During a speech to an audience of trainee teachers in 2014, Gove stated that 'one in seven children still can't read and write properly' and that there were 'around 500 primary schools where more than a third of children can't read and write properly' (Gove, 2014: speech to Brighton College).

Gove's view contrasted to the (then) most recent Progress in International Reading Study (Twist *et al.*, 2012), detailing the United Kingdom (UK) pupil test results for reading achievement. The study compared UK reading test results with forty-five other countries. Key findings stated that England scored significantly higher than thirty-one countries, and significantly lower than just five countries. It stated that of the higher-achieving countries only two, 'the United States and Chinese Taipei, showed a greater improvement than England between 2006 and 2011' (Twist *et al.*, 2012: 1). Despite this global research evidence, Gove referred to literacy standards in UK schools as 'a scandal', justifying his changes to the English curriculum (Gove, 2014: speech to Brighton College), but then '[s]tatements that standards in our schools are falling are nothing new; often made in the absence of hard evidence' (Clark, 2014: 107).

The curriculum serves to frame which aspects of English are valued and impact on how English is taught. The current curriculum, implemented in 2014 (DfE, 2013), is heavily skills based and advocates technical understanding about language. The consequence of this is a loss of equilibrium in the curriculum between 'whole' English and its constituent parts: between the bigger picture of language learning and the details which comprise it (Laugharne, 2007). Despite the lengthy, technical appendices, there is little for teachers to use to plan the English learning. If the NLS Framework took away the need for teachers to use their own English subject knowledge, the new 2014 curriculum (DfE, 2013) brought it back with alarming contrast.

Years of teaching to the NLS Framework resulted in a 'lack of clarity' (Cambridge Assessment Review, 2013: 6) about the purpose of English among the teaching profession. This, combined with high-stakes assessment processes, resulted in many schools becoming less focused on meeting the needs of pupils through the provision of a 'dynamic and productive curriculum' (Cambridge Assessment Review: 2013: 6).

It is therefore *essential* that the effective English subject leader has a clear understanding of the purpose of English and can determine a rich English curriculum for the school: a curriculum that provides much more than the means to meet English assessment. Whilst it is important for the English subject leader to understand that policy and curriculum change will usually involve some level of 'number-driven education system reform' (Moss, 2017: 56), it is equally important that the English subject leader understands that they are left to navigate *how* this will play out in school. Having good subject knowledge in English and a strong and secure philosophical approach to English teaching is key to this.

Defining your philosophical approach

Defining your own philosophical approach to English teaching begins with exploring what *you* define as important to quality primary English teaching. Literacy as social practice denotes language skills as useful for functioning within society; however, in the context of the current National Curriculum, the term literacy has its own definition understood as schooled literacy. Policy compels teachers to ensure pupils master these literacies, but it is important to remember that these definitions are fluid, as national guidance and political influence change the learning requirements of schooled literacy. Much of the new curriculum has little content and, therefore, it is still the case that the 'real *Programme of Study* has to be devised' by the subject leader (Waters and Martin, 1999: 11).

Reflection on the very terms 'literacy' and 'English' is a good place to begin. The two terms often appear interchangeable; however, they are loaded with different connotations.

Consider each of the five terms below. Try to rank them in order of importance. Which aspect of literacy would you give priority to? Remember, there is no right answer.

- Literacy in the digital age/media literacy;
- Functional literacy;
- Cultural literacy;
- Critical literacy;
- English as an aesthetic, a medium and a message.

Reflect on your ranking order and consider the reasons behind your decisions. Each decision will reveal something about your beliefs and values regarding English teaching. These values and beliefs will inform your philosophical approach to subject leadership and the wider English goals you are likely to want to achieve through your leadership of the subject.

Hopefully, by understanding how the English curriculum has evolved, you will begin to reflect on how power, literacy, language and the English curriculum are tightly bound in an educational relationship. As the English subject leader it is important that you can perceive this relationship and understand how it impacts on your role and the required pupil knowledge. The demographic you are supporting should shape *what* and *how* you deliver English. The good subject leader of English will find ways to deliver the curriculum through meaningful contexts. It is helpful to consider how good leaders of English determine a curriculum content and approach that meets pupil needs and government requirements.

Shaping the English curriculum

 Good subject leaders will consider how to shape the curriculum to meet the needs of the pupils. Careful consideration is given to approaches, resources and attitudes that the subject leader wants to underpin English.

The range of texts used to deliver the curriculum

- Do the texts that are used to teach English cover a broad and rich range of genre and culture?
- Are digital, multimedia approaches included in curriculum design?

- What current mapping procedures are in place to audit the use of texts across the school?

School culture, creativity and pleasure within the curriculum

- How does the school ensure that children have choice over the books they read?
- Does the school encourage children to recommend and share books for pleasure?
- Does the school hold author visits or celebrate World Book Day?

Culture and curriculum

- Does the school assume that children's home literacies are supportive or unsupportive to school literacies?
- Does the school believe parents and carers require more support to understand how to help their child?
- How does the school currently engage with parents?

The English curriculum: What experiences do children need?

The National Curriculum (DfE, 2013) currently favours technical learning approaches to English. Mastery of certain technical aspects of language (grammar and spelling) is a component required for successful literacy in the present context. Component elements of literacy are more easily measured and assessed, and these are arguably the less important aspects of English (Goodman, 2013). There is also the risk that technical components of language are taught in decontextualised ways. The isolation of literacy learning from meaningful practice is problematic for all children, but it is more acute for those groups of pupils who are socially disengaged from reading and writing. The acquisition of school literacies can easily become purposeless and de-motivating because of a failure to provide writing opportunities that make links between school literacy and language in a social and cultural context relevant to pupils (Bearne, 2017; Cremin et al., 2015). The good English subject leader knows that language acquisition is much more than the learning of isolated skills, and they know that language is influenced by social practice and culture.

Hall and Harding (2003) remind us that the effective teacher of literacy provides pupils with a 'balance between the direct teaching of skills and more holistic approaches' to English teaching (2003: 3). Ofsted (2009) articulate the view that effective teachers of English need to reflect on their own philosophy of teaching, and 'decide what English should look like as a subject in the 21st century' in order to successfully 'provide a ... dynamic and productive curriculum ... that reflects the changing nature of society and pupils' literacy needs' (2009: 54).

Sound pedagogic evidence should inform the subject leader's decisions about practice and provide clear underlying principles to move practice on in English. As the subject leader it will be important to make the right decisions about teaching approaches and ensure that you can confidently support colleagues to embrace new teaching methods. Chapter 6 provides further detail about how good English subject leaders approach pedagogical decision making and the following texts are recommended as essential reading for different aspects of English teaching. They are written by respected experts in the field and will provide both subject knowledge and pedagogic understanding to inform the decisions you make.

Early reading – decoding and encoding

Dombey, H. and colleagues in the UKLA (2010) *Teaching Reading: What the evidence says.* Leicester: UKLA.

Goouch, K. and Lambirth, A. (eds) (2007) *Understanding Phonics and the Teaching of Reading: Critical perspectives.* UK: Open University Press.

Jolliffe, W. and Waugh, D., with Carss, A. (eds) (2015) *Teaching Systematic Synthetic Phonics in Primary Schools.* 2nd edn. London: Sage.

Martin, T. (2010) *Talk for Spelling.* Leicester: UKLA.

Reading comprehension

Clarke, P. J., Truelove, E., Hulme, C. and Snowling, M. J. (2014) *Developing Reading Comprehension.* Chichester: John Wiley.

Horton, S., Beattie, L. and Bingle, B. (2015) *Lessons in Teaching Reading Comprehension in Primary Schools.* London: Sage.

Oakhill, J., Cain, K. and Elbro, C. (2015) *Understanding and Teaching Reading Comprehension.* Oxon: Routledge.

Tennent, W., Reedy, D., Hobsbaum, A. and Gamble, N. (2016) *Guided Readers – Layers of Meaning.* London: UCL Institution of Education Press.

Picture books and visual image

Bearne, E. and Wolstencroft, H. (2007) *Visual Approaches to Teaching Writing.* London: Sage.

Roche, M. (2015) *Developing Children's Critical Thinking through Picturebooks.* Oxon: Routledge.

Salisbury, M. and Styles, M. (2012) *Children's Picturebooks: The art of visual storytelling.* London: Laurence King.

Writing

Chamberlain, L. (2016) *Inspiring Writing in Primary Schools*. London: Sage.

Graham, J. and Kelly, A. (2009) *Writing Under Control*. London: David Fulton.

Myhill, D., Jones, S., Watson, A. and Lines, H. (2013) 'Playful explicitness with grammar: A pedagogy for writing.' In: *Literacy*, 47 (2), 103–11.

Grammar, punctuation and spelling

Horton, S. and Bingle, B. (2014) *Lessons in Teaching Grammar in Primary Schools*. London: Sage.

Reedy, D. and Bearne, E. (2013) *Teaching Grammar Effectively in Primary Schools*. Leicester: UKLA.

Waugh, D., Warner, C. and Waugh, R. (2016) *Teaching Grammar, Punctuation and Spelling in Primary Schools*. 2nd edn. London: Sage.

Talk

Barnes, D. (2008) 'Exploratory talk for learning.' In: Mercer, N. and Hodgkinson, S. (eds), *Exploring Talk in School*. London: Sage.

Gross, J. (2013) *Time to Talk*. Oxon: Routledge.

Mercer, N. and Dawes, L. (2008) 'The value of exploratory talk.' In: Mercer, N. and Hodgkinson, S. (eds), *Exploring Talk in School*. London: Sage.

General English

Brien, J. (2012) *Teaching Primary English*. London: Sage.

Cremin, T. (2015) *Teaching English Creatively*. Oxon: Routledge.

Mallett, M. (2016) *A Guided Reader to Early Years and Primary English*. London: Routledge.

Wyse, D., Jones, H., Bradford, H. and Wolpert, M. A. (2013) *Teaching English, Language and Literacy*. Oxon: Routledge.

Professional development and enrichment

As well as ensuring your own personal professional development through reading, it is important to regularly exchange ideas and practice with other teachers. One of the best ways to seek support in achieving curriculum goals and developing pedagogy is to work with other, like-minded English subject leaders. Such groups might already exist in your geographical area. Clusters of schools tend to work closely together to innovate practice and share experience across schools. Action research projects can also benefit from the impetus of joint working. Piloting new teaching methods and reflecting on impact in a collegiate way can also help invigorate subject development. You may also find this support through your local authority (LA), with some LAs retaining subject-specific advisory teachers.

Professional associations

Another good way to ensure that your practice remains invigorated, and your subject knowledge up to date, is through membership to subject associations. Below are four of the best journals that consistently include useful articles on English research and classroom practice:

1. *English in Education* (NATE journal)
2. *The Primary English Magazine* (NATE journal)
3. *Literacy* (UKLA journal)
4. *English 4–11* (UKLA journal)

United Kingdom Literacy Association (UKLA) membership provides access to the research journal *Literacy*. This journal is highly regarded by teachers, researchers and advisors of English, and it is guaranteed to keep you abreast of current thought and practice. UKLA membership also provides access to the practitioner-focused magazine *English 4–11*. This publication is filled with creative approaches and action research projects that will inspire and support the development of your own school's pedagogic practice.

References

Alexander, R. J. (ed.) (2009) *Children, their World, their Education: Final Report and Recommendations of the Cambridge Primary Review*. London: Routledge.

Beard, R. (2011) 'The origins, evaluations and implications of the National Literacy Strategy in England.' In: Goodwyn, A. and Fuller, C. (eds), *The Great Literacy Debate: A critical response to the Literacy Strategy and the Framework for English*. London: Routledge.

Bearne, E. (2017) 'Assessing children's written texts: A framework for equity.' *Literacy*, 51 (2), 74–83.

Becta (2010) *Digital Literacy: Teaching critical thinking for our digital world*. Coventry: Becta.

Beverton, S. (2001) 'Whatever happened to primary English knowledge and understanding?' *Evaluation and Research in Education*, 15 (3), 128–35.

Cambridge Assessment Review (2013) 'What is literacy? An investigation into definitions of English as a subject and the relationship between English, literacy and being literate.' A research report commissioned by Cambridge Assessment.

Clark, M. M. (2014) *Learning to be Literate: Insights from research for policy and practice*. Birmingham: Glendale Education.

Cremin, T., Mottram, M., Collins, F., Powell, S. and Drury, R. (2015) *Researching Literacy Lives: Building communities between home and school*. Abingdon, Oxon: Routledge.

Dearing, R. (1994) *The National Curriculum and its Assessment: Final report*. London: School Curriculum and Assessment Authority.

Deeqa, J. and Dugdale, G. (2012) 'Literacy: State of the nation. A picture of literacy in the UK today.' The National Literacy Trust. Available at: https://files.eric.ed.gov/fulltext/ED541407.pdf [accessed 10 March 2018].

Department for Education (DfE) (2013) 'English programmes of study: Key Stages 1 and 2 National Curriculum in England.' Available at: https://assets.publishing.service.gov.uk/government/uploads/system/uploads/attachment_data/file/335186/PRIMARY_national_curriculum_-_English_220714.pdf [accessed 3 July 2018].

Gee, J. P. (2000) 'The New Literacy Studies; from "socially situated" to the work of the social.' In: Barton, D., Hamilton, M. and Ivanic, R. (eds), *Situated Literacies: Reading and writing in context*. London: Routledge, 180–96.

Goodman, K. S., Calfee, R. C. and Goodman, Y. M. (2013) *Whose Knowledge Counts in Government Literacy Policies?: Why expertise matters*. London: Routledge.

Goodwyn, A. and Fuller, C. (eds) (2011) *The Great Literacy Debate: A critical response to the Literacy Strategy and the Framework for English*. London: Routledge.

Gove, M. (2014) 'Education Secretary Michael Gove's speech to Brighton College.' Available at: www.gov.uk/government/speeches/education-secretary-michael-goves-speech-to-brighton-college [accessed 10 February 2015].

Hall, K. and Harding, A. (2003) 'A systematic review of effective literacy teaching in the 4 to 14 age range of mainstream schooling.' In: *Research Evidence in Education Library*. London: EPPI-Centre, Social Science Research Unit, Institute of Education.

Holbrook, D. (1961) *English for Maturity*. Cambridge: Cambridge University Press.

Laugharne, J. (2007) 'The personal, the community and society: A response to Section 1.' In: Ellis, V., Fox, C. and Street, B. (eds), *Rethinking English in Schools*. London: Continuum.

Limbrick, L. and Aikman, M. (2005) 'Literacy and English.' A discussion document prepared for the Ministry of Education, Faculty of Education, University of Auckland.

Meek, M. (1991) *On Being Literate*. London: Bodley Head.

Moss, G. (2017) 'Assessment, accountability and the literacy curriculum: Reimagining the future in the light of the past.' *Literacy*, 51 (2), 56–64.

Office for Standards in Education, Children's Services and Skills (Ofsted) (2009) *English at the Crossroads*. Manchester: Ofsted.

Street, B. (2003) 'What's "new" in New Literacy Studies? Critical approaches to literacy in theory and practice.' *Current Issues in Comparative Education*, 5 (2), 77–91.

Twist, L., Sizmur, J., Bartlett, S. and Lynn, L. (2012) 'PIRLS 2011: Reading achievement in England.' DfE. Available at: www.nfer.ac.uk/publications/PRTZ01/PRTZ01.pdf [accessed 10 March 2018].

United Nations Educational Scientific and Cultural Organization (UNESCO) (2006) 'Understandings of literacy.' In: *Education for All: Literacies for life*. Paris: UNESCO Publishing, 147–59.

United Nations Educational Scientific and Cultural Organization (UNESCO) (2015) *Education for All: 2000–2015: Achievements and challenges*. Paris: UNESCO Publishing.

Waters, M. and Martin, T. (1999) *Coordinating English at Key Stage 2: The subject leader's handbook*. London: Falmer Press.

A shared vision for English

Lisa Baldwin

This chapter will explore how schools decide on their vision for a subject and how this vision evolves into school policy. Questions will be asked about what makes a good English policy: what needs to be included and what is its key purpose? There will be discussion about how to move an existing policy forward by considering what works well and how it is interpreted by the whole staff. There will also be practical advice for rewriting a policy and its core components. Suggestions will be made about how to involve teaching staff, and how to report policy to a range of audiences to ensure your ambitions for English are realised.

Vision for English

To write a vision for English is to create and define what you aspire to achieve as the leader of English in your school. The vision should be ambitious for all pupils and in accord with both the school's values and your own philosophy of English teaching.

As a trainee teacher, or a recently qualified teacher, you will have begun to assume your own professional identity. Professional identity is crucial to being able to make decisions and judgements about teaching and learning. During the course of their career teachers develop the ability to become pragmatic practitioners: practitioners who are true to their values (Catling, 2013; Goodson and Gill, 2014). This growing sense of professional judgement comes from thinking critically about education and developing working practices that support personal philosophical views about teaching.

As the English subject leader, your values and beliefs about English will shape both the kind of vision you intend to achieve and the means through which you implement it. These values will underpin the school curriculum that you shape and determine pupils' learning experiences under your subject leadership.

Define your vision for English

Davies and Brighouse (2008) and Fullan (2003) identify the link between effective leadership and passion. With this in mind, the effective subject leader needs to consider what it is about English that constitutes their passion. Below are some questions that might frame your thinking and provide responses that help to shape your vision statement.

 Defining your vision

- What is English? What is literacy? What is the difference?
- Are there short-term aims that meet primary curriculum requirements and long-term aims that are important beyond primary schooling?
- What is imperative about English learning?
- What knowledge do you want to impart to pupils?
- How do you envisage English learning for pupils at your school?
- What do you want the pupils doing, saying and feeling about English?
- How do you want the school staff to deliver English teaching?
- What is the pupil demographic and community context for language learning?
- How is this important and what does it bring to the whole-school vision?

When starting to shape your ideas it can be helpful to look at examples of school English vision statements. Vision statements can also be the 'rationale' or 'philosophy' statement in a policy document. Considering statements from other schools can help you reflect on whether the content is in accord with your own beliefs.

 Consider the two vision statements for English below:

At **primary school A** we believe that literacy is an essential life skill. Success in English enables children to communicate effectively at school, at home and in the wider world, leading to improved life opportunities. The skills of listening, speaking, reading and writing enable children to organise and express their own thoughts and to access the knowledge and ideas of others. These skills, together with confidence in the use of ICT, are increasingly necessary in today's world. In addition to this, the ability to respond to literature, at a personal and aesthetic level, enriches our children's lives.

At **primary school B** we believe that all pupils should be taught English at a level appropriate to their age and ability. We consider it important to ensure a progression of literacy skills and provide opportunities for children to develop and apply their knowledge and understanding of the English language in many forms.

- What does each vision statement reveal to you about the values and beliefs of the school?
- What language is used and to what effect?
- What is included in the statement and what is omitted?
- What assumptions do these inclusions and omissions lead us to make about the school each vision represents?

Firstly, let's consider vision statement A. This statement refers to literacy as an 'essential life-skill', making immediate reference to the value of English beyond school life. The statement then goes on to illustrate a range of contexts where English is of importance. This further embeds the idea that school A's vision of English teaching goes beyond children doing well in their school literacy lessons. The key skills of 'listening, speaking, reading and writing' are listed as important to a child's ability to communicate personal viewpoints and opinions. This indicates that there is a clear understanding of how these three strands of English are interrelated. The final sentence alludes to the cultural and aesthetic nature of language learning. The vision statement strongly conveys the principles that English is a subject important to deep, life-long learning and is key to a cultured understanding of language as an art form.

In contrast, statement B defines the vision and purpose of English teaching solely within the pupils' school life. Language such as 'level', 'age-appropriate' and 'progression' echoes the vocabulary associated with government policy. Arguably, statement B offers a more realistic vision for English in a school, compared to the lofty ideals of statement A. However, it is important to consider if statement B provides a long-term ambition for the school to strive to achieve, or if this is something that might already have been achieved.

Fullan (2003) stresses the importance of vision communicating a 'moral imperative' to spur continuous, transformational improvement (Fullan, 2003: 29). Fullan describes four levels of 'moral imperative' that categorise change at different levels. He describes change at:

- an individual level;
- a school level;
- a regional level;
- a societal level.

He relates effective leadership (leadership that makes significant impact) with the higher levels of change.

If we relate these levels of change to the vision statements for schools A and B we can see that they operate at different levels. Statement B articulates the desire to make a difference within the first two levels (individual and school levels), whilst statement A strives to articulate a desire to teach the children skills useful to school and wider society (regional and societal levels).

- Which of the two vision statements do you consider to be the most inspirational?
- Which of the two vision statements do you consider to be the most realistic for schools to achieve?
- Which vision statement is nearest to the government's Purpose of Study, as outlined in the National Curriculum (see below)?

English has a pre-eminent place in education and in society. A high-quality education in English will teach pupils to speak and write fluently so that they can communicate their ideas and emotions to others and through their reading and listening, others can communicate with them. Through reading in particular, pupils have a chance to develop culturally, emotionally, intellectually, socially and spiritually. Literature, especially, plays a key role in such development. Reading also enables pupils both to acquire knowledge and to build on what they already know. All the skills of language are essential to participating fully as a member of society; pupils, therefore, who do not learn to speak, read and write fluently and confidently are effectively disenfranchised.

(DfE, 2013: 3)

- Does the wording in the Purpose of Study change your view of the two vision statements?
- Do current assessment and accountability processes in English teaching embrace the sentiments of the Purpose of Study, or is there a tension?
- Which is more likely to spur effective change?

Draw on your critique of statements A and B and begin to define the values you want to express in your vision. When you have drafted your vision, consider where there are similarities, differences and tensions between your own views, government policy and vision statements A and B.

Bush (2011) notes that the articulation of a school leader's vision is unlikely to be radically different from any other school. Bush's (2011) concern is that because the government specifies curriculum content and purpose, school leaders are unable to make any significant attempt to shape their own, unique vision. As much as possible the English vision *should* be specific to your school and it *should* be unique to the children you work with. It will be important to remember that a vision for English should have a longevity that will extend beyond existing statutory requirements. Statutory curriculum content will always change over time, but if your vision reflects core values about English teaching it should withstand most variations to official curriculum content.

Vision and leadership: Getting started and getting others involved

Effective leaders engage with staff to create energy about English teaching (Davies and Brighouse, 2008). An autocratic, commanding leader is likely to impose their vision on a staff team, and in some circumstances this can be the best approach to improve the quality of teaching. In the instance of a newly appointed, relatively recent member of staff, it is unlikely that such an approach would be suitable. It is better to encourage staff to commit to aspirational goals for English through involving them in the vision process.

Whether you are redefining an existing vision and policy statement for English, or writing from scratch, it is important to invite views and responses from other staff members. Share your own draft vision statement or revisit the existing statement inherited from a previous post-holder. Adopt an approach that enables the whole-school staff to contribute their ideas. It is important to remember to include support staff, as they are often involved in the teaching of English: hearing readers, delivering intervention programmes and providing general support in the classroom.

 ## What do good subject leaders do to involve others?

- Create a staff working-wall that provides informal opportunities for staff to add their own statements about the purpose of English;
- Lead a staff meeting that raises questions for staff to consider about the purpose and vision for English;
- Allow time for staff to discuss differences of opinions and explore alternative viewpoints;
- Group staff contributions into themes and highlight common language important to the school;

- Consider similarities and differences between contributions. Use the range of contributions to shape and refine a statement;
- Shape a draft school statement and share it with the whole staff for comment;
- Make any further refinements as necessary.

Your vision statement for English is key in providing a rationale for changes in practice. It is also the means to motivate staff towards a common goal and purpose. One factor determining whether or not you achieve your goals will be how successfully you can motivate staff to make the relevant changes to their practice. The collegiate process described above will lead to greater, whole-school staff ownership of the vision and a collective will to achieve it.

From vision to strategy: A policy for English

After the vision statement has been devised, you should next write (or revise) the school English policy. An English policy is not a mandatory requirement but it is recommended. The purpose of the policy is to provide guidance on approaches the school will adopt in order to achieve the vision. The vision defines *what* the school aims to achieve, and the policy defines *how* you will achieve it. Documenting the strategy for English teaching aims to ensure a consistent whole-school approach to English teaching. The policy will serve as a guide for teachers, focusing on the planning, teaching and assessment of English. However, the intended audience is often much wider, encompassing parents and carers, governors and support staff. School inspection teams are also usually interested in viewing a policy for mathematics and English.

In order that a policy remains an effective guide it should be reviewed on a regular basis, usually every one to three years. This is to ensure it is updated to reflect current educational practice and acknowledge any changes to the curriculum or government policy.

Stages to policy writing or rewriting

Prior to writing the policy it will be important to review current practice in your school. This is essential whether you are revising the school policy or writing one from scratch. Before you can begin to revise the policy guidance you need to gain knowledge of:

- current pupil attainment and achievement in English;
- how teachers currently plan for English;
- any schemes and approaches adopted;
- resources available to staff.

To gain this knowledge you need to draw on school self-evaluation data, familiarise yourself with staff planning, engage with staff and pupil views and review English resources. An audit of current practice is a good place to start and this is likely to focus on aspects of English that require improvement and changes in practice.

Talking to staff and pupils will help you to gain a picture of English across the school. Once the current picture has been understood, the aspects requiring change need to be defined in your policy, ready for implementation.

Case study: Moving forward with an inherited English policy

Hampden Gurney Church of England Primary School, Central London

Hannah was recently appointed to the post of English subject leader. Her first steps were to try to work out what needed doing to move English forward. Hannah inherited an existing English action plan from the previous post-holder and she also had direction from the head teacher. Both sources of information directed her to consider how to progress the teaching of reading comprehension. Before she could devise what to do to progress this aspect of English she first needed to understand teaching approaches across the school and discover potential areas for improvement. To do this Hannah conducted an audit of resources and practice.

Hannah's audit was conducted through formal and informal conversations with staff. Staff meetings provided a formal setting for whole-school discussion. Hannah also approached staff individually. Based in a Year 4 class, Hannah had limited understanding of what happened in Key Stage 1. She therefore sought to find out the current approaches to reading comprehension across the school. Staff supported Hannah by sharing their understanding and resources with her. Hannah listened and took on board their opinions and experience, and collected together the resources and tools they used to plan and assess reading comprehension.

The audit process gave Hannah new information about guided reading practice. It gave her knowledge beyond her own class experience and it provided feedback confirming the school's need to embrace a new, consistent approach. During her individual conversations she was able to suggest the new ideas she was thinking of introducing. This gave time for staff to hear about proposed changes and they were able to raise issues and ask questions. Hannah actively listened to staff views and was able to foresee issues that may have prevented policy change being realised in every classroom.

Equipped with this information Hannah was ready to devise a way forward for the whole school. She knew what changes to policy she would make and had a better idea of how to support teachers to adopt the new approach. Her initial collaboration with the staff team ensured that she had them on board from the beginning. They understood the need for policy change and were ready to work with Hannah to implement it.

Case study learning points

✓ **Conduct an audit.** The subject leader needed to widen her knowledge in order to have a full understanding of the resources and approaches adopted by teachers throughout the whole school.

✓ **Use formal and informal approaches.** The subject leader made use of staff meetings and informal conversations. Both methods were fruitful approaches to gather information and discuss ways forward.

✓ **Seek consensus.** Hannah's approach to rewriting the policy for reading comprehension is important to note. She sought consensus and evidence for change right from the beginning.

The case study school already ensured excellent pupil outcomes for English, yet despite their success the school was not complacent. Hannah benefited from working in a culture of improvement: one that embraced change. In some schools the practice evident in classrooms can be far removed from the rhetoric in the policy statement (Waters and Martin, 1999). A lack of connection between written procedures in the policy document and the reality of actions undertaken by staff will result in failure. If actions do not change in the classroom, then policy is not going to transform pupil learning or outcomes. So, how do good subject leaders work to ensure policy effects change?

Steps to successful policy change

- Limit policy change to one or two aspects of English. This will make policy change more purposeful and more manageable. The focus should link to where the school's development areas lie – identified through data monitoring processes.
- Review and audit current practice in the focus area of teaching and learning. This will determine what practice currently exists across the school.

- Understand what is working and what is not working. Canvass staff opinion as well as examining your own perception of the issues.
- Use your knowledge of high-quality emerging practice to propose potential ideas for new teaching approaches.
- Continue to communicate and collaborate with staff whilst you shape the new policy statement.

The success of your policy depends on your colleagues being able to implement the changes. By reviewing practice and rewriting policy through the suggested 'steps to successful policy change', it is more likely that your policy changes will have a positive impact on teaching practice.

Sometimes new policy approaches are imposed on schools, through changes at government level, but a good subject leader is also proactive about introducing new, emerging practice as a way to improve English teaching. New policy approaches, whether imposed or self-instigated, should be discussed, possibly trialled and always supported by professional development.

Policy: What needs to be included?

The English policy will detail the procedures and practices that underpin all aspects of English teaching: clarifying the school's approaches and methods. The policy needs to articulate the school's aims and objectives for reading and writing before unpicking how these aims will be achieved.

Possible aims for reading

A. To develop a culture of enjoyment of reading across the school
B. To enable all children to read accurately, fluently and with expression

The two example aims above link to National Curriculum outcomes but they are broad, generic statements, relevant across the whole school. Your policy does not need to include everything from the National Curriculum document but it can be a good source of reference when determining what you want to achieve for each aspect of English, particularly when considering progression across the school.

Once you have articulated the school's aims you then need to identify the procedures, practices and teaching approaches that will support them in being achieved. Practice should embody high-quality pedagogic approaches, proven to support pupil learning in reading and writing. Below is an example of how policy builds from the two suggested aims for reading, defining *what* the policy aims to achieve and *how* the school intends to do this.

Example policy for statements for reading for pleasure

The following policy statements are examples of how you might detail the procedures, practices and teaching approaches that underpin reading aim A.

Aim A: To develop a culture of enjoyment in reading across the school

- Children throughout the school will read a range of text types, genres and styles. (You might have a curriculum overview that provides information on texts used across the school.)
- There are regular, timetabled opportunities for teachers to read aloud to their class, sharing a book for enjoyment.
- Teachers will plan opportunities for children to engage in informal, child-led discussion about their reading (book-talk).
- Teachers will provide planned opportunities for independent reading from a book of the child's choice.
- There will be regular, timetabled class visits to the school library.
- Teachers will create exciting book corners in their classroom and provide opportunities for the children to use the area for both quiet, independent reading and social interaction.
- Regular rotation of shared display areas will include the celebration of whole-school reading for pleasure and children's responses to texts.
- Author visits and whole-school reading and writing days are planned to celebrate and inspire reading and writing in the school.
- World Book Day is celebrated every year.
- There are planned activities that support communities of readers (book clubs for pupils, book clubs for teachers, events that develop relationships with librarians, parents and carers).

 Consider the policy examples for reading aim A:

- Which statements focus on defining regular, planned teaching and learning opportunities that teachers must ensure their class receives?
- Which statements focus on the delivery of evidence-based teaching approaches?

- Which statements focus on the learning environment and access to resources?
- Which statements focus on wider, whole-school curriculum enrichment activities?
- Finally, drawing on your own experience, can you think of anything else that would be relevant to supporting reading for pleasure?

Example policy for statements for reading accurately, fluently and with expression

The following policy statements are examples of how you might detail the procedures, practices and teaching approaches that underpin reading aim B.

Aim B: To enable all children to read accurately, fluently and with expression

- Phonics is taught daily across Key Stage 1. (Include details of any phonic scheme the school uses, differentiation, lesson structure and frequency of teaching.)
- Children are taught the phonics skills required to decode unfamiliar words by blending known phoneme/grapheme correspondences.
- Children are supported to develop sight vocabulary of high frequency words.
- Regular planned provision of shared and guided reading will provide opportunities for the teacher to develop children's regard for punctuation and model how to read with expression.
- Regular planned provision of shared and guided reading will provide opportunities for the teacher to model strategies that encourage children to tackle new vocabulary through the application of phonic skills, and syntactic and semantic strategies.
- Reading schemes and book banding approaches support children's progression in word reading and comprehension.
- Guidance is available to parents and carers to support pupils' reading experiences at home.
- Home–school reading link-books enable a shared understanding of the child as a reader.

 Consider the policy examples for reading aim B:

- Which statements focus on defining regular, planned teaching and learning opportunities that teachers should ensure their class receives?
- Which statements focus on the delivery of evidence-based teaching approaches?

- Which statements focus on word reading?
- Which statements focus on reading for meaning?
- Finally, drawing on your own experience, can you think of any other practice relevant to supporting this aim?

Possible aims for writing

A. To enable children to write fluently and develop competence in spelling and handwriting
B. To develop pupils' understanding of how good writers use techniques and use a range of language features effectively in their own writing

The following policy statements are examples of how you might achieve the two example aims for writing, detailing the procedures, practices and teaching approaches that underpin the writing aims.

Example policy statements: Write fluently and develop competence in spelling and handwriting

The following policy statements are examples of how you might detail the procedures, practices and teaching approaches that underpin writing aim A.

Aim A: To enable children to write fluently and develop competence in spelling and handwriting

- The teaching of spelling is integral to daily phonics sessions in Key Stage 1. Teachers will provide children with regular opportunities to practise and apply their encoding skills.
- Children are encouraged to apply their phonics knowledge when reading and spelling new words across the curriculum, throughout the age-phases.
- Throughout the school children are taught to learn an increasingly wide range of words from memory. Teaching approaches include visual, kinaesthetic and mnemonic strategies, and recognising word analogies.
- The learning of spelling rules is supported through opportunities to investigate words and recognise patterns in spelling.
- Pupils are taught to use dictionaries and other aids to support vocabulary, word choice and spelling.
- Teachers provide opportunities for pupils to proofread and edit their writing, with a focus on spelling.
- Writing opportunities encourage creativity and ambitious use of vocabulary.

- Teacher modelling will demonstrate cursive script and pupils will have regular opportunities to practise joined writing.
- Classroom environments will display word banks to support the learning of spellings, e.g. high frequency words or vocabulary related to topics.

Consider the policy examples for writing aim A:

- Which statements focus on defining regular, planned teaching and learning opportunities that teachers must ensure their class receives?
- Which statements focus on the delivery of evidence-based teaching approaches? Which statements focus on the learning environment provision?
- Which statements would you need more detail about if you were a new member of staff at this school?
- Finally, can you think of any other practice relevant to supporting this aim?

Example policy for statements for writing: Grammatical language features

The following policy statements are examples of how you might detail the procedures, practices and teaching approaches that underpin writing aim B.

Aim B: Understand a range of grammatical language features and be able to use them effectively in their writing

- Teachers make use of high-quality texts to teach language features and provide models of effective writing in a range of styles.
- Children are taught the features of a range of writing forms and genres. (Include any curriculum plan with an overview of writing genres.)
- Grammar and punctuation are introduced within the context of writing lessons and planning will make clear connections between the aspect of grammar and punctuation being taught, and the learning focus for the writing.
- Quality texts will provide teachers with opportunities to discuss how good writers use grammar and punctuation to create certain effects that impact on the reader.
- Teacher-led demonstration writing will emphasise how good writers review and edit their work, drawing attention to language choices, and aspects of grammar and punctuation.

- Teachers will consistently use grammar terms in accordance with the National Curriculum guidance to support the children's knowledge of terminology.

Other important policy issues to consider

The interdependent nature of reading, writing, and speaking and listening means it is important to highlight the links in your policy. The example policy statements reflect the importance of integrating the teaching of grammar, spelling, handwriting and phonics into meaningful reading and writing contexts. Arguably, to ensure your policy will provide consistency across the school, there might also be a need to exemplify some aspects in greater detail. Your policy might therefore include specific information under the headings of phonics, spelling and handwriting. Other important policy links to consider are as follows:

Cross-curricular planning. As well as helping to alleviate pressure on the teaching timetable, planned opportunities for cross-curricular activities provide authentic contexts for reading, writing, and speaking and listening activities.

ICT. Opportunities for the pupils to use technology in literacy learning will serve to increase pupil engagement and are highly beneficial to pupils with particular barriers to literacy.

Home–school links. You may want to encourage parents and carers to support children's literacy at home. Effective communication systems for reading at home, helping with homework and involvement during Book Week can really assist in this.

Intervention programmes. You may wish to detail how literacy intervention programmes are delivered in the school and list any materials and resources that underpin intervention teaching.

Assessment. You might include details of summative assessments in English and how this will be reported to parents. It is also useful to summarise the formative assessment processes that are used to monitor pupil progress and inform the English planning and teaching.

It may be helpful to append documentation that illustrates or supports teaching and learning in English. School planning overviews, curriculum maps, schemes of work, planning templates, details of resources and intervention programmes are all useful. Finally, you should date the policy document and record how often the policy will be reviewed.

Making policy links

It is important to remember that the English policy does not stand in isolation: it needs to be in line with other school policies and read in conjunction. Documentation that might overlap with the English policy includes assessment, marking and feedback, Additional Educational Needs, and teaching and learning. Of course there is no requirement for schools to have all of these policy documents and the titles may well vary, but knowledge of policy guidance that already exists in your school will ensure that you consider any overlapping points and avoid differences.

Communicating your policy

It is widely understood that parents and carers have significant influence on a child's learning. Professor John Hattie found that 'parent engagement in the educational development of their children improves attainment more than any other single factor' (Lucas, 2010: 1). It is therefore highly important for schools to communicate their way of working to parents and carers.

Policy will often appear on the school website, but effective communication involves much more than just making a document public. Governors can play an important role in transmitting information and they can support you in communicating the English policy to parents.

Some schools have a parent council, or forum, which enables parents to meet, share ideas, hear news and feed back to the school. Parent councils provide a valuable, regular forum for parents to have a voice within the school and to support the school.

Presenting your policy to the governors should be an important part of the policy being understood throughout the school community. It is likely that the governing body will review all policy changes as part of a review cycle. In some cases you may be invited to talk about the policy changes.

* What are the key elements (or changes) in the English policy that parents and governors need to be informed of?
* What mechanisms exist in your school to communicate with governors and parents? This might include governor working groups, individual governor roles and responsibilities, Parent–Teacher Associations, Parent Councils or Forums, and wider community forums and groups.

(Based on National Governors' Association (NGA) guidance, 2016)

Personally inviting parents into school for a structured discussion, a learning walk or other opportunities for them to see how children are being taught English is a good way to build understanding. Offering these opportunities will help to establish better relationships and secure parent and carer support for the school's policies.

Reporting to wider audiences

Policies might also need to be presented to wider audiences, such as the local authority, an academy trust board or an Ofsted inspection team. In such instances talking the audience through your 'steps to successful policy change' will enable you to communicate a clear rationale for your policy and ensure you have adopted an evidence-based approach to the practices within the policy. If you are clear on all of these steps, then reporting to any audience should be an opportunity, rather than something to fear.

References

Bush, T. (2011) *Theories of Educational Leadership & Management*. 4th edn. London: Sage.

Catling, S. (2013) 'Teachers' perspectives on curriculum making in Primary Geography in England.' *The Curriculum Journal*, 24 (3), 427–453.

Davies, B. and Brighouse, T. (eds) (2008) *Passionate Leadership in Education*. London: Sage.

Department for Education (DfE) (2013) *English Programmes of Study: Key Stages 1 and 2, National Curriculum in England*. London: DfE.

Fullan, M. (2003) *The Moral Imperative of School Leadership*. London: Sage.

Goodson, I. and Gill, S. (2014) *Critical Narrative as Pedagogy*. London: Bloomsbury.

Lucas, B. (2010) 'The impact of parent engagement on learner success: A digest of research for parents and teachers.' *Research into Practice*, Centre for Real-World Learning and the University of Winchester, Spring, 1. Available at: www. thehampshireschoolchelsea.co.uk/userfiles/files/For%20Parents/Parental% 20Engagement/The-Impact-of-Parental-Engagement-on-Learner-Suc cess613583.pdf [accessed 20 January 2018].

National Governors' Association (NGA) (2016) 'Knowing your school – engaging parents.' 2nd edn. Briefing note 3, NGA. Available at: www.nga.org.uk/News/ NGA-News/May-Sept-2016/Knowing-your-school-Engaging-Parents.aspx [accessed 4 July 2018].

Waters, M. and Martin, T. (1999) *Coordinating English at Key Stage 2*. London: Falmer Press.

Documentation supporting English

Lisa Baldwin

This chapter will explore the themes across school documentation to support understanding of how priorities are established both at a strategic, whole-school level and class level. It will further explore the processes through which English documentation and planning develop. Examples of action planning will include a school's self-evaluation and school development plan, together with the subject leader's action plan. There will be discussion about identifying areas for development and a case study will exemplify one school's paper trail.

Key documents and the relationship between them

In order to lead English effectively the subject leader needs to consider three key areas: curriculum development, staff development and children's progress. These areas cannot be considered in isolation, as all three aspects are interrelated. The success of pupil learning in English is dependent upon the quality of teaching they receive and the effectiveness of the curriculum in engaging the learner. In turn, the quality of teaching is reliant upon a teacher's ability to plan and deliver English, utilising their understanding of subject development and pedagogy. The ongoing improvement of subject knowledge and pedagogy is only brought about through professional development opportunities.

Figure 5.1 serves as an attempt to capture the many processes and documents that inform school planning procedures. The process is a cycle of actions that begin with the school's own evaluation of its successes and areas for development.

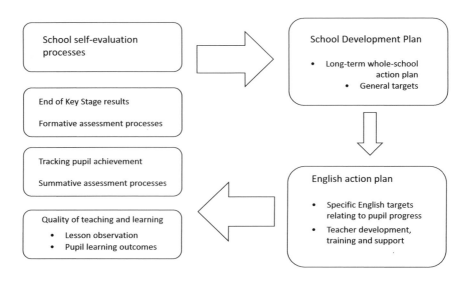

Figure 5.1 Overview of the school plans, processes and procedures

School improvement and school self-evaluation

The school self-evaluation (SSE) process is a school's own assessment of its effectiveness: an ongoing pursuit that is the responsibility of the head teacher and the senior leadership team. The SSE process seeks to evaluate a range of indicators such as pupil achievement and attainment, quality of teaching and learning, and curriculum design. The SSE process makes use of internal and external monitoring data to evaluate where the school believes itself to be in terms of the quality of educational provision. Ultimately, the SSE process serves to identify where the school needs to develop and grow in order to improve.

The School Development Plan (SDP) is a long-term, whole-school plan that encompasses a wide range of planned actions covering every aspect of the school improvement journey. The SDP (sometimes also known as the School Improvement Plan or SIP) draws from the SSE process and identifies targets and actions needed to address identified areas for improvement. As well as defining teaching and learning goals, the SDP will encompass diverse targets beyond the curriculum, such as plans for the school building, provision for equipping the outside environment, planning for significant resource spending, development of wider community activities and future staffing plans.

Monitoring processes enable schools to analyse pupil achievement and attainment as part of the whole-school self-evaluation process. Online database platforms currently provide attainment data for schools, detailing results for each new academic year, enabling evaluation against data from previous years, and comparison against statistically similar schools. The statistical information provided is used on an annual basis to evaluate effectiveness and determine a school's actions and priorities. The use of data to inform strategic planning is discussed in greater detail in Chapter 11.

As well as the school's monitoring information, statutory regulations and guidance from outside bodies (such as government legislation and OfSTED inspection reports) will also impact on this whole-school planning document. Within the SDP strategic goals for English will be outlined in the broadest sense. Below is an example extract of a school inspection summary report from OfSTED:

The school is not yet an outstanding school because:

* Too few pupils make more than expected progress.
* Teaching does not encourage enough pupils to deepen learning, including the most able and least able.

The summary statement does not mention English specifically, but the reference is to pupil performance in reading, writing and mathematics.

 Defining the actions for improvement:

* Consider the two statements from the school's Ofsted report.
* How do you think this report will influence English priorities in the school?
* What aspects of teaching and learning does the school need to develop?

Whole-school action planning and general curriculum targets

Having considered monitoring information and other information about pupil progress, school priorities are agreed by school leadership teams (SLTs) and then refined to become whole-school targets. Targets are likely to include areas of development deemed important for *all* children in the school, as well as additional targets to meet the needs of *groups* of children. Targets might include goals for specific groupings of pupils defined by gender, ethnicity, disadvantaged pupil groups, year group trends or community-specific goals, and this is usually determined through scrutiny of the performance data.

The SDP takes the Ofsted feedback, along with the school's own monitoring information and data analysis, and clarifies the target more specifically within the strategic plan.

Table 5.1 Extract from the School Development Plan

Key priorities for pupil outcomes:

1a) Increase pupil progress and attainment in reading, writing and mathematics

1b) Increase the percentage of disadvantaged pupils achieving age-related expectations in reading, writing and mathematics

1c) Increase the percentage of pupils exceeding expected progress in reading, writing and mathematics

Key priorities for teaching and learning:

2a) Ensure teachers are secure in their understanding of the new National Curriculum requirements

2b) Develop teachers' understanding of effective strategies that will support pupil achievement in reading, writing and mathematics

2c) Increase the percentage of outstanding teaching to ensure the most able pupils are challenged and disadvantaged pupils are supported

In the extract in Table 5.1 you can see how the whole-school targets relate to the Ofsted report and use other monitoring information to discern more specific curriculum targets.

The English action plan

Once a school has identified the English targets, the next step is to consider the actions needed to bring about the required goals. It is the English subject leader's role to determine these actions. The action plan will detail a list of tasks and responsibilities to be undertaken by the English subject leader over the course of a year.

The action plan will clearly define the priorities for English as specific, measurable targets. The plan will define these targets in terms of year group and age-phase appropriateness. It will detail the support and professional development staff will receive to implement and achieve the targets, and it should detail evidence that will form the basis for monitoring and evaluating the impact of the actions. Success should be measured in terms of what the school staff will be doing differently, and in terms of what the children will be able to demonstrate. Each action should also have a timescale for the target to be achieved by and a possible resourcing allocation. Good targets are therefore SMART: *S*pecific, *M*easurable, *A*chievable within the timescale, *R*ealistic and *T*ime-bound.

There may be a budgetary or resource implication attached to some actions. Resources in most schools (be they financial or human resources) are an important consideration when defining realistic goals in an English action plan. Whilst it might be highly desirable to be out of class conducting peer teaching, or monitoring teaching, the reality is that many schools cannot afford for a class teacher to be released from the classroom. The same is true of staff development and training

Table 5.2 Extract from the English subject leader's action plan

Overall aim: (SDP priority / issue for development)

- *Increase pupil progress and attainment in reading (priority 1a)*
- *Increase the percentage of disadvantaged pupils achieving age-related expectations in reading (priority 1b)*
- *Increase the percentage of pupils exceeding expected progress in reading (priority 1c)*
- *Develop teachers' understanding of effective strategies that will support pupil achievement in reading (priority 2b)*

Action to be taken and by whom	Success criteria	Resources / cost	Timescale	Evaluation of impact
Provide staff with training on effective questioning, range of reading experience, reading comprehension skills and age-related expectations	*Teachers are secure in their understanding of how to plan questions designed to develop pupils' comprehension skills using a range of text types*	*INSETsession Purchase of high-quality texts*	*Sept*	*Pupils make expected or better than expected progress in reading Pupils are enthusiastic about reading Quality of reading comprehension teaching is consistently high across the school*
Share existing good practice on how to support reading comprehension, and recommend new approaches (English subject leader)	*High-quality activities and approaches are disseminated across the school New approaches are trialled and evaluated*	*Staff meeting*	*Sept*	
Planning scrutiny (English subject leader)	*Planning will specify questioning that supports children to develop their understanding and response to literature*			
Audit texts used across the school (English subject leader)	*Mapping will ensure that children encounter a rich and varied breadth of literature across the school*		*June/July*	
Monitor planning and pupil progress in reading comprehension through book scrutiny(English subject leader)	*Marking will accurately identify what pupils have achieved and how they need to develop*	*Subject leader release*	*Nov Feb May/June*	

courses. Again, whilst this might be a highly desirable action, cost often prohibits investment in external training.

In the extract from the English action plan (see Table 5.2) you can see how some of the SDP targets become the overall aim for the subject leader. This extract only focuses on reading and another part of the plan will consider the overall writing targets. The English subject leader takes the overall aims and identifies specific actions that will support the school in developing practice. The actions focus on making changes that will impact on pupil outcomes. An effective plan is straightforward to work from, avoids jargon and lists step-by-step what you and the staff need to do in order to develop the aspect of English (Waters and Martin, 1999).

Deciding on the right actions

When considering how good subject leaders ascertain the right actions to support English development one cannot underestimate the importance of subject knowledge. If the subject leader doesn't understand reading comprehension development, then it will be difficult to identify how pupil learning in this area can be strengthened. As stated throughout this book, subject knowledge and pedagogical understanding are absolutely crucial to effective English subject leadership. So how does the English subject leader go about identifying next steps? How do they know exactly what needs to happen in order to bring about improved learning experiences for the pupils that will result in better levels of achievement?

- What do I know about the teaching of the priority area? (Reading comprehension/writing/spelling/grammar or phonics);
- What information do I already have from monitoring processes that indicate possible routes to improve this area?
- What information do I need to find out more about?
- Is the policy guidance on the teaching approach for this aspect of English clear and up to date?

The good subject leader might need to refresh or deepen their understanding of the current school practice in this aspect of English. They have to discover what the challenges and issues are for staff and for pupils in this area before being able to produce the plan.

Prior to writing an action plan:

- talk to teachers about how they feel about the planning and teaching of this aspect;
- talk to pupils about their learning;
- look at planning and children's work;
- talk to other successful schools to find out what they do that works;
- read about this aspect to refresh subject knowledge and inform themselves of current teaching approaches in this area.

Communicating your plan

Once the English action plan is drawn up it is key to share the headlines with staff. Effective communication of the targets, training and support, and the measure of success is crucial to the realisation of the plan. Today all class teachers are expected to take ownership of pupil progression and therefore shared ownership of targets is relatively standard. Ultimately, it will be the responsibility of the subject leader to understand the whole-school picture for English in the priority area. Monitoring activities intended to support your understanding of how things are developing should be integral to the action plan. The monitoring process should also be communicated to staff so they know how success will be measured. It must also be stressed that monitoring will be used to review progress towards the targets and to reflect on training and support requirements, with the emphasis on using monitoring information to provide support when and where it is required.

Monitoring your plan

Monitoring and evaluation are likely to involve both the subject leader and the SLT, but it might not always work this way. It will be essential that you understand what monitoring senior leaders in your school will conduct and what aspects of monitoring you will be personally responsible for. Greater detail about the monitoring process is discussed in Chapter 11.

It is likely that there is an overlap between usual SLT monitoring processes and your own responsibilities. The example in Table 5.3 illustrates how the English action plan and the SLT's strategic monitoring and evaluation processes might sit alongside each other, complementing and informing each other.

Table 5.3 Monitoring by the SLT and by the English subject leader

Reading goals	SLT monitoring	SL monitoring
Pupils make expected or better than expected progress in reading	Pupil progress-meetings SLT/year leader meetings	Book scrutiny
Quality of reading comprehension teaching is consistently high across the school	Lesson observation	Lesson observation, team teaching, scrutiny of planning
Pupils are enthusiastic about reading		Observations of pupils' attitude to learning during lesson observation Pupil interview

Where there is an overlap between the SLT and the subject leader's monitoring there is a need to share information.

 The English action plan should detail activities that will support the implementation of new approaches. The good subject leader will:

- coach and team teach in the focused aspect of English;
- give suggestions and ideas about how to improve planning;
- review teachers' perceptions of the new approach;
- review pupils' perceptions of learning;
- review planning and children's work.

It is important to remember that every school is different, but the general principles of action planning remain the same. The examples above are designed to give you an idea of how the paper trail might work in your school. The following case study will relay the complete journey one school took in a year, focusing on one aspect of English. From target setting to action planning, the case study provides an explanation of the step-by-step procedures the subject leader undertook to implement the school's English targets.

Case study: The paper trail of English development

Hurstbourne Tarrant Church of England Primary School, Hampshire

Chris is the head teacher of a small, rural school. He works closely with subject leaders to support development of the curriculum across the school.

Whilst the English subject leader role and action planning falls to another member of staff, Chris works in partnership with them to formulate the strategic planning for English. He also supports the monitoring processes that feed the evaluation of English action plan priorities. This collegiate approach to planning and setting targets is common in most schools where the English subject leader is not a member of the Senior Leadership Team (SLT).

The school have focused on guided reading as one of their English action plan points. Guided reading happens across the school on a daily basis. The general approach is for the teacher to offer a range of reading activities and rotate pupil groups throughout the week to enable teachers to work with a guided group a day. The teacher will hear pupils in the guided group read, and support them to develop their responses to the text. Whilst the teacher focuses on supporting the guided group, other pupils will be working on reading-related tasks.

Through the school's self-evaluation processes Chris identified reading comprehension as an area to be improved. Knowing that this was a target determined by SLT, the English subject leader examined school assessment tracking data to explore pupil progression in relation to reading skills. His findings were that pupils' ability to retrieve information and give responses to literal questioning was assessed as better than their ability to infer meaning from a text. The head teacher and the English subject leader then agreed that they needed to find out more, so they conducted monitoring visits that incorporated focused reviews of the learning environment, resourcing and lesson observations. Through monitoring processes they identified that during guided reading lessons the teachers focused well on the literal questioning of the children, but not so well with regard to inference and deduction. With this information it was clear that in order to improve pupils' skills in inference, teachers needed to refine their questioning in this area of reading.

The monitoring process also highlighted a second development focus for the guided reading sessions. Tasks given to children who were not working with the class teacher needed to be independently undertaken by the pupils but also needed to be meaningful and challenging. The lesson observations and scrutiny of plans revealed that getting the balance between these two elements was difficult. Staff either needed to leave the guided group to help another table with their independent task, or pupils were set work that did not fully challenge their learning.

Case study learning points

✓ **Action planning can be fine-tuning.** Developing practice does not need to be a complete change. The case study example of action planning sought to retain what was good practice whilst making some tweaks to refine and make things better. There is no need to start from scratch. The English subject leader and staff retained the good, existing practice but made adjustments to improve pupil outcome.

Equipped with this information the English subject leader ran a staff meeting. He asked staff to bring a guided reading text of their choice to share at the meeting and a copy of their guided reading planning. They initially spent time sharing their chosen texts with colleagues and discussing the type of questions they had planned to ask the children as they read. The English subject leader next led an input that focused on the key comprehension skills children needed to acquire in order to develop their reading skills. Staff were then asked to match the reading comprehension skills to the guided reading plan brought to the meeting. Teachers embarked on discussing and categorising the reading skills required of the children to answer to their planned questions. Staff then reflected on the range of questions and skills their original plan had provided. The exercise revealed to staff that their planning focused readily on literal understanding but less so on inference and deduction. The whole staff agreed that incorporating more inferential and deductive questioning into their planning would improve pupil performance in reading.

The subject leader then led a staff meeting input on quality talk and open questioning, modelling some examples for the staff from a text. Next, staff worked together to add questions to their original guided reading plan, developing the questions they could use with their chosen text to illicit pupil response.

At the end of the meeting the English subject leader worked in collaboration with staff to define the expected elements of future guided reading planning.

Case study learning points

✓ **Plan for staff to understand the reason for targets.** You might know what target you want to meet but you have to give staff time to know this too.

Build time and opportunity into your action plan to enable staff to analyse and reflect on the issue. Instead of telling staff the areas they needed to improve on, staff were encouraged to see for themselves the aspects of their planning that needed changing. This approach resulted in all staff understanding the reason for the shift in practice and shared ownership of the targets.

✓ **Ensure a shared understanding and ownership of change.** All staff left the meeting with a clear, shared understanding of the new approach to guided reading, a clear rationale for why they were focusing on making these changes and a model of the types of questions that should be incorporated into their guided reading planning.

Over the coming weeks staff tried out their new approach to guided reading planning, focusing on developing quality questions. After a month the English subject leader began to drop in to classes to see the English teaching and offer support. During these drop-ins the English subject leader would respond to teachers' varying support needs. In some instances the subject leader modelled a guided reading lesson to demonstrate the level of challenge, appropriate task design and classroom organisation. In other classes the subject leader team taught alongside the class teacher. Alternatively, some staff wanted support at the planning stage or in identifying quality texts.

Case study learning points

✓ **Plan time to give support for all, and vary the approach.** In the case study the support provided by the subject leader was varied in approach. Some teachers expressed the need to see someone else teach and model guided reading whilst others wanted the subject leader to support them through a team teaching approach. Some staff required less class support and just needed to discuss their plans.

After another six weeks the subject leader carried out further team teaching and conducted observations to determine if teacher questioning had improved and if pupils' inference skills were being challenged. Chris and members of the SLT also carried out lesson observations as part of the regular whole-school monitoring process.

Once staff had got to grips with refining their questioning, the next stage was to focus on improving the task design for the non-guided groups. In another staff meeting teachers shared their ideas of tasks that could be offered to children not working with the guided group. Teachers evaluated the purpose and challenge incorporated into the suggested tasks and made suggestions of how the task might be adapted for different year groups. These shared ideas developed into a checklist of meaningful tasks. This checklist was not an exhaustive list, nor was it meant to be prescriptive, but it offered a starting point for teachers to draw from when planning their guided reading sessions. Both the head teacher and the subject leader felt it was essential that teachers understood the list was just a starting point so that a teacher's individual creativity was not limited. Guided reading became a regular briefing item at staff meetings. This was a regular opportunity for teachers to talk about how guided reading was going, discuss problems they were encountering, share experiences and suggest ways forward.

Case study learning points

✓ **Ensure teachers understand that checklists and guidance are not an exhaustive list.** It is important to retain an element of teacher autonomy, whilst ensuring that underlying principles in practice are shared and understood. This approach will ensure the quality of learning and teaching for pupils and retain the creativity of individual staff members.

✓ **Plan regular opportunities for staff to discuss how implementation is going and share progress.** This maintains the profile of your action plan goals and it enables the regular sharing of good practice. Having a recurring update opportunity in staff meetings doesn't take much time but provides a valuable chance to troubleshoot issues before they accumulate and demotivate staff.

The progress of quality teaching in guided reading was measured throughout the year with ongoing monitoring processes such as learning walks, looking at planning, book scrutiny and lesson observations. Both the head teacher and the subject leader carried out the monitoring process at different times. The impact in terms of pupil learning was measured through the examination of pupils' work, talking to pupils during lesson observations, the observation of pupil engagement during lessons and regular analysis of pupil tracking data.

Towards the end of the year the tracking data indicated that pupil progress was better in a range of reading skills. Teachers reported that they were more confident assessing pupils' abilities in reading comprehension. Teachers spoke of increased awareness of which reading skills their questioning challenged, and this meant that they felt more secure in assessing when pupils demonstrated specific reading skills. Teachers felt confident that they had evidence of pupils' inference and deduction skills across a range of texts. Teachers articulated that the refocus on reading comprehension skills enabled them to better assess pupil progress and identify the reading skills that needed further development through their planning and questioning.

The result of the subject leader's action was that Assessment for Learning in guided reading became more responsive and precise, and that pupil achievement in reading comprehension increased. The whole school had successfully progressed with reading comprehension. The effective identification of the issues behind the data and supportive approaches to improve planning and teaching generated better learning opportunities for the children.

Case study learning points

✓ **Pace the timings between input, delivery and monitoring of the new target.** In the case study, staff were given time to try things out and make mistakes. The delay between the staff meeting, the lesson observations and subject leader support meant that teachers had some freedom to make mistakes, take risks and discover what worked for them. When subject leader development was offered, the teachers knew what further support they needed.

✓ **Celebrate success.** It was important to evaluate the impact of the changes, not only in terms of the pupils' performance but also in terms of the impact on staff. The subject leader knew how the changes had impacted on the staff and this success was shared with the staff.

Reference

Waters, M. and Martin, T. (1999) *Coordinating English at Key Stage 2: The subject leader's handbook.* London: Falmer Press.

Pedagogical choices in primary English

Liz Chamberlain

This chapter focuses on the importance of subject leaders developing an awareness and understanding of effective literacy pedagogy in order to articulate and make visible the choices they make as they lead English in their schools. In some countries, student teachers learn to be pedagogues, whilst in other countries, pedagogy is a subject in and of itself. Over the last twenty years, educationalists like Robin Alexander have made the case for teachers reclaiming the language of teaching and making visible the basis of their decision-making. The chapter also outlines the characteristics of effective teachers of literacy, many of whom go on to lead English within their schools.

Pedagogy and pedagogues

If teaching is the classroom act narrowly defined, pedagogy is that act together with the ideas that inform it.

(Alexander, 2010: 280)

Robin Alexander (2004) refers to pedagogy as being 'both the act of teaching and its attendant discourse' (Alexander, 2004: 11); in essence, it is what teachers do combined with what they say and how they justify what they do. A teacher's pedagogy is about more than what they do or say in the classroom, it comprises their 'ideas, beliefs, attitudes, knowledge and understanding about the curriculum, the teaching and learning process and their students' (Westbrook *et al.*, 2013: 7).

We know from research that literacy outcomes for pupils can be boosted if they are taught by 'very effective' teachers, in some cases, by as much as a third of an examination grade (Machin and Murphy, 2011: 5). However, the National College for School Leadership (2012) argues that little attention has been given to what constitutes effective teaching, which they define as 'the behaviours and actions of good teachers; what good teachers do to promote good learning' (NCSL, 2012: 1). Pedagogy is sometimes referred to as the 'science' of teaching, and educationalists like Ken Robinson talk of teaching as an 'art' form. Whilst this sounds creative and interesting, it doesn't necessarily get to the heart of what it is that subject leaders need to know and do to enact good practice in English. The concept of 'pedagogy' feels relatively new to teachers in this country and there has been an absence of 'critical accounts of pedagogy' (Murphy, 2008: 28). In other countries, the study of pedagogy is taken for granted, with students learning a subject called 'pedagogy' and teachers referring to themselves as 'pedagogues'. In Denmark, a pedagogue is usually an early years teacher, whilst in Hungary the words *teachers* (of all ages) and *pedagogues* are used synonymously.

As a subject leader, you may be asked by teachers or governors what your rationale is for a new initiative or change in policy. In your response to them, you will be basing your explanations on your understanding of pedagogy – you just might not have called it that before. For example, you might refer to 'active' pedagogy or 'child-centred' pedagogy, or you might just have a passion or enthusiasm for a particular approach to the teaching of English. You may hear an inspirational speaker explain talk for writing or attend a stimulating course on the use of picture books in Key Stage 2 and just know that's the right approach for your children. What the speaker and course are tapping into are your beliefs and attitudes about what constitutes good English learning and teaching.

If you're finding it difficult to articulate your pedagogy, then don't be too disheartened; over recent decades, the focus in England has been on the curriculum rather than on a shared discourse about teaching methods (Alexander, 2004). The implementation of the National Literacy Strategy in the late 1990s, and the subsequent twenty years of ever-changing government guidance, resulted in teachers seeing themselves as deliverers of a transmission model of learning rather than as teachers who were enablers using the very best evidence-based teaching approaches to match the needs of their pupils (Alexander, 2010). However, effective teachers of literacy have always been clear about how they interpret policy and national initiatives by ensuring that they plan for purposeful reading and writing activities (Fox *et al.*, 2001). This would suggest that there are teachers who have a clear sense of the necessary subject knowledge and ideas for literacy practices that are embedded in their classroom practice. For other teachers this process is more of a struggle and this can cause issues for you as a subject leader. As Robin Alexander (2010: 412) asserted, 'if we are unable to define teaching then we are unable to say what kinds of expertise it requires'.

83

As an English subject leader, you need to ensure that your practice is constantly reviewed so that the way in which you lead English across the school is based on the latest evidence. Knowing where to find this information can feel challenging – English reports from Ofsted like 'Moving English Forward' (2013) are a useful starting point, as they highlight effective practice gathered from observations and findings of outstanding schools. More recently, one of the Chartered College of Teaching's aims is to support teachers and subject leaders by signposting evidence-based approaches through their online research digests and research hubs. Making explicit the evidence and values on which you base your decision-making will further support you in creating a vision for outstanding English learning and teaching across your school.

Evidence-informed practice

As the subject leader, you will often be involved in interpreting government policy or guidance, often through a process that Alexander (2009) refers to as 'curriculum metamorphosis' (Alexander, 2009: 8). It is possible to track this process through the ways in which teachers talk about their practice. Bruning and Horn's (2000) research into writing motivation highlighted that teachers' views and beliefs about writing (and reading) are often made visible through their planning and teaching. Teachers who plan activities designed to motivate developing writers were able to understand 'the power and pleasure of writing (and reading)' (Bruning and Horn, 2000: 35).

In the following examples of teachers' reflections on their practice, you may wish to consider two questions:

1. To what extent is the language of policy explicit in the teachers' explanation of their practice?
2. How do the teachers express their beliefs, values and ideas about English through their descriptions of classroom practice?

You may find it useful to work with your own school staff in a similar way: asking teachers about their practice in a professional conversation before reviewing what they say often makes visible their pedagogical beliefs and practices. This is especially useful if you are supporting a teacher to improve or refine their practice.

Professional testimonies – talking about practice

Here, two teachers, Sam, who's been teaching in Key Stage 1 for six years, and Terrie, a Reception teacher with twenty years' experience, reflect on their approach to the teaching of reading (Chamberlain, 2010).

Uncertainty about practice

Sam, Year 2 teacher

I suppose ... well ... hopefully an inviting book corner as much as I can, even if it means I'm on at them about keeping it nice, looking after things and putting things away. In the morning they often come in and choose a book and sit and do sort of quiet reading on the carpet and I might have some words of the week or something like that up that they can try and find them in books. So it's kind of like a nice reading experience. Well, I have reading once a week and it's just something that I find really difficult to do, to manage. I think because I don't really know how to do it properly. If you could sit in a room with a group of five children that would probably be much easier ... I find really difficult to do on a regular basis. Lots of bits around the room with words up in the role play area and lots of things like that and trying to get them to ... if they've got to find something they need to look at labels on things, those sorts of things.

For Sam, the key points here appear to be about the organisational issues associated with reading and not the process of reading itself; therefore, we don't get a clear sense of what she thinks is important. However, despite the lack of reading pedagogy, Sam is able to reflect on where the difficulties lie – and that in itself demonstrates an awareness that the practice of her classroom is not necessarily aligned with what she knows good teaching of reading should look like. Sam was responding to the question, 'What's your approach to reading?' and her responses suggest a difficulty in knowing how to explain her practice – there's a meta-language that she's struggling to find. Now compare Sam's response with Terrie, a more experienced teacher.

An awareness of practice

Terrie, Reception teacher

We usually do the literacy appreciation, so we do a book, just on reading it but I do lots of questioning and we talk about the comprehending and thinking about what's in the book, not just what I'm hearing. So we look at pictures, we do picture talk, so then if I don't do that then I alternate it with a picture talk lesson where we do the same thing, where we're looking for things and doing language concepts.

Even though Terrie's response is shorter, we know more about her pedagogy, both in terms of her beliefs and attitudes but also how this translates into practice in her classroom. Unlike Sam, she has the meta-language, and she talks of literacy appreciation, questioning, comprehending, thinking, picture talk, picture talk lesson and language concepts. Note also the nuance in her reference between *picture talk* and a *picture talk lesson*. If you were to describe your approach to reading, or maybe the school's approach, what would the listener learn about your reading pedagogy?

Effective teachers of literacy

We learned at the start of this chapter that children learn better if very 'effective' teachers teach them. We have also learned that in order to be that very effective teacher, you need to understand what it is that you are basing your classroom practice on, your pedagogical approach. Flutter and Rudduck (2004) argue that teachers need to do more to help pupils engage in a 'focused discussion' about learning and themselves as learners. The same could be said to be true of teachers; as Anthea Millett (ex-Head of the then Teacher Training Agency) asserted at the turn of the century, 'teachers must start talking about teaching not learning' (Millett, 1998).

Shifting practice

However, there are many teachers who have always been able to do both. For example, in a small-scale study of teachers across Australia and England (Chamberlain, 2010) there was evidence of subject leaders who had begun to anticipate rather than wait for policy change that led to shifts in practice. For example, three years before the writing curriculum changed its focus from 'genre' to 'purpose' (DfE, 2013), these teachers were already ahead of the game.

> Our main shift has been teaching kids about the fact that we write for different purposes, that authors write for different purposes and these are the reasons why you write ... but if you're writing to entertain, not just narratives, they might be poems, they might be this, they might be that.

One of the key factors in understanding how effective teachers of literacy operate is knowing that what underpins their practice is an understanding of not only subject knowledge but also what it means to be a developing reader and writer. Alexander

(2010) suggests that to help children articulate their desire to know what and why they are engaged in a task they need to be brought 'inside the thinking that informs the teacher's decisions on their behalf' (Alexander, 2010: 282). This awareness of the value in communicating ideas and making explicit belief systems about the teaching of literacy were found to be key factors in Wray *et al.*'s (2000) research into effective teachers of literacy. Of note to subject leaders when planning the English curriculum is that effective teachers 'made the purposes and processes of literacy explicit for their pupils' (Wray *et al.*, 2000: 83). Naomi Flynn's (2007) case study of three teachers in an inner-city school also highlights that effective literacy teachers (that means you as the English subject leader) have an awareness of the complexity of literacy teaching. Furthermore, what is essential is an understanding of the interconnectivity of 'teacher behaviour, teacher subject knowledge and teacher–pupil interaction (Flynn, 2007: 145). In short, to explain all three aspects is to articulate effective literacy pedagogy.

An embedded teacher of literacy

Pedagogy is central to learning. It is a dynamic relationship between 'learning, teacher and culture' (Livingstone *et al.*, 2017) and this is illustrated in the following case study of Richard, a teacher in his seventh year of teaching. He trained as a primary teacher with a specialism in PE before, in his first school, developing and leading in Computing and ICT. His route into English is not a traditional one but, as you reflect on what he knows about literacy pedagogy, consider the following:

* his ideas, beliefs and attitudes;
* his knowledge and understanding about the curriculum;
* his knowledge of the teaching and learning process;
* his awareness of his pupils and their learning needs.

Case study: Richard – Pedagogical choices in Primary English

Grove Park Primary School, West London

Walking into Mr Charlesworth's Year 3 classroom it's clear to any visitor that this is a class that loves English. There's a book corner, text-rich classroom displays and language prompts that pop out from every wall. The available resources are culturally diverse and the lives of the children in the class are reflected in the range of texts they read. The lesson prompt sheets are beautifully presented, offering children a model of what quality work looks like. Other displays in the classroom become more visible the more you look – there are messages to the children such as 'How can I improve my work?' and there are topic words to support new vocabulary in maths and science. Each class at the school is named

---

after a native British tree. Richard's is called 'Aspen', which he has linked to a line by Meg Murry, the main character in *A Wrinkle in Time*, in which she says 'she was completely unaware that her voice was trembling like an Aspen leaf'. This is a class teacher who knows his children's literature. The other featured author is Beverley Naidoo, and in guided reading the children explore *The Ice Palace* by Robert Swindells.

'English is certainly a strength of mine, and one I enjoy teaching. Its multifaceted nature and constant evolution mean that there is always new literature to use in the classrooms and new approaches to try out in practice. I have never been one to stop learning. It's the joy behind the job and the reason I teach.'

In their literacy lesson, the children are learning how to structure a non-chronological report in the form of a cold weather survival guide, and they use their knowledge of the guided reading text to justify their choices. The discussion between Mr Charlesworth and the children is lively and genuine. He asks questions about the text, he asks for reasons behind responses and both he and the children know this story well. The children are confident in their book talk; they give their reasons predicated on 'the way he describes it' (as if Robert Swindells is known to them personally). The conversations and book talk are carefully managed through a structured conversation – Mr Charlesworth knows where he's headed, and this is not a 'guess what's in the teacher's mind' conversation. As the children set to work, they read through a pre-prepared modelled example of a non-chronological report. In this class, a final draft is always shared with the children – the children do not produce a paragraph or section a day across the week, but instead are encouraged from the outset to work towards the final piece. Mr Charlesworth says this is 'letting the children in on the game'.

* What is your initial reaction to the idea of sharing a final modelled writing exemplar to children?

- If this isn't the approach you adopt, can you explain to Richard why you would instead scaffold the exemplar over the course of the week?
- Are you confident that staff in your school are knowledgeable about children's literature and are able to explain why it is important for teachers to be readers?

At the end of the lesson, Richard (Mr Charlesworth) takes time to explain the choices that he's made both in the planning and in the teaching of the lesson. He is currently studying for an MA in children's literature – his tutor is Michael Rosen. This is a teacher who knows his stuff. Richard is in the seventh year of his career and he's taught across Key Stage 2 but thinks Year 6 may be his favourite to teach. It is Richard's second job and he's as surprised as anyone that he has such passion and affinity for teaching English. He started out thinking that he would be a maths teacher, but found himself at the end of his three-year course being so inspired by his English tutor that he wrote his dissertation on picture books and critical thinking. He explains that much of his curriculum planning is literacy-based and with an emphasis on immersing the children in language and structure. He talks of the type of activities that develop the children as young readers and writers; he mentions his classroom displays and how he draws out good examples of language, and he encourages children to magpie ideas and explains to them why this is a useful strategy. Richard explains his approach to the teaching of reading in a class of varied ability but shared positive attitudes. He lists a range of strategies, including the embedding of grammar across reading and writing tasks, and the integration of texts from the imagined world and the real world.

'St Anthony's Primary School in Renfrewshire, Scotland was the UKLA Literacy School of the Year (2018). All the school's teachers attend a monthly children's book club and the majority of the school staff have completed a Master's-level module in children's literature.'

Richard talks with passion about reading for pleasure and the importance of children making their own book choices when selecting a library book. The children all read on a 1:1 weekly basis to Richard, regardless of whether they are an experienced or a struggling reader. He reads aloud on a daily basis and these are texts in addition to the agreed texts linked to each year group's curriculum maps. In Year 3, the children study *The Ice Palace, Charlotte's Web, Stone Age Boy, Danny the Champion of the World, Norse Myths* and *The Village that*

Vanished. The choice of texts exemplifies a teacher who knows literature – there are familiar texts, picture books, favourite authors, as well as texts highlighting diverse cultures. The children are enjoying a rich literary diet. Across the school, reading buddies work across year groups to talk about books and reading choices. Richard uses Aidan Chambers' approach (1993) to encourage purposeful book talk and uses the PEE principle – Point, Evidence, Explain – to develop children's skills in reading comprehension. He adds one more – Linking – to create the acronym PEEL, making the case once more that reading and writing are inextricably interconnected. Richard talks confidently about his pedagogical practices – he refers to models of personal growth, of a teacher's internal narrative and the importance of meaning-making and citizenship.

- How would you define Richard's literacy pedagogy?
- Are you confident that Richard is able to explain the practice in his classroom beyond describing the children's learning?
- As English subject leader, what goals or targets would you set for Richard?

Richard chose to pursue his Master's in children's literature, and as well as this formal learning, he also seeks out informal professional development opportunities. He follows authors and other teachers on Twitter, he has completed courses (self-funded) at CLPE (Centre for Literacy in Primary Education) and he is a member of UKLA (United Kingdom Literacy Association). His good work has been acknowledged by both his head teacher and across the local schools cluster, and he has led workshops with teachers and parents where he emphasises collaboration and shared experiences.

- Teachers need access to both informal and formal professional development.
- Collaborating across school clusters informs and supports all teachers.

- Knowledge of literacy organisations, networks and associations is crucial in supporting the school in taking an evidence-based approach to English teaching.

Teachers in the school are given creative freedom in their planning – there are no commercial or published schemes, just a curriculum vision of what the children in this school should be learning. Richard explains that he puts his efforts into producing quality resources and marking children's work rather than producing polished plans. He is firm in his commitment that each child, regardless of their background, should be set high expectations and that all children should see themselves as authors and readers. When asked to explain the importance of children becoming competent language users, he answers, 'Where don't you need reading in your life?'

 Creative approaches that seek to inspire further reading/research from the children, alongside a variety of writing opportunities, allow children the best possible chance to succeed and view themselves as accomplished readers and writers.

His practice has been influenced by his head teacher, Darren, who shares a passion for English and who himself is research-active and widely read. When Darren joined the school, he encouraged team teaching and modelled this himself by teaching every class using picture books. This approach became adopted into the school's repertoire, as every two weeks picture books are used as a stimulus for creative writing – for children and teachers. For this school, a contextualised curriculum means that English is a living, breathing subject – children go on trips, welcome visitors and are given experiences, which means they have something important to write about and a ready audience of staff, children and parents to share it with.

- What is the role of the head teacher in ensuring there is shared school vision for English?

- How are the expectations communicated to staff?
- What was the support offered to staff?
- How would you, as the English subject leader, measure and evaluate impact and success?

Case study learning points

✓ **Define and articulate your pedagogy for English.** Seek out ways to make explicit the dynamic relationship between the learning, the teacher and your school's culture. Share your vision of English with the children, staff, governors and wider community and be confident about the ideas, beliefs and attitudes that underpin your decisions. Demonstrate excellent subject knowledge, and know how this translates into an English curriculum that reflects both an awareness of the importance of purposeful reading and writing experiences and your understanding of the teaching and learning process that best meets the needs of your school's pupils.

References

Alexander, R. (2004) 'Still no pedagogy? Principle, pragmatism and compliance in primary education.' *Cambridge Journal of Education*, 34 (1), 7–33.

Alexander, R. (2009) 'Towards a comparative pedagogy.' In: Cowen, R. and Kazamias, A. M. (eds), *International Handbook of Comparative Education*. New York, USA: Springer, 923–942.

Alexander, R. (2010) *Children, their World, their Education*. Oxford: Routledge.

Bruning, R. and Horn, C. (2000) 'Developing motivation to write.' *Educational Psychologist*, 35 (1), 5–37.

Chamberlain, L. (2010) 'Where are we now in our approach to the teaching of writing?' UKLA Conference paper Winchester, July 2010.

Chambers, A. (1993) *Tell Me: Children, reading and talk*. Portland, ME: Stenhouse Publishers.

Department for Education (DfE) (2013) *National Curriculum*. London: DfE.

Flutter, J. and Ruddock, J. (2004) *Consulting Pupils: What's in it for schools?* London: Routledge.

Flynn, N. (2007) 'What do effective teachers of literacy do? Subject knowledge and pedagogical choices for literacy.' *Literacy*, 41 (3), 137–146.

Fox, R., Poulson, L., Medwell, J. and Wray, D. (2001) *Teaching Literacy Effectively in the Primary School*. London: Routledge.

Livingstone, K., Schweisfurth, M., Brace, G. and Nash, M. (2017) 'Why pedagogy matters: The role of pedagogy in education 2030.' Policy Advice Paper.

Machin, S. and Murphy, S. (2011) *Improving the Impact of Teachers on Pupil Achievement in the UK: Interim findings*. London: Sutton Trust.

Millett, A. (1998) 'Let's get pedagogical.' Times Educational Supplement. Available at: www.tes.com/news/tes-archive/tes-publication/lets-get-pedagogicalbriefing school-management [accessed 15 March 2018].

Murphy, P. (2008) 'Defining pedagogy.' In: Hall, K. Murphy, P. and Soler, J. (eds), *Pedagogy and Practice: Culture and identities*. London: Open University/Sage.

National College for School Leadership (NCSL) (2012) *What Makes Great Pedagogy? Nine claims from research*. Nottingham: NCSL.

Ofsted (2013) *Moving English Forward*. London: Ofsted.

Westbrook, J., Durrani, N., Brown, R., Orr, D., Pryor, J., Boddy, J. and Salvi, F. (2013) *Pedagogy, Curriculum, Teaching Practices and Teacher Education in Developing Countries. Final report. Education rigorous literature review*. London: Department for International Development.

Wray, D., Medwell, J., Poulson, L. and Fox, R. (2000) 'The teaching practices of effective teachers of literacy.' *Educational Review*, 52 (1), 75–84.

7 | Literacy in the 21st century

Sandy Stockwell

This chapter explores the potential opportunities offered by new literacy practices in the 21st century, including using multimodal approaches, and digital and visual literacies. It will consider how to value children's use of technology within their home literacies in order to enhance traditional teaching approaches. A discussion of theoretical perspectives will lead to an understanding of how new technologies and media can stimulate and scaffold children's reading, writing, speaking and listening, whilst simultaneously increasing motivation and engagement. Guidance will identify challenges and implications for your school's English curriculum, enabling you to make informed choices. Helpful sources will also be shared.

The social and cultural practices of literacy in the 21st century

As discussed in earlier chapters, being literate is more than reading and writing the written word; it is a socio-cultural practice which equips citizens to be able to fully participate and function in their society (Marsh, 2010a). Being literate enables us to keep informed, maintain relationships, communicate with others and express ourselves. How we choose to do these things forms part of our identity.

> **REFLECTION**
> Think for a moment about how *you* complete each of these tasks. It is likely that you will use the Internet to keep informed, searching for information on websites, reading blogs and watching clips on YouTube. Perhaps you use email, messaging apps or social media to keep in touch with friends and

family; you might even write a blog or upload your own videos to YouTube. If you were denied access to these different media, you might feel out of touch with your peers and with society in the broader context. Our society's social practices include access to Facebook, Twitter, mobile phones, tablets and computers. Increasingly this is also true for the social and cultural practices of children.

On an annual basis, Ofcom produces an accessible report exploring the media use, attitudes and understanding of children. Ofcom define media literacy as 'the ability to use, understand and create media and communications in a variety of contexts' (Ofcom, 2017). The report's headlines about children's usage of media for 2017 are detailed in Table 7.1. The full report provides interesting detail behind these figures. For example:

Children's use of tablets

Increased numbers of children aged 3–15 now have their own tablet, which has resulted in increased Internet use.

Children's television viewing

The majority of young children's media usage is spent watching TV, with older children spending more time on their mobile phones and online. Popular family viewing includes Britain's Got Talent, Strictly Come Dancing and Bake Off, which are among the top ten

Table 7.1 Ofcom report on children's usage of media 2017

	% of 3–4 year olds	% of 5–7 year olds	% of 8–11 year olds	% of 12–15 year olds
Own a smartphone	1	5	39	83
Own a tablet	21	35	52	55
Watch TV on a TV set	96	95	95	91
Watch TV on other devices	41, usually on tablets	49, usually on tablets	55, usually on tablets	68, usually on tablets or mobiles
Play games	40	66	81	77
Go online	53	79	94, usually on tablets or mobiles	99, usually on tablets or mobiles
Use YouTube	48 (Half of these only use YouTube Kids app)	71 (Quarter of these only use YouTube Kids app)	81	90
Have a social media/ messaging profile	0	3	23	74
The device they'd miss the most		TV set	TV set or tablet	Mobile phone

most watched programmes for 4–15 year olds. Children trust the news viewed on the TV as more truthful than news shared via social media and similarly believe that TV adverts mostly tell the truth.

Children's online activity

The percentage of children aged 3–15 engaging in online activity has grown due to the increased use of tablets. Around a quarter of 8–15 year olds believe that they can trust websites listed by a search engine. Children can find it hard to identify online advertising, including personalised adverts, endorsements made by vloggers and sponsored links on search engines.

Children's use of YouTube

Increasing numbers of children of all ages now watch YouTube, with younger children watching cartoons, mini-movies and songs while older children's preferred content is music videos and humorous content, followed by clips to relax them, to talk about with friends, to learn things from and to make them think. Children and young people aged between 12 and 15 years perceive themselves to be YouTube's target audience. This age group uses YouTube as their 'go to' source for all content that is important to them.

Children's use of social media

Despite minimum age requirements, almost a quarter of 8–11 year olds and three-quarters of 12–15 year olds have a social media profile; their favoured sites are Snapchat, Snapstreaks, Instagram, WhatsApp, Facebook and Facebook Messenger. An increasing number of older children have used live streaming services to share their own content. Children struggle to differentiate between true and fake news stories on social media sites. They also report feeling social pressure from being on these sites. Whilst recognising some content as being inappropriate for their age group, many children see social media as a tool for challenging unkind comments and for sharing more positive messages.

This report provides a timely summary of the social and cultural practices of children. It is beneficial to explore the literacies which your pupils choose to engage with beyond school. Respecting and valuing children's home literacies and welcoming them into the classroom builds bridges between home and school literacy practices; it has a positive impact on children's motivation and engagement, especially for those 'hard to reach' pupils, potentially increasing their progress and attainment (Marsh *et al.*, 2005; UKLA/PNS, 2005). As children are experts in their own cultural capital they will be more confident to contribute when in class (DCSF, 2009). This knowledge also enables you to provide a culturally relevant curriculum which includes reading and writing across a range of media, complementing and enhancing traditional literacies (Marsh, 2010b).

Created in conjunction with Childnet, Ofcom provides an engaging 'Children's Online Content' worksheet aimed at children aged 8–11. It explores their online activity and preferences and provides prompts for discussion. You might want to use this as a survey tool for your own school or adapt it to meet your local needs. Access the 2017 Ofcom report and survey worksheet here: https://www.ofcom.org.uk/__data/assets/pdf_file/0026/97226/Childrens-online-worksheet-2016-17.pdf

- Which aspects of the report are most relevant to your pupils?
- How can you use the data from the report and your own survey to inform your English curriculum?
- Which forms of literacy are going to support your children in becoming competent and safe users of an ever-increasing range of technologies and their associated practices?

Recognising multi-literacies in the 21st century

So where do you currently stand on using new technologies in the English curriculum? Can you justify your response in relation to pedagogy, pupil engagement and pupil attainment? Do you see children's increased use of technology as a positive step forward? Is this an inevitable outcome of our increasingly digital society or is it something to be resisted within the primary classroom? Have your opinions influenced your school's English curriculum and practices?

Thinking about the range of media practices, digital tools and technologies which children engage with, it is evident that they need to develop a broad range of literacy skills. As consumers and creators of digital content, they need to be able to both comprehend and compose information in a range of forms which are often multimodal. These modes can be:

- **visual**, including still and moving image;
- **audio**, including music, sound effects and the spoken word;
- **linguistic**, including vocabulary, grammar, and oral and written language;
- **gestural**, including body language and facial expression;
- **spatial**, including the design and layout of a text, and typography.

(Bull and Anstey, 2010; Kress, 2010)

These elements can be weighted differently, in any combination to make meaning. Children therefore need to develop skills across a range of literacies: digital, visual, media, multimodal and traditional.

It can be assumed that children are naturally able to use new technologies; we might refer to 'digital natives' (Prensky, 2001: 1) who have grown up with access to the Internet and social media, and use of mobile phones and tablets. However, in addition to having access to such digital technologies, digital natives also need to have the skills and knowledge to use them (Palfrey and Gasser, 2008). A child might have the skills to play their favourite game on an iPad but not those necessary to create a multimodal text to express themselves; they might be able to find a chosen clip on YouTube but not know how to create and edit their own video.

The UKLA (2011) appealed for the current National Curriculum (DfE, 2013) to make explicit reference to 21st-century forms of communication, including digital, online and moving image media. They asserted that children were entitled to read, write and evaluate these sources in order to participate fully in society, both as a child and in preparation for adulthood. The British Film Institute (2008) called for a 21st-century literacy curriculum focusing on children's ability to read, interpret, analyse and create a range of media, including moving image and audio. As part of its 'Film: 21st Century Literacy' strategy it advocated that children need to enjoy and under-stand moving images in the same way that they do the written word in order to be 'not just … technically capable but to be culturally literate too' (Brooks *et al.*, 2012: 2).

Despite such pleas, the current National Curriculum for Primary English (DfE, 2013) appears to refer to a traditional view of literacy, making reference to books and print-based texts only. There is no direct reference to multimodal texts, including moving image and audio. However, if read alongside the curriculum for Primary Computing (DfE, 2013), exciting opportunities arise, as it calls for pupils to 'become digitally literate', able to 'express themselves and develop their ideas through information and communication technology at a level suitable for the future workplace and as active participants in a digital world' (DfE, 2013: 178). Its aim is for pupils to be 'responsible, competent, confident and creative users of information and communication technology' (DfE, 2013: 178). Working in conjunction with your school's Computing subject leader, there are multiple opportunities for identifying relevant and meaningful links between the two curriculums, fulfilling the aims of both.

- Work with the Computing subject leader to identify meaningful links and opportunities;
- Identify a progression of skills for both English and Computing for each year group. This is likely to exist within planning, assessment and tracking documentation for both subjects;
- Make use of exemplar documentation from the Local Authority;
- Attend local Subject Leader Networking events to share good practice;
- Match identified opportunities to relevant software and apps to resource the teaching;
- Consider how to assess, moderate and track progress of children's digital multimodal texts. Children's videos provide valuable evidence of progress from year to year.

Beyond the English and computing curriculum

Preparing children for the digital age requires mastery of a range of broad and essential skills. In the 2000s, a raft of curriculum reviews and government reports recommended revision of the primary curriculum (Alexander *et al.*, 2010; Becta, 2009; DCSF, 2009; DfES, 2006). They argued that learning should be:

- connected to what children know and do outside of the classroom;
- active;
- cross-curricular.

They focused on developing:

- communication skills, including oral communication;
- collaboration and teamwork;
- critical thinking and evaluation;
- creative thinking;
- problem solving.

The European Charter for Media Literacy (2004) also placed emphasis on the potential for developing collaboration and communication skills; this is reflected in the current Key Stage 2 Computing curriculum (DfE, 2013). The curriculum reviews intended teaching to be engaging and exciting, leading to innovation and inventiveness and to a love of learning. Teaching multi-literacies enables children to develop these skills within meaningful contexts, preparing them for life in the 21st century. For example, working in small groups to create an animation, children develop communication, presentation and teamwork skills; through collaboration, they have to make decisions and solve problems.

Critical literacy

Due to the nature of digital communication, children also need to develop critical literacy. Children potentially have constant access to digital information, much of it unregulated, with sources which are not always transparent. Children need to be discerning and critical consumers of texts, able to assess and evaluate content in order to make informed choices, remain safe and benefit from the opportunities offered (Alexander *et al.*, 2010; DfE, 2013). The features of critical literacy include:

Authorial intent:

Knowing that texts are constructed with an intention and that they have the power to inform, entertain or persuade, provoking the reader into action; that the text producer has made sophisticated choices over how to achieve this; that the content will be influenced by the author's own viewpoints and that therefore no texts are neutral; they represent values and opinions.

Interpretation:

Recognising that all readers and viewers of a text will interpret it differently based on their own prior experience, knowledge, beliefs and values.

Making meaning:

Recognising text features which create meaning, e.g. capital letters to indicate shouting in a text message, sentence construction within a written text, camera angle within a still image, and sound effects and colour within moving image.

Active engagement:

Examining and challenging the text's message through questioning.

(Janks *et al.*, 2013; LNS, 2009)

Does your English and wider curriculum provide opportunities for children to engage critically with printed, audio, visual and multimodal texts?

During shared and guided reading and through exploratory talk, are children encouraged to discuss responses to critical questions such as:

Who produced this text and what is their motive?
What is the purpose of the text and who will benefit from it?

What message is the text giving?

What does the producer want us to think and feel?

Whose perspective and viewpoints are being voiced and whose are missing?

What might an alternative viewpoint be?

What information has been included and excluded?

What assumptions have been made?

Who is the intended audience and is the text suitable for its audience and purpose?

Are pupils encouraged to compare the text against their own experiences and to discuss whether they agree with it?

Are pupils encouraged to consider point of view by comparing the text against other texts they have read or seen, including alternative versions?

Are children enabled to recognise relevant, cross-curricular and age-appropriate text types and their purposes, such as stories, magazines and comics, newspapers and online news sites, TV shows, instructions, packaging, text messages, podcasts, adverts, information texts, websites, films and animations? Do they critically examine hybrid texts such as a vlog which incorporates an advert?

Do children deconstruct texts in order to identify and evaluate their design features? Why were they included? What is their impact on the reader/viewer? E.g. comparing the persuasive features of adverts on television, in magazines and on the Internet, including within blogs, vlogs and social media.

Developing new literacies within the primary English classroom

Integrating new literacies into the curriculum signals a move in focus from print-based texts to multimodality. Increasingly children engage with digital texts outside of school, and if we are to keep them engaged in class, we need to embed these texts within our provision. The implication for teachers is that pupils need to develop skills across multiple literacies. This places demands on the subject knowledge of teachers and has resource implications.

You may already feel confident that your school provides and uses multimodal texts such as picture books, comics, graphic novels and children's newspapers; however, it is important to audit the digital texts which teachers use within their teaching and those which children have access to.

 Good subject leaders consider using the following:

* **Reading scheme e-texts.** Many reading schemes now include ebooks. These interactive texts feature games, puzzles and animations. Highlighted

words are read aloud and children can record themselves reading. Often texts can be accessed from home, encouraging home–school links and reading for pleasure. Some publishers' websites and apps also enable children to make their own digital stories.

- **E-comics** such as The Beano.
- **Appropriate websites** such as First News (www.firstnews.co.uk) and BBC Newsround (www.bbc.co.uk/newsround).
- **Multimodal apps** incorporating image, text and sound. You will need an Educational licence for these.
- **Short films and animations** available from sources including: The Literacy Shed, the British Film Institute (BFI), Pixar Story Shorts, Teachers Media (Primary Lesson Starters), KidsTV on YouTube.
- **TV programmes.**
- **Audio books.** Texts combined with an audio retelling on CD-Rom and children's audio books available on Audible (www.audible.co.uk/).

Children need to be explicitly taught how to access, navigate and interpret these highly complex texts. Through discussion using metalanguage and teacher modelling, children need to become aware of their structure and organisation (Bearne, 2003).

As required by the National Curriculum (DfE, 2013), children need to be creators as well as consumers of multimodal texts. This requires an understanding of the contribution and effect of each mode, audio, visual and written. Teachers need to discuss with children how each contributes to a text's meaning. The skills needed to produce a multimodal text extend into design and layout, and children will need support in making appropriate choices of how to combine the different modes to suit the purpose and audience of the text (Bearne, 2003). Clear steps for success need to be set, and when introducing a new skill, children will benefit from working in groups with the teacher and additional adults, all of whom need sufficient training. With experience, children will become increasingly independent, needing less support from adults.

Further to auditing the resources used within school, you will also want to audit the range of multimodal texts which children produce and their audiences. This could be achieved through reading teachers' schemes of work and planning, observing lessons and sharing examples of children's multimodal texts within staff meetings. Appropriate texts could include:

- **Blogs.** These enable collaborative research, writing and editing (Zawilinski, 2009); use them for encouraging discussion between pupils, teachers and parents and as digital newsletters. Use a closed site, within the confines of your school e-safety policy.

- **Podcasts.** Record presentations, discussions, interviews, audio diaries and children reading their own stories; use these to generate dialogue and narration. Sound effects and music can be added using a multitrack facility.
- **Emails** between pupils in local and distant locations, between fictional and historical characters.
- **Text messages.** For example, using the Threads app enables you to generate dialogue between characters.
- **Video.** Short films, film trailers, video diaries, documentaries, news reports, historical or scientific enactments or interviews. Layer different elements such as image, sound effect and music using iMovie.
- **Animation** of a short story, poem, a chapter of the class text or a scientific process.
- **Multimodal texts** using apps which combine text, image and sound.
- **Twitter messages.** Use individual class accounts to facilitate discussion, share ideas and receive feedback in real-time; communicate with real-world audiences, including authors and politicians, pupils and parents, the school community and beyond.

(Becker and Bishop, 2016; Henthorn and Cammack, 2017; Waller, 2010; Waller, 2011)

Digital technologies make it easier than ever to extend the participation of children, parents and the school community, especially when they are integrated into school practice and used on a regular basis. Moderate children's work and then publish it on your school blog or website, play them on a screen in the school reception area, share them during assemblies, and make them available in class and school libraries.

Developing visual literacy through the use of film

Film is a shared and motivating medium which plays a major part in most children's cultural lives (Bazalgette, 2010). The BFI refer to the Cs and Ss of film grammar: Camera shots, Colour and lighting, Character, Setting, Story and Sound. Through film, children can explore the impact of these features, combining images, sounds and words to express meaning. They explore how setting is created, and how character is portrayed through action, dialogue or appearance, together with identifying the narrative structure of the film text (British Film Institute, 2008).

When creating film with children, organise small teams with a range of roles: camera person; director; actor; interviewer; newsreader; researcher; prop maker;

script writer; editor; title and credit writer. Swap these across the year so children develop a range of skills. Also, take children through the process from storyboarding to identify the plotline, scenes, props and dialogue, to script writing, prop making, rehearsal, production and editing.

Whilst developing visual literacy, film can also improve traditional literacy skills. Spoken language and vocabulary can be developed through the use of exploratory talk and drama strategies in response to the text. Comprehension skills are developed as children explore narrative structure, characterisation and themes. When watching film, children still use the skills of hypothesis, deduction and inference; as they actively engage with the text, they draw on prior knowledge, respond to character and predict events (Bazalgette, 2010; Todd, 2013). This can be particularly beneficial when comparing a film version with a children's book, identifying the similarities and differences, discussing the director's interpretation of the film and exploring how the book's meaning has been portrayed through the Cs and Ss.

Film also acts as a scaffold for writing: character descriptions draw on evidence from the film; thought and speech bubbles are generated; sequencing still images is a stimulus for captions or acts as a storyboard for written narrative; diary entries can be written for characters; listening to a short clip of the sound track can stimulate creative writing; focusing on the Cs and Ss can lead to writing informed by camera angle or colour; and stopping the film at a strategic point can lead to writing story endings. Research would suggest that film increases children's motivation, improves visuality in their writing and leads to more sustained writing (UKLA/PNS, 2005).

Throughout these activities, children practise and develop storytelling and narrative skills as they engage in oral rehearsal, retell and innovate on known texts, and use story language.

The challenges of embedding new literacies within your English curriculum

The nature of digital technologies is that they are constantly evolving. It can feel daunting to keep abreast of this and it is important to make wise purchases when spending limited budgets. Where you can, keep it cheap and simple. Keep up to date by speaking to your pupils and observing what they choose to engage with, regularly visit websites which share and model the use of apps for educational purposes, follow online blogs, attend Local Authority events such as TeachMeets, attend professional conferences such as those organised by TEAN (Teacher Education Advancement Network) (www.cumbria.ac.uk/research/enterprise/tean/) and look at school and Local Authority websites.

It is also important to recognise that there can be a digital divide between pupils, their parents, their teachers and their peers who may or may not have access to digital technologies at home. Adults brought up in a print-dominated world may feel that the traditional skills of English are more important and should take precedence in the classroom or that digital texts are inferior and dumb down the curriculum, believing that children 'get enough of that at home' (Lambirth, 2003). Others, born before the advent of the digital age, may be described as 'digital immigrants' (Palfrey and Gasser, 2008). Having engaged with technology later in life, their limited knowledge and experience may lead to a lack of confidence. For teachers, this can mean that their pupils are more digitally literate than they are. Actually allowing children to be the expert in the room offers an opportunity to change the power dynamics, resulting in children and teachers learning alongside each other. However, consider the need for professional development required in order for teachers and teaching assistants to feel confident and competent in subject knowledge, pedagogy and technical competence.

 Steps to take to support your school community in engaging with new literacies:

- Ensure that your vision statement and School Development Plan reflect your school's stance on new literacies; identify priorities and budget requirements
- Purchase essential resources: video cameras, tablets, USB cameras, mics, portable green screen, stands, tripods
- Create animation sets
- Collect props, models and characters
- Provide training for equipment, core software and apps
- Keep productions short and simple
- Use copyright-free sites for images, music and sound effects or collect your own images
- Celebrate children's work in local and national competitions
- Increase enthusiasm and participation through extra-curricular activities, such as Animation Clubs
- Provide workshops for parents, demonstrating and justifying the activities their children are doing

- Your SMT might set performance management targets referring to specific foci, e.g. creating an animation; set clear success criteria and an agreed timescale

> • Monitor progress and share ideas regularly during workshops, staff meetings and via a Staff Learning Wall; do paired teaching; observe teaching and learning
> • Monitor impact: assess children's progress against National Curriculum expectations (DfE, 2013) and your school's assessment tracking systems

Where to go for inspiration and advice

Key texts in addition to those in the References list:

- Barber, D. and Cooper, L. (2012) *Using New Web Tools in the Primary Classroom: A practical guide for enhancing teaching and learning.* London: Routledge.
- Bearne, E. and Wolstencroft, H. (2007) *Visual Approaches to Teaching Writing.* London: Paul Chapman.
- Carpenter, J. P. and Krutka, D. G. (2014) 'How and why educators use Twitter: A survey of the field.' *Journal of Research on Technology in Education,* 46 (4), 414–34.
- Charles, M. and Boyle, B. (2014) *Using Multiliteracies and Multimodalities to Support Young Children's Learning.* London: Sage.
- Children's Commissioner (2017) 'Growing up digital: A report of the Growing Up Digital Taskforce.' https://www.childrenscommissioner.gov.uk/publication/growing-up-digital/ [accessed 4 September 2018].
- Davies, J. and Merchant, G. (2009) *Web 2.0 for Schools.* New York: Peter Lang.
- Frey, N. E. and Fisher, D. B. (2008) *Teaching Visual Literacy.* London: Sage.
- Henry, M. (2015) *Learning in the Digital Age: Developing critical, creative and collaborative skills.* In: Younie, S. Leask, M. and Burden, K. (eds), *Teaching and Learning with ICT in the Primary School.* Abingdon: Routledge.
- Kuznekoff, J. H., Munz, S. and Titsworth, S. (2015) 'Mobile phones in the classroom: Examining the effects of texting, Twitter, and message content on student learning.' *Communication Education,* 64 (3), 344–65.
- Lankshear, C. and Knobel, M. (eds) (2008) *Digital Literacies: Concepts, policies and practices.* New York: Peter Lang Publishing.
- Merchant, G., Gillen, J., Marsh, J. and Davies, J. (eds) (2012) *Virtual Literacies: Interactive spaces for children and young people.* New York, NY: Routledge.
- Savage, M. and Barnett, A. (2015) *Digital Literacy for Primary Teachers.* Northwich: Critical Teaching.
- Stafford, T. (2011) *Teaching Visual Literacy in the Primary Classroom.* Abingdon: Routledge.

Suggested websites:

EuroMediaLiteracy: provides links to useful resources to support media education
https://euromedialiteracy.eu/resources.php
Media Smart: free educational materials to help children think critically about advertising
http://mediasmart.uk.com/
Tim Rylands – Using ICT to Inspire: a very comprehensive collection of engaging and motivating ways to use ICT for teaching and learning
http://www.timrylands.com/
Mr P's ICT Blog – Tech to raise standards: creative approaches to supporting learning with technology across the curriculum, including ideas for English
http://mrparkinsonict.blogspot.co.uk/

Popular apps/software:

* Filming: Windows Movie Maker, iMovie, Adobe Premier Elements
* DV Prompter – teleprompter
* Green screen: Veescope, DoInk
* Animation: I Can Animate, Animate It, Toontastic, Sock Puppets, Puppet Pals
* Multimodal capability: PowerPoint, Prezi, My Story, Book Creator, Comic Life, SonicPics, Photostory, Tellagami, Morfo, Skitch, Explain Everything, Shadow Puppet Edu

References

Alexander, R., Armstrong, M., Flutter, J., Hargreaves, L., Harrison, D., Harlen, W., Hartley-Brewer, E., Kershner, R., MacBeath, J., Mayall, B., Northen, S., Pugh, G., Richards, C. and Utting, D. (2010) *Children, their World, their Education: Final report and recommendations of the Cambridge Primary Review.* London: Routledge.

Bazalgette, C. (ed.) (2010) *Teaching Media in Primary Schools.* London: Sage Publications.

Bearne, E. (2003) *Rethinking Literacy: Communication, representation and text in reading.* Leicester: UKLA.

Becker, R. and Bishop, P. (2016) 'Think bigger about science: Using Twitter for learning in the middle grades.' *Middle School Journal*, 47 (3), 4–16.

Becta (2009) 'Curriculum and teaching innovation.' Bristol: Futurelab. Available at: www.creativetallis.com/uploads/2/2/8/7/2287089/futurelab_-_curriculum_and_teaching_innovation.pdf [accessed 4 September 2018].

British Film Institute (BFI) (2008) 'Reframing literacy: A film pitch for the twenty-first century.' Available at: https://www.bfi.org.uk/sites/bfi.org.uk/files/downloads/bfi-education-reframing-literacy-2013-04.pdf [accessed 4 September 2018].

Brooks, R., Cooper, A. and Penke, L. (2012) 'Film: 21st-century literacy teaching using film – statistical evidence.' Available at: https://www.bfi.org.uk/sites/bfi.org.uk/files/downloads/film-21st-century-literacy-teaching-using-film-statistical-evidence.pdf [accessed 4 September 2018].

Bull, G. and Anstey, M. (2010) *Evolving Pedagogies: Reading and writing in a multimodal world*. Carlton, South Australia: Education Services Australia Ltd.

DCSF (2009) *Independent Review of the Primary Curriculum*. Nottingham: DCSF.

Department for Education (DfE) (2013) *The National Curriculum in England Key Stages 1 and 2 Framework Document*. London: DfE Publications.

Department for Education and Skills (DfES) (2006) *2020 Vision Report of the Teaching and Learning in 2020 Review Group*. London: DfES Publications.

EuroMediaLiteracy (2004) *European Charter for Media Literacy*. Available at: https://euromedialiteracy.eu [accessed 28 March 2018].

Henthorn, J. and Cammack, P. (2017) 'Blogging and tweeting in the classroom: Exploring how effective use of new media can help teaching and learning in primary schools.' *TEAN Journal*, 9 (2), 3–13.

Janks, H., Dixon, K., Ferreira, A. and Granville, S. (2013) *Doing Critical Literacy: Texts and activities for students and teachers*. Abingdon: Routledge.

Kress, G. (2010) *Multimodality: A social semiotic approach to contemporary communication*. New York: Routledge.

Lambirth, A. (2003) '"They get enough of that at home": Understanding aversion to popular culture in schools.' *Reading, Language & Literacy*, 37 (1), 119–133.

LNS (2009) 'Capacity Building Series: Critical literacy: available Ontario: LNS.' Available at: http://www.edu.gov.on.ca/eng/literacynumeracy/inspire/research/Critical_Literacy.pdf [accessed 4 September 2018].

Marsh, J. (2010a) 'Social networking practices in homes and schools.' In: Bazalgette, C. (ed.), *Teaching Media in Primary Classrooms*. London: Sage.

Marsh, J. (2010b) *Childhood, Culture and Creativity: A literature review*. Newcastle: Creativity, Culture and Education.

Marsh, J., Brooks, G., Hughes, J., Ritchie, L., Roberts, S. and Wright, K. (2005) 'Digital beginnings: Young children's use of popular culture, media and new technologies.' Report of the 'Young Children's Use of Popular Culture, Media and New Technologies' Study. Available at: https://www.researchgate.net/publication/265183910_Digital_beginnings_Young_children's_use_of_popular_culture_media_and_new_technologies [accessed 4 September 2018].

Ofcom (2017) 'Children and parents: Media use and attitudes report.' Available at: https://www.ofcom.org.uk/research-and-data/media-literacy-research/childrens/children-parents-2017 [accessed 4 September 2018].

Palfrey, J. and Gasser, U. (2008) *Born Digital: Understanding the first generation of digital natives*. New York: Basic Books.

Prensky, M. (2001) 'Digital natives, digital immigrants.' *On the Horizon*, 9 (5), 1–6.

Todd, I. (2013) 'Visual literacy.' In: Metcalfe, J., Simpson, D., Todd, I. and Toyn, M. (eds), *Thinking through New Literacies for Primary and Early Years*. London: Sage.

UKLA (2011) 'UKLA response to the Review of the English National Curriculum.' Available at: https://ukla.org/news/story/ukla_response_to_the_review_of_the_english_national_curriculum [accessed 4 September 2018].

UKLA/PNS (2005) *Raising Boys' Achievement in Writing*. London: HMSO.

Waller, M. (2010) 'It's very, very fun and exciting – using Twitter in the primary classroom.' *English, 4–11*, 39 (1), 14–18.

Waller, M. (2011) 'Everyone in the world can see it – developing pupil voice through online social networks in the primary classroom.' In: Czerniawski, G. and Kidd, W. (eds), *The Student Voice Handbook: Bridging the academic/practitioner divide*. Bingley: Emerald Group Publishing.

Zawilinski, L. (2009) 'HOT Blogging: A framework for blogging to promote higher order thinking.' *The Reading Teacher*, 62 (8), 650–661.

Working in teams and managing change

Neil Suggett

In this chapter we will consider the nature of successful teamwork and the components of effective change management. Managing change involves finding the answers to three basic questions and you will be introduced to two change management models to support this process. We will then address the complementary skills triangle required by an English subject leader: leadership, management and coaching. The judgement call is to select a 'leadership style' that is appropriate to the demands of the situation. The final part of the chapter addresses the challenge of developing your team, with an emphasis upon positive self-talk and optimism.

Working in teams

It is a truism that nobody is perfect, but a team can be. As the English subject leader one of your biggest challenges is to facilitate people working together as an effective team. We all have an intuitive understanding of what good team-work looks and feels like and there are many and various definitions of the term *team*. Katzenbach and Smith (1998) capture the essence of teamwork in their definition:

> A team is a small number of people with complementary skills who are committed to a common purpose, performance goals, and approach for which they are mutually accountable.
>
> *(Katzenbach and Smith, 1998: 45)*

The quotation sounds deceptively simple at first sight, but when the definition is broken down into its component parts it may be slightly more complex:

- a small group of people;
- commitment to a common purpose;
- shared performance goals and approach;
- mutual accountability.

A small group of people

The English subject leader is ultimately responsible for everybody in the school who has a part to play in delivering effective English teaching. In a large school this will be a substantial number of adults, while in a one-form entry primary school it will be eight teachers and designated support staff. From the child's perspective, regardless of the size of the school, this should be a seamless and stimulating learning experience, with each adult playing their part in the delivery process. The English subject leader has the responsibility of shaping the vision and living it out on a daily basis.

A commitment to a common purpose

Teamwork is most effective when everybody knows what they are seeking to achieve and understands their part in the process. A clearly articulated vision provides a picture of where the school is going and what outstanding teaching and learning look like. The subject leader is both the architect and guardian of this vision. Developing and maintaining a shared vision takes time and commitment, especially as the curriculum and the staff change. The subject leader needs to have a finger on the pulse of the school and constantly monitor team performance.

Shared performance goals and approach

The starting point for effective practice is to know precisely what you seek to achieve. There is room for professional autonomy and creativity in *how* (approach) lessons are delivered, but there should be absolute clarity on *what* (performance goals) needs to be achieved by each group of children. The subject leader will be responsible for authoring the policy and practice documents for English that support shared performance goals. These documents will reflect national policy and the collective thinking of the team involved in delivering the subject within the school.

Mutual accountability

Every adult in the school has a myriad of accountabilities: to senior leaders, to other colleagues and most importantly to the children. In an ideal world everyone would accept these accountabilities and perform accordingly, although in reality individuals may need to understand personal accountability and know that performance will be monitored. Monitoring is a significant part of the role of the English subject leader. Through regular monitoring, a subject overview can be maintained, individual teacher performance analysed and pupil progress tracked. This monitoring should include learning walks, classroom observations, book scrutiny, pupil voice interviews and data analysis. Evidence of teacher underperformance has to be addressed quickly and decisively.

Managing change

> 'The only constant in the universe is change.'
>
> (Heraclitus, c. 535 BC–475 BC)

Nothing stays the same for long, and the English subject leader is responsible for analysing what actually needs to be done to systematically move the subject forward. When managing change, the following broad principles apply:

- the *what* of change is not difficult to ascertain, provided that you are tracking national policy changes and in-school performance;
- transforming this knowledge into effective team action requires leadership skill and staff development time;
- the *how* of implementation is the real challenge in a busy school environment – it is demanding to get colleagues to embrace new ideas that might initially involve more work.

The components of managing change successfully

Henry Ford, American founder of the Ford Motor Company, once said, 'If you always do what you have always done, you will always get what you have always got.' Managing change successfully is a foundational component of any leadership role, not least for those who manage change in a key subject such as English.

- Create a compelling vision and have the energy and resilience to make it a reality;
- Deliver a relentless focus on learning and teaching, the starting point for everything in the school;

- Determine a strategy for motivating staff and ensuring the continuing professional development of the whole-school workforce;
- Establish clear procedures and ways of holding people to account;
- Have mechanisms for celebrating and sharing success widely and quickly, and addressing underperformance directly.

Where to start

As a new English subject leader it is very important to establish a clear starting point when managing change. Two change management models that have been used with great success are MIC (Maintain, Improve, Change) and SWOT (Strengths, Weaknesses, Opportunities, Strengths).

MIC is a three-part model that can be employed widely with staff, children and parents (see Table 8.1).

A SWOT analysis is a very commonly used tool that has both a current and a future dimension (see Table 8.2).

This model was used in Chapter 1 to help you to determine your own strengths and weaknesses as an English subject leader. The judicious application of these two models to the wider context of English across the school will provide the data to establish a starting point for future development and will answer the question: *Where are we now?*

Three basic questions

The simplest management of change strategy is based around this and two further questions:

- Where are we now?
- Where do we want to be?
- How do we get from one to the other?

Moving from the current reality to the ideal, desired future state requires an appropriate balance of visionary leadership, conscientious management and developmental coaching.

Table 8.1 Maintain, Improve and Change (MIC) – a three-part model

Maintain	*What are we doing that is working well and we need to maintain?*
Improve	*What are we doing that we need to keep doing, but needs some improvement and modification?*
Change	*What needs to be changed fundamentally because it is not working?*

Table 8.2 SWOT (Strengths, Weaknesses, Opportunities and Threats) analysis for managing change

SWOT Analysis

Strengths	**Weaknesses**
• *What are the best things about our English teaching that we should hang on to at all costs?*	• *What are our collective weaknesses in English?*
• *Which three strengths of our English teaching should we be publicising widely?*	• *Which three weaknesses in priority order should we be addressing first?*
Opportunities	**Threats**
• *In five years' time our English teaching will be...*	• *The threats to our English teaching from national and local changes in the next five years are...*
• *If I were a parent considering sending my child to our school I would want...*	• *We can deal with these threats by...*

The complementary skills triangle

Cashman suggests that 'leadership is authentic influence that creates value' (Cashman, 2008: 24). Let's consider the three complementary skills of leadership, management and coaching (see Figure 8.1).

Leadership is not simply something we do, rather it is an intimate expression of who we are and reflects our values, principles and life experiences (Cashman, 2008). The English subject leader is required to generate and implement a vision for high-quality English learning and teaching that is appropriate to your school and the needs of your children. A good leader is also acutely aware of the needs of her or his followers: the other members of the team.

Management was once described by William Henry Koontz, the United States congressman, as 'getting things done through and with other people'. The challenge is to get the whole team working towards the same vision and playing their part in the smooth delivery of the English curriculum. This will require visionary leadership and careful management. Policy documents enshrine the vision and the day-to-day challenges, and ensure that all staff members comply with the agreed ways of working. Leadership may sound more exciting than the grind of systematic monitoring but the two activities are complementary.

Coaching provides the third side of the subject leader's skills triangle. Whitmore defines coaching as a way to unlock an individual's 'potential' (Whitmore, 2009: 10). Coaching supports people to develop their own potential rather than instructing them in what they need to learn (Whitmore, 2009).

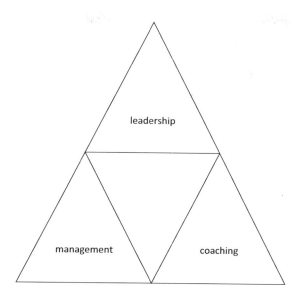

Figure 8.1 The complementary skills triangle

Coaching for successful change

The educational world is constantly changing and educators have to grow and develop in order to keep abreast of this change. The subject leader has a responsibility to provide continuing professional development both to the team and to individuals. Individual coaching is an excellent way of helping colleagues reach their full potential (Suggett, 2017).

In summary, leadership provides vision, management ensures compliance and coaching facilitates team and individual development.

Employ an appropriate leadership style

A great deal has been written about leadership styles and, as discussed in Chapter 1, it is sensible to have a range of styles at your disposal in order to deal with whatever challenge comes your way.

Goleman's six leadership styles

1. Commanding
2. Visionary
3. Affiliative
4. Democratic

5. Pacesetting
6. Coaching

(Goleman, 2000)

You may have a preferred style, but it is advisable to have other approaches in your locker in case your preferred style does not work. Your choice of style will be influenced by the particular individual or situation you are working with. It will also be affected by the culture of your school and where it is in its organisational life cycle. Style choice is always a judgement call and the key criterion is 'does it get the job done in the most effective way?'.

Subject leadership is a marathon rather than a sprint, with the twin imperatives of getting the job done and growing the people in the process. There are positive and negative aspects to each of Goleman's (2000) leadership styles, and his work highlights when different leadership styles work best and considers the overall impact of each style on the climate of the team.

It is preferable to adopt a *coaching* style, with *visionary, democratic* and *affiliative* components (see Chapter 1 for leadership definitions). This way of working would ensure that leadership worked with colleagues in a highly supportive and collaborative way. However, this blend of styles is unlikely to be appropriate in the aftermath of an unsuccessful Ofsted Inspection, when a mixture of *commanding* and *pacesetting* may be more suited to the demands of the situation.

The leadership cycle

Vision

The importance of a clear and compelling vision cannot be overemphasised. As Charles Handy says, 'Vision grabs' (Handy, 1993: 116). As discussed earlier, the vision may have been established by employing a blend of *democratic* and *affiliative* leadership styles. It should also reflect systematic evidence-based research and best pedagogical practice. This vision should encapsulate a shared anticipation of the future and make clear what will be happening at three levels: the individual teacher, the English team and the whole school. The subject leader should model best practice on a daily basis, providing an exemplar of how to make the vision a living reality.

Envision

One of the basic tenets of a coaching approach is that people are much more likely to implement a plan they have had a hand in shaping. This will be the case in designing a new policy or approach with the current staff team. The challenge arises as staff change and new members, who were not part of the original design team, come on

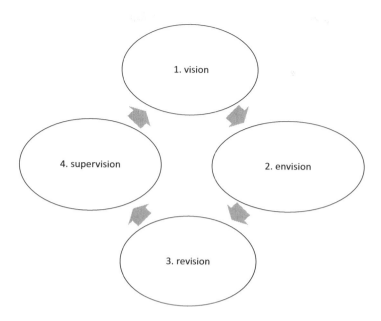

Figure 8.2 The leadership cycle

board. Bringing the vision alive for new colleagues is a challenge that requires consistency and subtlety. Even for long-standing members of the team there is a periodic need to bring the approach 'back to the boil'. This may be done at both the individual and team levels. The positive role model of the subject leader is crucial.

Supervision

The literal meaning of *supervision* is to look over. This is part of the role of the English subject leader: to look over the quality of learning and teaching across the school and to hold people to account. This is often the part that new subject leaders find quite uncomfortable, to oversee the work of colleagues, especially those who are more experienced. Nevertheless, it is vital that the subject leader has a comprehensive picture of what is going on in all parts of the school in order to ensure consistency and progression. The more comprehensive the picture that can be established, the better the opportunities to highlight good practice and address underperformance early. It might not be comfortable, but it is a very important part of the accountability of the subject leader.

Revision

Policy and practice will continue to evolve over time. National guidelines change and people grow and develop. Most importantly, the nature and preferences of the learners may also change. It is important to revisit the MIC and SWOT tools on an annual basis in order to keep your finger on the pulse of your subject. Some things will be working very well and you can capitalise on these successes by doing more of these things or using these approaches more widely. Conversely, some things will not be working as well as you might have hoped and corrective action might need to be taken. At the very simplest level, the effective subject leader will promote what is working well and change what is not working. The English subject leader is the repository of this overview.

Developing your team

As English subject leader, your task is to promote learning and teaching in English, and in order to do this you need to be aware of the process of how to get people to work together successfully. There are two fundamental skills of team literacy that you need to develop: process observation, and giving and receiving feedback.

 Effective subject leaders carry out effective observation processes, which requires:

- skill in accurate observation;
- identification of the things that are done and said that help the team make progress;
- the ability to pin-point blockers and blockages in team process;
- awareness of your own behaviour as a team member.

They give and receive feedback successfully, which involves:

- a focus on developing each individual, the team and the whole school;
- supplying usable information in a timely manner;
- being specific and citing evidence for your feedback;
- providing a balance of support and challenge.

The importance of the team's self-talk

Self-talk is the mental evaluation of what you have done, what you are doing and what you are about to do. Each conversation you have with yourself and with other people has a potential impact upon your self-image. The nature of your team's self-talk has a profound effect upon the quality of your performance and merits careful attention.

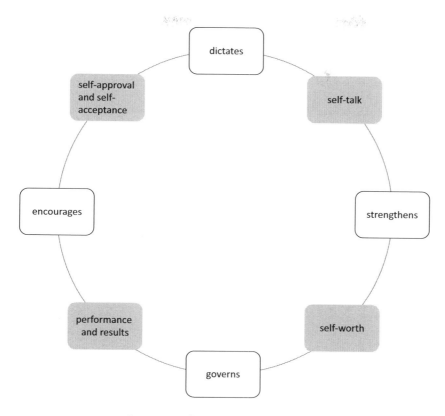

Figure 8.3 The importance of self-talk

Self-talk comes in two basic varieties: negative and positive. Negative self-talk is destructive and engenders disappointment and underperformance. On the other hand, positive self-talk predisposes us to success and generates optimism and resourcefulness. We choose!

Self-talk strengthens self-worth and governs performance and results. Performance and results encourage self-approval and self-acceptance. It is therefore important that as the English subject leader you dictate and promote positive self-talk, helping the cycle of positivity, performance and results to move on.

- 'This is a great team, I enjoy working with these people.'
- 'Our children are great to work with, we are so lucky.'

They NEVER say...

> • 'What is a nice person like me doing working in a team like this?'
> • 'These children are hopeless, they have no rich experiences to underpin their writing.'

Listen to your team's self-talk scripts in a conscious and deliberate way. Observe what you hear and reflect upon what you have written. Which frequently voiced scripts are hampering the team and which ones are serving you well?

Invest in relentless optimism

As the English subject leader, you have a fundamental choice in the way you approach the future. You can be pessimistic and see the future as a threat to be endured. Alternatively, you can see the future as an opportunity and embrace the possibilities it offers. The conventional wisdom is that successful teamwork results from a combination of talent and desire, and failure reflects a lack of talent or motivation. Martin Seligman (2006) suggests that failure could occur when talent and desire are both present but optimism is missing. Optimism is the key, and it is your job to personify it.

Martyn Newman's twenty-three years of research in psychology confirm optimism as the emotional competency that is the most robust predictor of success in life (and teams). Optimism isn't the passive expectation that things will get better. On the contrary, it is a conviction that we can choose to make things better (Newman, 2008).

Team review

Where is your team in Tuckman's (1965) four stages of team development (see Figure 8.4)? Is the team forming, storming, norming or performing?

It is part of the role of the English subject leader to move the team through to the performing stage. The question is: *'How do I do that?'*

 Develop a clear strategy for moving the team and the subject forward:

• Establish a shared vision and be clear about what is negotiable and non-negotiable;
• Divide the labour and ensure everybody understands their role in the team;
• Beef up communication and cohesion so that everybody knows what is going on;
• Emphasise shared leadership and shared accountability;

- Invest in people and their continuous development;
- Rely on their professional judgement, but seek advice where necessary.

Review the team in terms of:

- the results it is producing and its impact on children;
- the areas of strength and development;
- its membership and how it deals with high performers and challenging members;
- your own impact on the performance of the team.

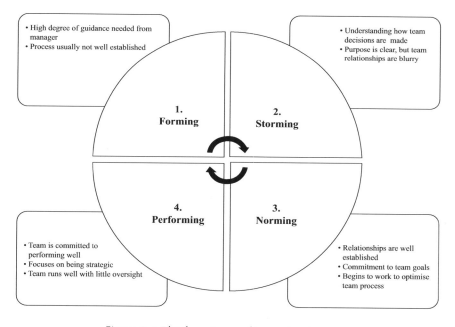

Figure 8.4 The four stages of team development

Use the following ten questions to shape a team and a personal action plan:

- What are our strengths as a team?
- What are our next development areas as a team?
- What are our successes?

- What do we need to do better?
- What is the quality of English learning and teaching in our school?
- How am I performing as English subject leader?
- How successfully do I influence the other members of my team?
- What is the quality of my leadership, management and coaching?
- What is the impact of staff development in English?
- What is my top priority?

Table 8.3 Actions for me

Actions for me	Actions for team	My learning about teams

Coaching and change

High levels of change in education make constant demands on school leaders. As the subject leader you will often be in the situation of asking staff to do more, or make changes to practice, in situations that are time and resource limited. In order to accommodate change and improve practice some managers will employ transactional methods to get things done. Coaching offers a different approach that shares the responsibility of finding solutions to the challenge of change. Coaching offers an approach to build capacity within the staff team.

The terms coaching and mentoring are often referenced together in leadership documentation but the terms are not interchangeable. Coaching is not mentoring: a mentor imparts knowledge accrued from expertise and experience. There is also an element of *telling* in the process of mentoring that is not required in coaching. Coaching is a more comfortable way of working for new post-holders because it does not assume a superiority of knowledge or expertise over the coachee (Passmore, 2017). Instead, coaching seeks to develop the coachee's own ability to see where the issues are with their performance and assist them in understanding how they can overcome them.

A coaching approach requires investment in colleagues and is not an approach that reaps results overnight. It might appear preferable to tell someone what to do, gain results quicker and spend less time working on solutions, but *telling* is a short-term solution that will reap limited results. Being told what to do is unproductive for two main reasons. Firstly, the employee is not encouraged to find solutions for themselves and, therefore, as the leader you will be required to provide answers and solutions to future issues. Secondly, it is harder to remember how to carry out something you have been told to do, rather than retaining information and knowledge gained through reflection on personal experience.

The English subject leader as coach

In order to coach successfully you need to embody the following key characteristics. The effective coach is:

- patient;
- detached;
- supportive;
- interested;
- a good listener;
- perceptive;
- aware;
- self-aware;
- attentive;
- retentive.

(Whitmore, 2009: 41–2)

The GROW model

The key to good coaching is to ask open questions that cause the coachee to reflect on their own performance. Whitmore (2009) suggests the following GROW model as a structure for asking the questions.

The framework above serves as a template for the subject leader to record their conversation with the coachee. Your role is to take notes and ask probing, open questions that require further thinking from the coachee. It may be hard at first for you to remain impassive in the coaching role and to not offer solutions or possible ways forward for the coachee. The form provides a record of the coaching session and should be given to the coachee for action. It is useful to retain a copy ready to bring to the next coaching

Table 8.4 The GROW model

G	GOAL: Set the goal for the session. What is it that the coachee wants to explore and try to resolve? This can be a long-term or a short-term goal.
R	REALITY: Define the reality of the situation for the coachee. Allow them to explore and describe the issue as they experience it.
O	OPTIONS: Ask the coachee to consider what options they have to progress the issue. What strategies could they employ? How could they alter their actions? What could they do to move forward to progress their GOAL?
W	WHAT will they commit to do? Which of the OPTIONS will they carry out? WHEN will they do this and WHOM else does it involve?

session. You can then use it as a means to recap on previous discussion and reflect on progress made.

Successful coaching requires the coachee to take responsibility for their actions and for finding solutions. It requires them to be aware of the educational focus and the context they are working in. The coachee also needs to be self-aware of their ability to identify their personal strengths and areas for development. This links to a teacher's ability to self-reflect on teaching and learning and to consider how they can improve. Whitmore suggests a few helpful questions to use in coaching sessions.

Helpful coaching questions

- Is there anything else you'd like to add?
- Why do you say/think that?
- What advice would you give to someone else in this situation?
- What would be the consequences of doing/saying that for you or for others?
- What would you gain/lose by doing/saying that?
- What is the hardest part of this for you?
- Who else could help you with this? Where could you seek support?

(Based on Whitmore, 2009: 51–2)

Practice in coaching is the only way to improve your coaching skills. The model can be applied to any situation or context, not just education, and this means that you can try out your coaching skills in safer contexts. Have a go at using the GROW template with a friend, peer or colleague – someone you have a good relationship with. The GOAL can be a personal or work-related matter. Work through the GROW template thinking carefully about how to ask open questions. Record what the coachee says. Summarise your notes at points throughout the process to ensure that you are capturing what the coachee tells you. This gives the coachee time to reflect on what they have said and they may wish to add or change the notes.

 After you have conducted the coaching session, reflect on the role and the process:

- Were you attentive to the coachee? How did you attempt to communicate this? Think about your body language and verbal responses.
- How easy did you find it to pose open questions? Did you ask any leading questions?

- Did you use any of the helpful coaching questions? What response did they illicit?
- Did you reflect back on the key points you heard? Were you able to summarise the coachee's discussion?

References

Cashman, K. (2008) *Leadership from the Inside Out*. 2nd edn. California: Berret-Koehler Publishers Inc.

Goleman, D. (2000) 'Leadership that gets results.' *Harvard Business Review*. March–April. Available at: www.powerelectronics.ac.uk/documents/leadership-that-gets-results.pdf [accessed 9 July 2018].

Handy, C. (1993) *Understanding Organizations*. 4th edn. New York: Oxford University Press.

Katzenbach, J. R. and Smith, D. K. (1998) *The Wisdom of Teams*. London: McKinsey & Company, Inc.

Newman, M. (2008) *Emotional Capitalists: The new leaders*. London: RocheMartin.

Passmore, J. (ed.) (2017) *Leadership Coaching: Working with leaders to develop elite performance*. 2nd edn. London: Kogan Page.

Seligman, M. E. P. (2006) *Learned Optimism: How to change your life and your mind*. New York: Vintage Books.

Suggett, E. N. (2017) *Living a Coaching Lifestyle*. Amazon.

Tuckman, B. (1965) 'Developmental sequence in small groups.' *Psychological Bulletin*, 63 (6), 384–399.

Whitmore, J. (2009) *Coaching for Performance*. 4th edn. London: Nicholas Brealey Publishing.

Leading school development: One school's journey

South Baddesley Church of England Primary School, Hampshire

Lisa Baldwin

This case study focused chapter will be from a practitioner's perspective with a focus on improving attainment in writing. There will an opportunity to understand how policy is put into action and how subject development leads to changes in practice and staff development. Exemplification will be provided of how one school used an action research project to pave the way for whole-school change. Examples will be provided of how this school identified key areas for pupil development and trialled new approaches to support the children. Guidance will be given on how a school can assess the impact of action research on pupil progress before taking the step of wider action in light of the project's success.

The development focus

The action research project described in this chapter began in October 2015. It has been a long journey and it is important to remember that action research will not provide a quick fix for school development issues. Action research is about long-term change that considers the specific needs of the pupils and allows for the experimentation of teacher practice to enable children to achieve their full potential.

The new National Curriculum (DfE, 2013) had been in place for a year and the school had made adjustments, as most schools did, to ensure that new expectations were being met. The school was deliberating over pupil progress in light of the changes, and evidence showed that the school was gaining good pupil results in reading comprehension and in the grammar, punctuation and spelling (GPS) test, but writing was tailing behind. Lyndsey (the English subject leader) reflected on this evidence and knew that high standards of grammar, punctuation and spelling were not always evident in the children's written work despite the high attainment in the GPS test. Changes to the writing requirements meant that teacher assessment of writing necessitated evidence of component parts of language and specific grammatical features and punctuation. Such elements were essential to reaching national 'age-related' and 'greater depth' expectations for writing. It was Lyndsey's belief that the slower progress in writing was due to pupils' perception of their knowledge about grammar, punctuation and spelling being distinct from their experience of writing. She noted that the children's separation of the skills reflected the lack of an integrated approach to grammar and punctuation in writing lessons.

The school had an established approach to teaching writing through high-quality texts, and Lyndsey was passionate about advocating strong links between reading and writing. She felt that an integrated approach could also be the right way for the school to develop the teaching of grammar and punctuation. She wanted to make sure that pupils' writing developed the use of grammar, punctuation and language features in a way that was both creative and effective.

Pupil interviews

Lyndsey wanted to find out more about the children's view of writing. Her starting point to defining the action research project came through discussions about writing with the children in her class. A group of pupils (with ranging abilities) were selected from her mixed Years 3/4 class and were asked the following questions:

* Is writing important?
* What makes a good writer?
* What helps you to write well?
* What is difficult for you about writing?
* How could you improve your writing?

Lyndsey used a semi-structured interview approach, asking the predetermined questions but also following the flow of the children's conversation. Lyndsey noted the children's responses as the group talked, recording their points on post-it notes. After the discussion had taken place she considered where the children's feedback raised similar themes. She was then able to reflect on what the comments revealed about writing. She composed a themed mind-map of the comments.

127

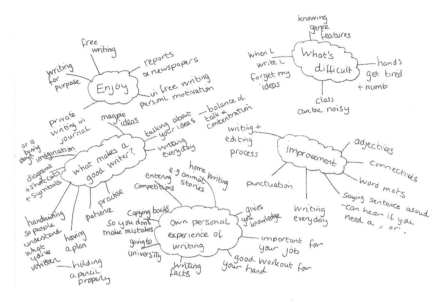

Figure 9.1 Pupil interview mind-map

Emerging themes: What was working?

The interview revealed that the children were aware of **what makes a good writer**. They talked about personal qualities and skills such as patience, motivation and imagination. They also talked about **transcriptional** elements, the importance of holding the pen properly and having clear handwriting so the teacher could read what they had written. One child said that writing was a good workout for your hand. They knew that good writers planned for writing, discussed thinking and often 'magpie' ideas. When the children spoke about the **enjoyment of writing** they enthused about private writing in their journals and the opportunity this gave them to 'free write'.

The interview revealed which experiences and methods the pupils valued and Lyndsey reflected on the success brought about by her established teaching approaches.

When the children talked about their own **personal experience** of writing they clearly understood the importance of being a good writer. They talked about writing as a purposeful activity and articulated this as a key skill in relation to their life outside of school. Entering competitions and writing stories were all given as reasons to write at home. They also talked about writing being important for getting a job and going to university. They clearly saw writing as an important life skill and understood how writing was useful beyond school.

Emerging themes: What could be improved?

When Lyndsey discussed how they could **improve** their writing the children said they needed more practice in order to get better. They said that checking punctuation and editing work was important, and they specifically talked about commas and full stops as something they needed to remember to do in their writing. They said that they sometimes forgot to use the prompts around the classroom (working walls and word mats) during the **writing and editing process**. They talked about their difficulty knowing **genre features** and when to use grammar such as **conjunctions** and **adjectives**. Some of the children also felt their **handwriting** was holding them back and this greatly affected some individuals, altering their perceptions of how successful they were at writing.

Lyndsey reflected on what the pupils' comments revealed about the strengths and weaknesses of her teaching of writing. She reflected that they valued the practices she regularly used to scaffold and model writing, such as the word wall and the use of talk. Their discussion indicated that the review of their written work, with a focus on accurate punctuation and better use of grammatical features, required improvement. Lyndsey was also troubled by the impact poor handwriting was having on a small number of pupils in the group and she felt this was something that needed specific intervention support.

Analysing pupils' written work

Next, Lyndsey took a close look at the children's writing in their English books. The books were analysed using the CLPE writing scale and key performance indicators (KPIs) used by the school to indicate progress towards National Curriculum age-related outcomes. A range of abilities was analysed to see how the pupils were doing. The books revealed that the children displayed many features indicative of a 'Moderately fluent writer' (CLPE, 2016). The children were able to write in a few known forms. They were developing their awareness of the reader, and including some expanded noun phrases and vocabulary for effect or description. Their sentence structure was beginning to be more varied, but use of adverbs and conjunctions was limited. Punctuation was not always used appropriately to support meaning and was either inaccurate or inconsistently used. The children were willing to take risks with composition but they found it difficult to sustain initial efforts over longer pieces of writing.

The book scrutiny and the pupil interviews formed a baseline of evidence that illustrated where pupil writing was prior to the research project taking place. A baseline is important, as it provides a reference for the end of the project, to 'help judge the effectiveness' (Bearne *et al.*, 2007: 6).

129

Case study learning points

✓ **Pupil interview.** Understand how the pupils think they need support.
✓ **Examine the evidence.** Look at pupil outcomes, reflect on ways of working and analyse children's work. This will give you a baseline to work from.

Planning the project

Formulating questions is a good way to define action research in school (Bearne *et al.*, 2007). Drawing on her analysis of the problems children faced, Lyndsey decided on the following two research questions:

Can integration of grammar and punctuation into shared discussion about reading, support pupils' writing?

Can peer review support pupils to effectively edit and review their writing?

Lyndsey decided to try out some different approaches to teaching writing. She wanted to try to deliver the grammar and punctuation requirements of the English curriculum through high-quality texts. She also wanted to emphasise the features of language and punctuation that were appropriate to different forms (or genres) of writing. She hoped that this would make clearer links between component knowledge and purposeful writing.

Lyndsey decided to adapt her English planning to highlight language features, punctuation and grammar when she discussed a quality text with the children. When planning her lessons she thought carefully about how the author had used specific language features and how to highlight this to the class through shared discussion about the text. When deciding on the writing outcome from her planning she also made efforts to link the taught grammar and punctuation to the writing form. An extract of Lyndsey's planning can be seen below:

Table 9.1 An example of integrated planning

Autumn term two Year 3 / 4 *Leon and the Place Between* by Grahame Baker-Smith		
Text types (writing outcomes)	**Reading skills**	**Writing skills**
Writing to entertain: fictional narrative / writing to describe	**Themes and conventions:** children can make simple links to other known texts or personal experience **Monitor and summarise:** discuss understanding as it develops and explain the meaning of vocabulary in context	**Transcription:** See English Appendix 1 Apply spelling patterns and common exception words, taught so far, within writing **Composition:** Pupils can work with a partner or a small

(Continued)

Table 9.1 (Cont).

Autumn term two Year 3 / 4 *Leon and the Place Between* by Grahame Baker-Smith

Text types (writing outcomes)	Reading skills	Writing skills
	Reason and explain: Why has the author used certain techniques? What is the effect on the reader? **Language for effect:** Identify how language, structure and presentation contribute to meaning. Identify specific techniques, e.g. simile, metaphor, repetition, exaggeration **Punctuation:** exclamation mark, question marks, ellipses	group to plan writing, contributing their own ideas and listening to and building on others' ideas Writing is clear in purpose and incorporates mostly relevant content to inform and interest the audience Events or ideas are developed using some appropriate vocabulary Writing is clear in purpose with viewpoint consistently maintained **Text structure and organisation** Organise writing into logical chunks and write a coherent series of linked sentences Narrative texts are paragraphed with an appropriately signalled opening and ending Nouns and pronouns are selected to create cohesion and achieve clarity **Sentence structure and presentation** Pupils can write an increasing range of sentences with more than one clause using conjunction taught so far Some sentence variation through sentence type (statement, question, exclamation, command), length and structure (simple, compound, complex) **Grammar and punctuation** Pupils can use punctuation, as indicated in English Appendix 2, accurately and consistently. This includes:

* compound sentences with coordinating conjunctions
* prepositions
* using the pronoun or noun in a sentence for cohesion

Next, Lyndsey wanted to see if the children could be encouraged to edit and improve their writing. Through the review of writing she wanted to ensure the children could check that they were using the grammar, features of language and punctuation appropriate to the writing form. She decided to give proper time and space to the editing process. She had read about the power of peer review and was keen to give it a try.

The research project aimed to trial two new approaches to teaching writing:

- *The integration of grammar into reading and writing experiences;*
- *Using peer review to support the editing process.*

The key changes in approach hoped to deliver these aims were as follows:

- *Shared reading, and the use of high-quality texts, will facilitate discussion to support children's understanding of the author's chosen grammatical techniques, sentence construction and punctuation;*
- *Peer review will support the editing process, with a focus on improving the children's use of language for effect, grammar and punctuation.*

A contextualised approach to grammar

The picture book *Leon and the Place Between* (McAllister and Baker-Smith, 2008) was chosen for its exciting themes of magic and imagination, and its use of descriptive language and illustration. Lyndsey shared the book, focusing on the use of language features, the illustrative text font, the sentence structure and the use of punctuation for effect. She planned a shared reading lesson using the double-page spread with three jugglers (McAllister and Baker-Smith, 2008). Lyndsey asked:

- What effect does the word BANG have on the reader?
- The word is written in capital letters. How does this help us to understand how we should read this word?
- What punctuation has the author used to emphasise the loudness of the BANG?
- Read aloud the phrase 'Skittles flew, fast and furious, BACK AND FORTH, UP AND OVER'. How does the use of the conjunction 'and' add to the sense of movement? Why doesn't the author use other connective words?
- Look at the language 'Flew, fast and furious'. What do you notice about the word choice? This is called alliteration. What effect does this have on how the reader says and hears the sentence?
- Look at the sentence 'THEN BANG THE SKITTLES WENT UP...' What does the use of an ellipsis do?
- How does the author build tension at the end of the page?

Lyndsey hoped that the discussion would not only draw the children's attention to the features of language and punctuation, but would also make the author's reason for using them clear. Next, she gave the children the opportunity to apply their understanding of the sentence structure, punctuation for effect and language choices in their own compositions. After having discussed the double-page spread, Lyndsey introduced her own idea of trapeze artists at the circus. Using a picture stimulus of the flying trapeze, the children planned and wrote their own page for the book. Examples of the children's writing are below:

Whoosh

Two trapeze artists **SWANG** over the cheering crowd! Twisting and turning, Flipping and swapping!
DRUMS BEGAN TO BANG!>
TAMBORINES BEAGN TO SHAKE…
BOTH TRAPEZE ARTISTS LET GO AND swaped…
The lights went out once again!
They had done it!

Figure 9.2 Example of child's writing in response to *Leon and the Place Between*

Terrific Trapeze
VOOM!

Two trapeze artists swung into action, gilding across the stage at a emaculate speed. Twisting, turning, flying, flipping non stop. Cheers and gasps broke out from the audience. Swinging high and low never stopping. The audience couldn't believe what was happening. They were mind blown. The trapeze artists were very daring and confident. They were so fast it was like a bold eagle hunting a mouse. Then the trapeze artists jumped down, took a bow and once more there was complete darkness.

Figure 9.3 Second example of child's writing in response to *Leon and the Place Between*

The children's writing drew from the shared reading experiences and applied the author's techniques to create wonderfully descriptive compositions. Throughout the lesson Lyndsey used terminology associated with the National Curriculum to define and discuss their writing. She felt pleased that her change in approach had enabled the children to accurately make use of the technical aspects of writing through appropriate and effective composition. She was also pleased to hear the children using increasingly technical language to discuss their own writing.

Lyndsey also noted that the children were much more engaged in their grammar learning when they discussed it in shared reading. She reflected that her own ability to discuss language choice and features of grammar was stronger when the discussion was in the context of a text. She felt that her explanations about grammar were clearer as a result, and that pupils became better at understanding how they could use grammar, language features and punctuation to good effect in their own writing.

 ## Pupil coaching: Peer review

The second element to the action research project focused on the editing and revision of writing. The class were reluctant to revisit their writing and had difficulty knowing how to improve their work. Lyndsey hoped that pairing the children with a carefully chosen peer partner would inspire and energise the process. She thought that it would be more motivational if suggestions for improvement were discussed with a peer, rather than with her during the lesson or through marked comments. This new approach would focus on editing as a collaborative process. Determining supportive pairings that would inspire the child was of crucial importance and took a great deal of consideration.

 ## Supporting the editing process

Lyndsey introduced the concept of peer review partners to the children. Through repeated modelling Lyndsey supported the pupils to develop their peer review skills. As well as frequent demonstration she also provided a clear framework for the children to use as they reflected and commented on their partner's writing. 'Steps to success' provided clear ground rules for the peer editing process. Each step detailed how the children should discuss someone else's writing, provided examples of what they could say, reminded them they should be positive in their talk and gave them key things to remember. The 'Steps for success' are listed below:

 Peer editing: Steps for success

Peer editing means working with someone in your class to help them improve their writing. It means making compliments, suggestions and corrections in relation to your partner's writing.

Step 1 Compliments

Say what is good about the writing.

- I really liked the way you. . .
- I liked it when you used the word. . .

- My favourite part was ... because...
- I liked the flowing details...

Step 2 Suggestions

Give your partner some ideas about how to make the writing better, but be positive. Instead of saying, 'This part doesn't make sense,' say, 'If you added in more detail after this sentence, then it would be clearer.' Instead of saying, 'Your word choice is boring,' say, 'Instead of using the word good, perhaps you could use the word exceptional.'

Think about:

- **Word choice.** Did your partner use interesting words?
- **Using details.** What else could you add? Sounds, smells, sights and description.
- **Organisation.** Does the writing flow? Have they used paragraphs?
- **Sentences.** Are sentences punctuated correctly? Are there any spelling mistakes, grammar mistakes, punctuation errors or omissions?

Step 3 Corrections

The third step is to read through the work with your partner and talk about:

- Spelling mistakes
- Grammar mistakes
- Missing punctuation

Next came the peer review grid

After two terms of trialling these changes, Lyndsey began to reflect further on what was working well and what could be improved. She began to think about how the peer review and the integrated approach to grammar could be extended. The result was a peer review grid, which enabled the writing form to be assessed by the peer in a more focused way. The grid gave the children key success criteria to look for and required the reviewer to identify examples of where the writer was successful. Lyndsey refined the peer feedback even further to ensure that pupils received specific praise for their writing as well as points to improve. Below is an example of a completed peer review grid:

Lyndsey reflected that the grid deepened the peer review process further. The children's understanding of learning objectives relevant to the writing form was reinforced through the act of reviewing another child's work. The peer review grid not only benefited the partner, it also empowered the peer reviewer, giving

Table 9.2 An example of a completed peer review grid

Writing task: To write a persuasive letter (peer review grid)

Has your partner included...?	Write the most persuasive sentence in your partner's writing	Write the different sentence openers your partner has used
An introduction that tells the writer why they are writing the letter? New paragraph for each different reason to save the rainforest. Questions for the reader to think about.	Trees are really important because they are helping people to live.	My first important point is...
What advice would you give to your partner to make their letter even better?	**How did this letter make you feel as a reader?**	**Write the different conjunctions your partner has used**
It is a great letter but is it finished? Could you use more conjunctions like therefore and moreover? Can you check **oxagon** in the dictionary please?	I have to stop rainforests being cut down! This is a really bad situation.	so and because
Name of peer reviewer: _____	**I was looking at** _____**'s writing.**	

them opportunities to apply their knowledge and understanding to the context of another child's writing. To review another child's work using the grid required the peer reviewer to know what to look for. In order to identify examples of success and suggest better use of language the peer reviewer had to judiciously read their partner's work. The review process therefore developed another layer of critical skills: of learning to read writing as a reader. The need to write well for your peer increased the children's awareness of the audience and purpose of their writing.

As Lyndsey's class became more practised in the process of peer review, she noticed that the children became better at making language choices and punctuating their writing for clarity. She also noticed that not all of the children could maintain concentration on editing for a whole lesson. She began to consider if editing could also happen more frequently and for shorter periods of time. She began to plan short opportunities to edit and review writing within her writing lessons. This meant that editing and review were happening both during the writing process and at the end of the writing process. Some pupils preferred to edit smaller amounts of their writing and others preferred to continue to the end and then review the whole work. The subject leader made efforts to accommodate both of these learning styles.

Evaluating the outcomes

Lyndsey had observed key changes in the pupils' confidence to edit and adapt their writing. She had witnessed renewed enthusiasm for the editing process, brought about by working with a friend. She also knew through ongoing assessment that the process was having a significant impact on the quality of the children's written work.

Figures 9.6 and 9.7 show a 'cold' writing sample of work (produced at the very beginning of the taught unit) and a 'hot' writing sample (produced at the end of the taught unit) in response to the story *The Miraculous Journey of Edward Tulane* (DiCamillo, 2008). By considering the two work samples Lyndsey was able to evaluate how the child had progressed their understanding of the required features of the taught genre. She compared the progress of the whole class and was pleased to see evidence of improved outcomes in writing by all pupils against the National Curriculum (DfE, 2013) age-related expectations for writing at Key Stage 2.

The influence of the peer review underpins the progression as well as the new, shared reading approach. Both pedagogies made a significant difference to the

> When I was waiting for adleen this un harey uninvited dog boxer dog calld rosy camin nd spraig on the crisp wiet table cloth I was furyas I hope I never se that dog again!!! Sudanly the dog pikt my up and shok me. I was sokt!

Figure 9.4 Typed version of child A's initial 'COLD' writing task based on the story *The Miraculous Journey of Edward Tulane*

> Dear Abiine,
>
> I am writing to tell you the series of unfortanate events that have happened in the last few months. I now have a different name. It's Susanna. You remember me s Edward. After ~~biei~~ being at the bottom of the ocean for weeks a kind fisherman scooped me up and brought me hoe with him. His name is Lawrence. He has a lovely wife called Nellie but she dressed me in pink, sparkly high heels and a polka dot dress. (It is extremly embarrassing!). Despite all that Nellie called me she! Anyway lately iv'e been thinking about my behaveir. I've beena bit self-centered. But I do wish we never went on that boat to England. I am just glad to be alive. Absolutely delighted.
>
> From Susanna (Edward)
>
> P.S.
> I think it was all Pellagrina's fault. Its like the story.

Figure 9.5 Typed version of child A's final independent 'HOT' writing task based on the story *The Miraculous Journey of Edward Tulane*

child's writing by the end of the taught unit. The peer review process helped the children to shape their writing in response to their partner's comments. This in turn provided a focus on the revision and editing process and aided the child's 'polishing' of their writing (CLPE, 2016). Lyndsey noticed that all pupils' writing was clearly shaped by their understanding of audience and purpose. In the writing sample in Figure 9.7 it is clear that the child understood the authorial voice required for the letter-writing task. The writing models a range of sentence types and appropriate punctuation such as statements, questions and exclamations that reveal the child's ability to engage with the reader and convey appropriate meaning. Lyndsey's observations, combined with further analysis of the children's writing, demonstrated the following outcomes from the new teaching approach:

- Enhanced use of grammar, punctuation and language techniques in children's writing, in a range of forms.
- Clearer links between reading, writing, grammar and punctuation.
- Children were empowered to make choices in their writing, facilitated by pupil-led editing and the peer review process.

Wider learning

In the summer of 2016 Lyndsey shared her learning with the whole-school staff. Having reflected on key learning from the action research project she was able to shape a new whole-school approach to the planning and teaching of writing. She shared videos of her pupils engaged in the peer review of writing. She provided staff with peer review templates and offered guidance on how to link quality texts with technical aspects of the National Curriculum.

The project was met with a buzz of excitement. This new way of working wasn't just a good idea that Lyndsey wanted the staff to try, it was a trialled approach proven to make a difference. The teachers were very excited to see and hear the children in the role of reviewers and to examine how it had impacted on the quality of their writing. Since September 2017 this has been key to the school's approach to teaching writing.

Case study learning points

✓ **Critically reflect on experiences** and constantly consider how your practice can be further refined to support the pupils.
✓ **Evaluate the outcomes.** Evaluate the success of the action research project before effecting wider change across the whole school.

✓ **Share success wider.** Reporting success and sharing the learning with your colleagues is important. Learning from action research will benefit the whole school and other schools too.

The action research example in this chapter illustrates how the English subject leader can work independently on projects within their own school. It is also possible for action research projects to be worked on collaboratively, across a 'community of practice' (Bearne *et al.*, 2007: 40). Today's English subject leader is no longer influenced by national literacy initiatives; therefore, action research has become a popular way for schools to approach subject development. Today's subject leader considers action research as the ideal way to take ownership over the evolution of teaching practice, through critical reflective practice and careful attention to pupils' needs.

References

Bearne, E., Graham, L. and Marsh, J. (2007) *Classroom Action Research in Literacy*. Leicester: UKLA.

Centre for Literacy in Primary Education (CLPE) (2016) 'The writing scale.' Available at: www.clpe.org.uk/library-and-resources/reading-and-writing-scales [accessed 13 March 2018].

Department for Education (DfE) (2013) *The National Curriculum in England: Key Stages 1 and 2 framework document*. London: DfE Publications.

DiCamillo, K. (2008) *The Miraculous Journey of Edward Tulane*. London: Walker Books.

McAllister, A. and Baker-Smith, G. (2008) *Leon and the Place Between*. London: Templar Publishing.

10 Observing key features of effective English lessons

Lisa Baldwin

Having identified the key features of an effective English lesson this chapter will further explore how to use these as the focus when observing lessons across the school. Practical examples will be used to unpick the following themes and to provide useful guidance as to what to look for:

- *planning for talk in the classroom;*
- *phonics and early reading;*
- *guided and shared reading;*
- *writing.*

Finally, consideration will be given to turning your reflections from lesson observation into development points for your colleagues.

Key features of effective literacy lessons

Lesson observation is a key way to ensure good standards of English teaching in your school. Monitoring through observation enables the subject leader to recognise and share good practice, as well as identify areas of support that teachers require. Lesson observations are also an effective way to check that the quality of teaching and learning is consistent across the classes. This is important, as evidence suggests that there often exists a larger pupil progress gap between classes in one school, than between one school and another of similar pupil demographic.

In order to be able to give good advice to the teachers you observe it is essential to understand what constitutes good English teaching in both reading and writing. This knowledge should be based on your combined understanding of subject knowledge and effective pedagogy.

Planning for talk

One effective pedagogy, common to all subject areas including English, is talk (Barnes, 2008). Effective, exploratory talk is underpinned by a classroom culture where children's ideas are shared and built upon. Effective literacy lessons should include planned time for exploratory talk, discussion and play with spoken language. Teachers should be confident in understanding how effective questioning and scaffolding supports pupils' purposeful talk. Good teachers also understand that planned opportunities for talk provide them with the chance to assess pupil understanding through overheard discussion (Eke and Lee, 2009).

Talk to support reading and writing

Open questioning fuels exploratory talk and is essential to the development of reading comprehension and meaning making (Medwell and Wray, 2017; Tennent *et al.*, 2016). Exploratory talk around a text will develop deeper understanding of character, action, setting and atmosphere, enabling children to explore text meanings. Through questioning the teacher can help children to communicate personal opinions, drawing on prior knowledge and experience to make connections with the text. Exploratory talk also encourages children to reflect on other pupils' ideas that might challenge, inform and enhance their own meaning making.

Talk is also a key pedagogic approach to support the teaching of writing. The importance of talk to support children's composition skills is endorsed by research into the cognitive demands made on children when they write. Talk should underpin children's composition processes through the generation of ideas and oral rehearsal prior to writing (Bearne, 2002). The creation of shared vocabulary during oral work should lead to word banks or working walls, which provide support for the children as they progress towards independent writing. Strategies such as talk-partners and think–pair–share also enable the children to rehearse composition and try out language before attempting to write. Oral rehearsal improves children's confidence and leads to improved outcomes in independent writing (Fisher *et al.*, 2010).

Drama

Drama is also an effective pedagogy that supports talk. Drama provides children with the opportunity to enhance vocabulary choices and explore situations through spoken language and action (Cremin, 2015; Wyse *et al.*, 2013). This enables children to formulate and adapt ideas, try out different language and rephrase their thoughts prior to writing composition. Drama also enables children to consider texts more deeply by experiencing a character's past, present and future. This enables children to consider different viewpoints (Crumpler, 2005). Drama also provides a creative context for writing.

Demonstration, modelling and scaffolds

Teacher modelling reveals to pupils the processes and strategies that good readers and writers employ. Effective modelling makes clear how the learner should approach the task in hand. To hear the thought process of a good reader will enhance a child's understanding of how to make meaning from a text (Myhill and Jones, 2009). To hear the thought processes of a good writer will enhance the child's understanding that writing involves constant review and change. The teacher should verbalise word choice, play with sentence construction and demonstrate the process of revision to writing such as re-reading sentences for clarity, sense and effect on the reader.

Teachers should consider what scaffolds will support children's success in the expected writing form. Provision of resources such as working walls, vocabulary banks and a writer's toolkit is an example of support that should be made available to children. Visual scaffolds can be helpful for pupils when they are writing a narrative plot line, planning a story and sequencing events. Resources that prompt the children to use particular language features, grammatical techniques and punctuation will also support pupils to use language and punctuation appropriate to the type of writing they are doing. The type and amount of scaffolds and support a child needs will vary and the teacher should make a judgement based on their knowledge of the child, about which children require additional support and which require further challenge and independence.

The teaching and learning of phonics and early reading

The *Independent Review of the Teaching of Early Reading* (Rose, 2006) underpins the current approach to the teaching of early reading. The Review proposes that there are two aspects of reading as illustrated by the Simple View of Reading model (Gough and Tunmer, 1986): language comprehension and word recognition processes. The government's 'Letters and Sounds' document (DfES, 2007) provided schools with non-statutory guidance for teaching phonics. This has since been superseded by the new National Curriculum documentation, which includes guidance on word reading (DfE, 2013).

Despite the change of government, the insistence on a phonics 'fast and first' approach to early reading remains (DfE, 2010: 2) and as such, phonics teaching retains a high profile in schools. As the subject leader you will be instrumental in ensuring the strong teaching of both phonics (*word reading*) and the less prescribed curriculum area of reading comprehension (*reading for meaning*). We will begin by considering phonics teaching and what constitutes an effective phonics lesson.

Phonics lesson structure and design

Ideally, a good phonics lesson will be planned around the four stages of *Revisit, Teach, Practise* and *Apply* (DfES, 2007: 49). *Revisit* is the first stage of the lesson and should recap children's previous learning and provide them with the opportunity to recall known phoneme grapheme correspondences. The lesson should then progress to new learning in the *Teach* stage.

At the *Teach* stage a new phoneme is usually introduced. Children should be able to hear and say the sound as well as being introduced to the visual representation of the phoneme (the grapheme). If a child has difficulty in discerning a phoneme, they will be unable to progress to the reading and writing of the grapheme without misconceptions arising.

With demands on time and pressure to get children to meet the required reading standard, there is a growing tendency for reception teaching to view activities that promote sound discernment, such as play and song, as less important than the instructional teaching of phonics. Skipping this developmental stage will have profound effects for some children. Pupils who have had limited opportunity to play with language through song, rhyme, games or dialogue prior to commencing school, are particularly disadvantaged if the school pursues phonics instruction at the detriment to sound discernment activities.

When teaching phonics the teacher should clearly and accurately articulate the phonemes. Modelling should include distinct articulation of the phonemes and demonstration of mouth movements and tongue shapes, and draw attention to the way in which air passes over, or through, the tongue, lips and teeth when the sound is articulated. Effective modelling will help pupils to overcome misconceptions in how they hear and say the sound. Simple games that provide opportunity for the identification of the new phoneme at the beginning, middle and end of words will enable the teacher to check for children who may have issues discerning new phonemes.

The *Teach* stage should also allow the children opportunity to articulate the sounds for themselves. Children should have the opportunity to articulate phonemes, blend words that contain the new phoneme and discern sounds by counting the number of phonemes in words that include the new sound. Once the articulation of the new phoneme is understood, teaching can progress to reading and writing. At this next stage the teacher should model reading and writing the new phoneme, reinforcing the sound, the letter name and any relevant language or terms associated with the learning, such as digraph, trigraph and split digraph. The teacher should model the process of blending for reading, emphasising how to combine the individual phonemes to pronounce a word. Modelling encoding skills should emphasise the segmentation skills required to spell words that contain the new phoneme. Use of visual or kinaesthetic strategies such as sound buttons, robotic talk and robot arm movement can further reinforce the learning. The teacher should observe the children's segmentation skills and their written representation of words and sounds. Continual assessment of the children's understanding should be implicit throughout the lesson and misconceptions should be quickly detected by the teacher and addressed.

At the *Practice* stage there should be opportunity for the children to read and spell words that contain the new phoneme. During the *Practice* stage children should be encouraged to use the strategies modelled to them by the teacher at the *Teach* stage.

Finally, the *Apply* stage should offer children the chance to apply their new learning to meaningful reading and writing tasks.

Effective planning and teaching of phonics will include appropriate pedagogies that encourage *all* the children to participate with the articulation of the phonemes and the reading and writing of corresponding phonemes and graphemes.

Active learning

Effective phonics teaching will be lively and well paced. It will make use of attractive resources to engage the children in the lesson. The use of real objects, visual aids or pictures will support the children to contextualise the meaning of words. The contextualisation of vocabulary is particularly helpful to additional language learners, but it is helpful to all children to make connections between phonics instruction and language meaning. The teaching of alien words is a significant challenge to this approach, however, and there is rightly some criticism about this aspect of the taught curriculum.

Many schools currently use a scheme to deliver phonics teaching. There are benefits to this approach, namely that planning is simpler for teachers to deliver and it ensures a consistent approach to phonics across the school. However, one significant limitation of phonic schemes is that they often result in highly repetitive teaching approaches, which can quickly become uninspiring and demotivating for both the children and the teacher. Your role as subject leader is to ensure that phonic fatigue is not endemic in your school. Considering new approaches and methods to support delivery of the scheme can pay dividends in reinvigorating the teaching and learning experience for both pupils and staff. Good-quality phonics teaching is multi-sensory in approach and promotes active, rather than passive, learning. It is worthwhile reflecting on whether a phonics scheme enables this level of engagement and variety in learning.

The characteristics of an effective phonics lesson

Planning and teaching

- The teacher ensures that children practise previously taught phonemes;
- The new phoneme (or phonic learning) is clearly introduced;
- The teacher articulates the phonemes correctly;
- All children are encouraged to participate and have the opportunity to practise saying the phoneme;
- The children are taught the name of the grapheme as well as the phoneme it is associated with;
- The children are clearly shown how to say, read and write the grapheme and are given opportunities to practise writing the letter;
- The children are taught how to blend and/or segment through effective teacher modelling;
- All children are encouraged to participate and have the opportunity to practise saying the phoneme, read the corresponding graphemes, blend phonemes to read words and segment words into phonemes/graphemes for spelling;
- Children have opportunities to apply their phonic knowledge and skills in purposeful reading and writing activities.

Delivery

- The lesson is lively and fast-paced throughout;
- The lesson is fun and interactive, short and focused;
- Visual aids, resources and objects are used effectively to support the teaching.

Learning and progress

- The teacher observes and questions learning throughout the lesson to assess individual children's progress;
- Pupil misconceptions are identified and addressed;
- Good progress is made by all of the pupils.

Observing pupil learning and progress

When observing a literacy lesson the subject leader should be constantly looking to determine the quality of *all* the children's learning. This can be done by talking to the pupils and checking that they can talk knowledgeably about the new learning in the lesson. During your observation you should listen to how well pupils answer questions and how engaged they are when completing tasks.

What do good subject leaders do when observing phonics teaching?

- Listen to the children's articulation of the phoneme for accuracy;
- Listen to and observe the children's application of blending skills for reading;
- Listen to and observe the children's accuracy of segmenting sounds for spelling (oral activities and written tasks);
- Talk to and observe the children to discover if they exhibit positive attitudes towards their phonics learning.

 What do subject leaders think when observing pupils' learning in phonics?

- Is the work in line with age-related expectations?
- Have the pupils acquired secure knowledge of letters and sounds at a level appropriate to age-related expectations?
- Is the lesson appropriately challenging for all the pupils?
- Is pupil progress **at least good** for different groups of children and **exemplary** for some children? Where is the evidence?

Following these prompts will ensure you focus on observing key information that will enable you to make a sound judgement about the quality of teaching and the impact on pupil learning. For ease of use, all lesson observation prompts are available as a checklist in Appendix 2.

Miss C teaches a phonics lesson to a Year 1 class. Her lesson aims to teach the new phoneme/sh/and support the children to read and write words with 'sh' in them. She begins the lesson by showing the children flash cards with a range of known graphemes written on them. As the cards are revealed, the children say the sounds together as a class. Next, she introduces the new phoneme/sh/to the class. She shows a card with 'sh' written on it and says the sound clearly. She asks the children to put up their hand and she picks John and Rowan to say the sound. Happy that the two children say the sound accurately, Miss C reads aloud the word cards 'shop' and 'ship' and the children use their fingers to count the phonemes. The children then move around the room on a word

146

hunt, looking for picture cards that depict the new phoneme and ruling out word cards that do not. The children take their whiteboards and excitedly move around the room looking for picture cards and writing down the words they find which contain /sh/. Cherrelle says she is using the picture on the word card to decide if she should write it down or not. Iman says he has recorded the words 'wish', 'fish' and 'witch'. At the end of the activity the children read out the words on their board and Miss C writes them in a list on the whiteboard. Together they compose some sentences that use three of the words.

Refer to the 'Characteristics of Effective Phonics Teaching' prompts and consider the following questions:

- What are the positive elements about Miss C's lesson?
- Did the planned activities support the new phonics learning?
- Did all the children have the opportunity to demonstrate and apply their learning?
- What do you think Miss C needs to develop in her phonics teaching?

The teaching and learning of reading comprehension

Reading comprehension skills can be taught in a number of ways. The most regularly used approaches are shared reading and guided reading. Increasingly schools also plan to deliver both reading and writing lessons around a key whole-class text. In Key Stage 2 in particular, this has led to the task design of reading and writing activities that encourage pupil response and develop deeper understanding of the text.

Teaching reading should focus on supporting pupils to develop strategies to support 'in the moment reading' as well as reflections after reading (Tennent *et al.*, 2016). 'In the moment reading skills' (Tennent *et al.*, 2016) enable the child to understand the constant comprehension monitoring skills that good readers undertake whilst they read, drawing on syntactic and semantic knowledge and understanding. Reflection after reading develops deeper comprehension skills that infer meaning and make connections to prior experience and other texts encountered by the child.

Shared reading

Shared reading is the sharing of a text with the whole class. During shared reading, all pupils should have a clear view of the text. This can be facilitated through use of a Big Book, the interactive whiteboard, copies of text extracts or poems, or sets of class readers. The teacher can lead the reading, or the children can take it in turns to read the text aloud. At points during the reading the class will stop and the teacher will check understanding. Together the whole class will be involved in clarifying and discussing vocabulary, plot and action, summarising events and answering a range of questions that support reading comprehension strategies for 'in the moment reading' and reflecting on reading (Tennent *et al.*, 2016).

Guided reading

Guided reading is usually delivered in smaller groups and groupings are often defined by the children having a shared development need. The class teacher provides specific support for one guided reading group. The need for the teacher to work closely with one group requires the planning of other meaningful reading activities for the rest of the class. Many teachers manage this through a carousel approach, which the children alternate to complete throughout a week. Carousel activities might include reading for pleasure, independent reading tasks, response to reading activities (such as character maps, diagrams, drawings, sequencing tasks), written response to text and vocabulary work. In many schools the use of reciprocal reading roles has been adopted to enable children to lead their own guided discussions around a text.

Quality texts

High-quality texts are key to the effective teaching of reading comprehension. The type of text selected for a lesson is crucial to the quality of discussion pupils engage in, the opportunities for exploring language and themes, and the potential for the text to inspire writing. A high-quality text will offer depths of interpretation that challenge a child's comprehension skills.

The characteristics of effective reading comprehension lessons

The effective teacher of reading comprehension will consider how they will support pupils to develop specific strategies when reading. Teachers will have planned opportunities for the children to engage in tasks that develop explicit reading skills such as prediction, making connections to personal experience, comparing texts, articulating preferences, inferring meaning and summarising the story. Planning should clearly link the learning objective (the reading comprehension skill being developed) with appropriate teacher-led discussion, modelling and activity.

Teacher planning and delivery

Planning and teaching

- The planning and teaching provide activities that support lower- and higher-order reading comprehension skills;
- The planning is clear about the purpose of teacher-led/child-led discussion of the text;
- The teacher plans appropriate questions and prompts that support the children in communicating and extending their responses to the text;
- Planned activities provide opportunities for the children to explicitly learn specific reading comprehension skills through scaffolded discussion and teacher modelling;
- The teacher enables exploratory talk through the use of effective, open questioning to pursue children's line of thought;
- There are opportunities for children to respond to each other;
- The teacher uses their subject knowledge of texts, and the technical features of language, to extend and deepen pupils' understanding;
- The teacher explains why a strategy is useful and supports the pupils in understanding how to apply it to the text.

Delivery

- Texts are engaging and appropriate for the pupils;
- The text is available and visible to all pupils;
- Children's ideas are captured for future reference;
- The classroom environment is respectful of children's ideas and response to the text;
- Shared reading is a lively and animated process.

Learning and progress

- Children's understanding is checked through effective questioning;
- Teacher-led talk develops the child's comprehension skills;
- A range of scaffolded support and challenge enables all the learners to make good progress.

Observing pupil learning and progress

 What do good subject leaders do when observing reading comprehension lessons?

- Listen to pupil-led and teacher-led discussion about the text;
- Observe the teacher modelling, questioning and explaining reading strategies;

- Listen to pupils read aloud;
- Observe and listen to pupils' responses to text;
- Talk to the pupils about the current text and gauge their attitudes to reading in general.

 What do subject leaders think when observing pupils' learning in reading comprehension?

- Do pupils offer personal responses to the text?
- Does teacher questioning probe pupils' understanding of language and scaffold the responses?
- Does the teacher challenge all pupils to make precise improvements to their written and oral work?
- Do pupils have a range of strategies that enable them to attempt unknown words, consider new vocabulary and make meaning from the text?
- What are pupil attitudes to reading? Are they keen to engage with the text and offer responses?
- Do the pupils demonstrate reading comprehension skills at a level appropriate to age-related expectations?

Following these prompts will ensure you focus on key information that will enable you to make judgements about the quality of teaching and the impact on pupil learning.

The teaching and learning of writing

Writing comprises two distinct skills: composition and transcription (Smith, 1982). Composition requires the child to generate ideas about what to write, give consideration to the audience they are writing for and identify the purpose of their writing. Transcription relates to spelling, handwriting and other secretarial aspects of writing. The new English curriculum defines a 'pedagogic shift' in the writing focus with increased emphasis on the learning of grammar, punctuation and spelling facts and explicit detail on transcriptional elements of writing (Chamberlain, 2016). It is important to recognise that skills in composition and transcription are very distinct and make significant cognitive demands on young children in the early stages of writing (Hayes and Flower, 1980). A young child may prioritise their handwriting and spelling at the detriment of composition, or they may prioritise getting their ideas down on paper at the expense of accurate spelling or neat handwriting. It is only as children get older, and their natural development in writing progresses, that they become able to deliver transcriptional aspects of writing with accuracy and fluency. Once handwriting and spelling have become more automatic the cognitive demands on the child become freer, enabling more of their working memory to focus on composition.

When planning for writing, teachers should aim to develop skills in both transcription and composition. It is important that teachers, particularly in the lower primary years, are mindful of the challenge pupils face trying to tackle both skills at the same time. Teaching transcription and composition skills separately, modelling effective approaches to both aspects and allowing the children time to focus on one element at a time are highly important (Medwell and Wray, 2017).

Teacher scribing is one approach that alleviates the cognitive demand on pupils when they write. As a scribe, the teacher's role is to write down the children's ideas in a group, whole class or one-to-one situation. By undertaking to perform the transcriptional elements of writing the children can concentrate solely on the compositional aspect of writing.

Time should also be planned into the writing lesson to provide opportunity for children to edit and review their writing. Teacher feedback also needs to be balanced and to value equally the transcriptional and the compositional aspects of children's writing (Medwell and Wray, 2017).

Stimulus for writing

Effective planning for writing will introduce the learning objective through a stimulus (Bearne, 2002). An effective stimulus for writing might include using a quality text, an illustration or image from a picture book, a short film, or a real or imagined scenario. The stimulus provides a context for the purpose and audience of the writing process. It should also stimulate the children's interest in the writing activity.

If a text is used within the lesson, the technical features of the writing form should be discussed. Teachers should examine with the class the author's technique and style and discuss the effect on the reader. Once the features of the writing are made explicit, opportunity should be provided for the feature to be practised and the terminology learnt. This can include punctuation, grammar and language features.

The characteristics of effective writing lessons

Planning and teaching

* The aims of the writing task are clear, with a focus on compositional and transcriptional aspects of writing;

- Quality texts are used to support the teaching of writing;
- The teacher discusses the features of language through shared reading, highlighting features relevant to the writing task;
- The lesson incorporates appropriate pedagogical opportunities that support the children with writing composition. This includes the teacher scribing, shared reading, opportunities for talk and drama;
- The teacher demonstrates to the children what successful writing looks like, through shared or modelled writing;
- Pupils are given the opportunity to plan and compose writing that enables them to practise using the taught features appropriate to the style and genre of the writing task;
- Pupils are given opportunity to apply taught grammar and technical language features appropriate to the writing task;
- There is planned opportunity for pupils to edit and improve (both elements of composition and transcription) through either peer review or self-review processes.

Delivery

- The teacher selects an appropriate stimulus for writing;
- There is a clear context and audience for the writing;
- Appropriate resources are provided to scaffold and support pupils' writing;
- Working walls and vocabulary banks display a record of the children's writing journey and provide a useful resource bank for them to draw from when writing;
- Children are excited by the choice and challenge of the lesson.

Learning and progress

- Pupils are provided with specific teaching support as identified by assessment for learning processes;
- All pupils make good progress and demonstrate writing skills in line with age-related expectations.

Observing the quality of pupil learning in writing

 What do subject leaders do to determine the quality of teaching and learning?

- Listen to teacher-led discussion about writing features;

- Observe the teacher demonstrate writing;
- Listen to pupil paired talk and oral composition;
- Watch how pupils use plans, resources or scaffolds to support their writing;
- Observe if pupils review and change their writing in light of clear success criteria appropriate to the writing task;
- Talk to the pupils about the writing activity.

What do subject leaders think when observing pupil learning?

- Is there a clear sense of purpose in the writing task?
- Do pupils understand the audience they are writing for?
- Are pupils provided with good-quality models for writing in the required style, form or genre?
- Do pupils understand language features and grammatical terms relevant to the writing and can they use them in their writing to good effect?
- Are appropriate scaffolds available to children to support the writing task?
- Does the teaching enable all pupils to show high levels of written work at a level appropriate to age-related expectations?

 An English subject leader has made the following notes during the lesson observation of a Year 2 teacher.

Mr B read the story 'Gorilla' to his class. Mr B stops every so often to ask the children questions about the story so far. He focuses his questions on how Hannah is feeling in the story. He tells them that they are going to write about Hannah's feelings towards her father in the story. Children go straight to their tables and work mainly independently. Mr B puts copies of some of the illustrations from the story on the tables. Mr B moves between the tables, trying to help the children with spellings. By the end of the lesson some children make a good attempt to write from Hannah's point of view, most have written only a few lines and the lower-attaining children have only written the date.

- What are the ways in which Mr B is struggling with his practice?
- How do you know this?
- How do you think Mr B can improve his teaching of writing?

- Prioritise what he needs to work on and explore how you could support him towards better planning and teaching of writing.

Conducting a lesson observation

Observation is often a stressful experience for teachers. Staff will usually put more effort into the planning and delivery of an observed lesson because they care that their lessons are deemed to be of a high quality. The raised status of the observed lesson means that tensions can run high and it is important to acknowledge this when observing your colleagues.

Before you conduct any lesson observation it is important to have a clear focus on what you intend to look for during the lesson. A clear focus will assist you in giving specific attention to an aspect of the English teaching and learning. It will also help the teacher being observed to understand exactly what is being observed, aiding their planning and delivery on the focus area.

Before the lesson observation date it is important to check that the teacher is clear about the focus of the observation. You should ask if they have any questions about the observation process and ask them if they need any support with the lesson planning. This professional courtesy will ensure that when the observation day arrives there will be a shared understanding of the purpose and process.

On arrival, ask the teacher where they would prefer you to sit to observe. It is likely that you will remain located in one position during the introductory teaching. However, after the main learning activity commences, be sure to move around the room, observing and listening to the children's interactions. Ask the children questions to help you gauge their understanding of the learning and to assess the level of engagement with the task.

You do not need to stay in the classroom for the whole duration of the lesson. Once you have seen enough of the lesson to enable you to make a judgement, exit the room and take time to write up your notes, reflecting on what you have seen. You can always re-enter the lesson towards the end of the teaching to see examples of pupil work resulting from the lesson.

The next stage of the process is to clarify what you will feed back to the observed teacher. Feedback will include those aspects of the lesson that went well and the aspects of the lesson that constitute development points.

Reflecting on the lesson observation

It is important to consider the links between the observed features of the lesson with the 'Characteristics of Effective Writing Lessons' prompts. Consider where you saw examples of effective teacher planning and delivery that relate to your observation points. For example, if you were to feed back to Mr B after having watched his English writing lesson you might link the following observation note – *Mr B reads the story 'Gorilla' to his class* – to:

- The teacher selects an appropriate stimulus for writing that provides a clear context for the audience and purpose of the task.

'Gorilla' is a high-quality text and offers rich possibilities to explore meaning. It is a well-chosen text to stimulate writing from the point of view of the main character. This is definitely a positive element from Mr B's observed lesson.

The observation notes continue – *Mr B stops every so often to ask the children questions about the story so far. He focuses his questions on how Hannah is feeling in the story. He tells them that they are going to write about Hannah's feelings towards her father in the story.* These notes link to the following characteristic of effective writing lessons:

- The teacher discusses the text through shared reading, highlighting features relevant to the writing task.

Mr B does discuss the text with the class, planning questions to develop the children's understanding of Hannah's feelings. This is in readiness for the writing task; however, Mr B misses the opportunity to develop the following characteristics:

- The lesson incorporates appropriate pedagogical opportunities that support the children with writing composition. This includes the teacher scribing, shared reading, opportunities for talk and drama.

This provides you with the first development point, and your discussion might include the need for him to have scribed children's responses to the questions, capturing vocabulary relevant to the writing task. Further opportunity for the children to orally compose sentences about how Hannah is feeling would have better prepared them for the writing task. Additionally you might consider the following characteristic:

- Working walls and vocabulary banks display a record of the children's writing journey and provide a useful resource bank for them to draw from when writing.

If Mr B had recorded the children's responses to the text, capturing their vocabulary in relation to Hannah's feelings, this would have provided support for the pupils' writing. By using the 'Characteristics of Effective Writing Lessons', you can consider which points from your observation are positive and which elements the teacher needs support to develop.

What do good subject leaders do when giving feedback on an observation?

- Maintain a professional and considerate manner;
- Give the observed teacher opportunity to reflect on their lesson first;
- Ask what they thought went well and what could have been improved;
- Summarise what they hear the observed teacher say and build on this to offer their viewpoint;
- Deliver positive feedback first before discussing developmental areas;
- Always finish the discussion by reiterating the positive points;
- Concentrate discussion on the observation focus;
- Provide written feedback that summarises points from the feedback discussion;
- Complete paperwork in a timely manner;
- Follow up identified development areas and ensure that any required support is provided.

References

Barnes, D. (2008) 'Exploratory talk for learning.' In: Mercer, N. and Hodgkinson, S. (eds), *Exploring Talk in Schools*. London: Sage, 1–12.

Bearne, E. (2002) *Making Progress in Writing*. London: Routledge.

Chamberlain, L. (2016) *Inspiring Writing in Primary Schools*. London: Sage.

Cremin, T. (2015) 'Developing creativity through drama.' In: Cremin, T. (ed.), *Teaching English Creatively*. 2nd edn. Oxon: Routledge, 25–34.

Crumpler, T. P. (2005) 'The role of educational drama in the composing processes of young writers.' *Research in Drama Education*, 10 (3), 357–363.

Department for Education (DfE) (2010) 'Phonics teaching materials: Core criteria and the self-assessment process.' Available at: www.gov.uk/government/uploads/system/uploads/attachment_data/file/298420/phonics_core_criteria_and_the_self-assessment_process.pdf [accessed 18 February 2018].

Department for Education (DfE) (2013) *The National Curriculum in England: Key Stages 1 and 2 framework document*. London: DfE Publications.

Department for Education and Skills (DfES) (2007) 'Letters and sounds: Principles and practice of high-quality phonics.' DfES Publications. Available at: www.gov.uk/government/uploads/system/uploads/attachment_data/file/190599/Letters_and_Sounds_-_DFES-00281-2007.pdf [accessed 17 February 2018].

Eke, R. and Lee, J. (2009) *Using Talk Effectively in the Primary Classroom*. Abingdon: Routledge.

Fisher, R., Jones, S., Larkin, S. and Myhill, D. (2010) *Using Talk to Support Writing*. London: Sage.

Gough, P. B. and Tunmer, W. B. (1986) 'Decoding, reading, and reading disability.' *Remedial and Special Education, 7*, 6–10.

Hayes, J. R. and Flower, L. S. (1980) 'Identifying the organization of writing processes.' In: Gregg L. W. and Steinberg, E. W. (eds), *Cognitive Processes in Writing*. Hillsdale, NJ: Lawrence Erlbaum Associates Inc.

Medwell, J. and Wray, D., with Griffiths, V. and Coates, E. (2017) *Primary English Teaching Theory and Practice*. 8th edn. London: Sage.

Myhill, D. and Jones, S. M. (2009) 'How talk becomes text: Investigating the concept of oral rehearsal in early years' classrooms.' *British Journal of Educational Studies, 57* (3), 265–284.

Rose, J. (2006) *Independent Review of the Teaching of Early Reading*. Nottingham: DfES Publications.

Smith, F. (1982) *Writing and the Writer*. London: Heinemann.

Tennent, W., Reedy, D., Hobsbaum, A. and Gamble, N. (2016) *Guiding Readers – Layers of Meaning: A handbook for teaching reading comprehension to 7–11 year olds*. London: UCL Institute of Education Press.

Wyse, D., Jones, R., Bradford, H. and Wolpert, M. A. (2013) *Teaching English, Language and Literacy*. London: Routledge.

Monitoring and evaluating progress

Lisa Baldwin

This chapter will focus on ways the English subject leader can monitor English teaching and learning. There will be a focus on how assessment data is used to determine the impact of new initiatives and set priorities. Practical examples will be used to illustrate how summative data can be interpreted for different groups of learners and how the subject leader needs an understanding of whole-school attainment. Using examples of pupil progress data we will explore how to use the information to set priorities for moving children's learning on. There will be guidance given on procedures that help ensure the effective implementation of English policy with a focus on pupil interviews, learning walks and book scrutiny. Finally, we reflect on the importance of each of these practices as part of the whole-school improvement process.

Why monitor?

In the current climate of high-stakes accountability, monitoring has become a regular pursuit in primary schools. Monitoring is a term that encompasses a range of different activities undertaken by class teachers and school leaders. Monitoring ensures a school has a clear understanding of the quality of teaching and the progress in learning. It is a term encompassing activities that all teachers engage with such as marking, pupil progress meetings, testing, assessment of pupil work and moderation. Monitoring also includes other tasks undertaken by the school senior leadership team and subject leaders, including book scrutiny, lesson observations, monitoring planning, learning walks and data analysis.

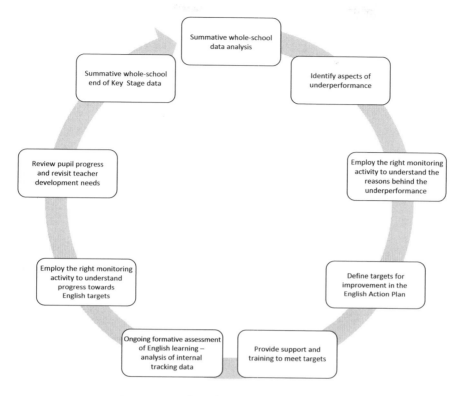

Figure 11.1 The school improvement cycle

It is important to understand that no single monitoring activity will provide complete information about the quality of teaching and learning in a school. Teaching is complex and each different monitoring activity aims to discover information about different parts of school life. Together the combined monitoring information provides a more complete understanding of teaching and learning across the school. Monitoring information is used to determine how well pupils are progressing and how well teachers are teaching, and these two strands of information feed the school's self-evaluation process. Figure 11.1 is a diagram that illustrates the relationship between monitoring and the school improvement cycle.

The role of monitoring in the school improvement cycle

Monitoring activities sound very official and onerous, but it is important to remember that monitoring isn't just conducted through prescribed routines. Waters and Martin (1999) remind us that monitoring also happens informally by 'simply ... keep[ing] an eye on things ... and being professionally nosy' (Waters and Martin, 1999: 131). Monitoring means giving time to thinking about English, 'standing back, having a look, and asking questions' (Waters and Martin, 1999: 131). Conversations with your colleagues, discussion in the staffroom and things you notice when you are in other classrooms, will all contribute to your understanding of English in the school. Good working relationships and an eager eye will allow you to give immediate feedback on any great practice you see. It enables you to celebrate success in English when you find it and share good practice with the whole staff. Such immediate, informal monitoring and feedback is akin to formative assessment processes used with pupils in the classroom. It enables you to act immediately on information, provide positive feedback and address issues in a timely fashion through the provision of suggestions, guidance and support.

A constant, informal flow of information will also enable you to continually shape your understanding of the school's next steps for English. Conversely, formal monitoring is akin to summative assessment processes used with pupils in the classroom. Formal monitoring usually requires dedicated subject leadership time to enable the leader to be in other classrooms, observing the teaching and learning of English and talking to pupils across the school.

- Use informal monitoring as a tool to motivate staff towards achieving English goals
- Praise good practice in English and acknowledge the progress and effort that teachers make through their contributions
- Share compliments publically with staff and ensure senior leaders get to hear about success

It is important to remember that 'consistent recognition helps people feel appreciated and motivated, knowing that their work is noticed and valued' (NCTL, 2015: 6–7).

Critical reflection

It is important to note that in the current high-stakes education culture, monitoring will bring some level of pressure to the teacher being monitored. Whilst lesson observations sit comfortably within formal monitoring procedures that impact on performance management, 'the status of learning walks, pupil feedback ... remain contested' (Page, 2016: 1000). This fact might inadvertently place the subject leader in an uncomfortable position when conducting subject monitoring. However, unless you are a member of staff with seniority in the leadership team, it is unlikely (and inappropriate) for your monitoring to contribute to the formal evaluation of a teacher's competence. The subject leader's role is to ensure the teaching of English is of high quality and monitoring should therefore focus on determining what and how you can support staff and pupils. The remit of any monitoring you carry out should be developmental, supportive and evaluative of policy implementation.

Using and understanding data

In terms of identifying the priorities for teaching and learning in English there is really only one overriding source to consult, and that is data. Data is a key tool for self-evaluation and good analysis of data is key to successful school development planning. There are, however, significant limitations in relying on data alone. What data doesn't provide is the story that sits behind the raw scores. This is where English subject knowledge, as well as an understanding of the school context, is essential. Contextual information, the importance of subject knowledge and other monitoring methods will be considered later, but first let's think about data.

Data comes from a range of external and internal sources, but most of the big picture data is summative data, reported by external bodies with a focus on pupils' end of key stage assessment results. The extent to which you will be required to understand this level of data will depend on the individual context of your subject leadership role. Unless you are a senior leader with responsibility for English it is unlikely that you will have full access to the whole-school data reported by government and local bodies. It is more likely that this information is communicated to you by members of the senior leadership team, through either meetings or shared documentation (such as the whole-school development plan). Either way, it is useful to know where big picture data exists and understand how this is used to inform your actions. Your role is pivotal in unpicking what the whole-school data picture means for the teaching and learning of English. The outcomes of whole-school data analysis will determine the targets in your subject leader plan and the focus of any subsequent monitoring activity you undertake.

External data: National data

National data is freely available to the public and will report a school's end of Key Stage 2 results for reading, writing and mathematics. Teacher assessment judgements and SATS test scores are converted into an overall scaled score that can be compared nationally. A school's Key Stage 2 scores are compared with the results of pupils in schools across England who started with similar assessment results at the end of Key Stage 1. The comparison of progression between Key Stages 1 and 2

Progress score in reading, writing and maths ❓

Reading	Writing	Maths
Below average -2.3	Above average +2.9	Average -1.1
More score details ❓	More score details ❓	More score details ❓

Figure 11.2 Progress score in reading, writing and maths (extract from national progress report for end of Key Stage 2)

provides a pupil progress score (STA, 2015). Alongside the reported progress score is a confidence interval. If the school's confidence interval is reported as greater than zero it means the year group has achieved greater than average progress, compared to pupils with similar national starting points. If the confidence rating is below zero, then the year group has made less than average progress. Where a confidence interval is reported as zero, the progress score is in line with the national average. You can see one element of the headline reported pupil progress for a school in Figure 11.2.

Pupil progress is reported for reading, writing and mathematics using colour to indicate progress. When pupil progress is well below average it is reported in red, below average in orange, average in yellow, above average in light green, and well above average in dark green.

 Consider the following statements and discuss **if and how** they are applicable to the data presented in Figure 11.2:

- In light of the headline pupil progress data it is likely that reading will be a target for improvement in the English subject leader's action plan.
- Pupils have progressed better in mathematics than in writing.
- Pupils have made better progress between Key Stage 1 and Key Stage 2 in mathematics than they have in reading.
- The pupils have made excellent progress in writing between Key Stage 1 and Key Stage 2.
- At the end of Key Stage 1 pupils had lower attainment in writing than in reading.

As well as pupil progress score data, the **percentage** of pupils achieving the *expected standard* and the *higher standard* for reading can also be viewed (see Figure 11.3). The bar charts offer a clear comparison of pupil achievement in relation to the national average and the local authority average.

Pupils meeting expected standard in reading, writing and maths ❔

School	55%
Local authority average	64%
England average	61%

Pupils achieving at a higher standard in reading, writing and maths ❔

School	2%
Local authority average	10%
England average	9%

Figure 11.3 Percentage of pupils meeting the expected standard and the higher standard in reading, writing and maths (extract from national progress report for end of Key Stage 2)

Pupil groups

Reported data sets about categories of **pupil groups** are also available. Detailed reporting on pupil groups is helpful for the school when considering the performance of particular pupil groups with specific learning or social needs. Reported groupings include gender, disadvantaged pupils, Free School Meal (FSM) pupils, looked after children, Special Educational Needs (SEN) pupils, English as an Additional Language (EAL) pupils and pupils with English as a first language.

The reported data presents the results in reading in Key Stage 1 with a clear breakdown of attainment by pupil groups. This data is presented alongside the National benchmark data to enable comparison to pupil attainment in reading across England, for both the *expected standard* and *greater depth*.

The example in Table 11.1 illustrates a condensed version of the data, with limited information on pupil groups.

 Consider the example data for reading in Key Stage 1 (Table 11.1). Compare the data for each pupil group shown and interpret the answer to the following questions:

* In the school population, what do you notice about the performance of pupil groups when compared to the National benchmark?
* What is the attainment of pupils for whom English is an Additional Language (EAL)?
* How does this compare to the attainment of pupils with English as a first language? How does the data compare to the National figures?
* Is there a difference in attainment between boys and girls at the school? How does this compare to the National picture?
* Look at all the pupil groups in turn and decide which require focused support for English.

The answer to these questions will inform targets in the subject leader plan, but the overall data covers a much wider range of pupil grouping.

 When considering all the information available about pupil groups, the subject leader considers the following questions:

* Which groups are underperforming in the school?
* How do disadvantaged children progress in comparison to other pupils?
* Does the ethnicity of a pupil affect their progress?
* Does the gender of a pupil affect their progress?
* How are EAL pupils performing in comparison to other pupils with English as a first language?

It is important to examine which groups of pupils are underachieving. Comparing pupil group performance is essential to identify pupil groups at risk of underachievement in relation to the rest of the school population. Pupil groups who are at risk will require a focused plan of support to improve their achievement.

Setting goals and planning ways forward

If we consider the data in Table 11.1, it is reasonable to conclude that the subject leader in this school might focus on the overall reading attainment of boys, and in particular the number of boys achieving *greater depth*. Boys' achievements are reported as lower than the national benchmark, particularly at *greater depth*. The subject leader might also consider the needs of FSM

Table 11.1 An example of pupil group reporting in external data

| Breakdown | Cohort | Achieving the expected standard | | Achieving greater depth | |
		School %	National benchmark	School %	National benchmark
Male	40	61	70	4	25
Female	48	80	78	19	21
FSM	21	73	78	5	25
English first language	83	87	74	17	25
English additional language	5	54	74	0	25

pupils. Whilst the percentage meeting the expected standard is similar to the national benchmark, the percentage gaining *greater depth* is significantly lower than the national benchmark figure. The subject leader might look at how all teaching can better support the number of pupils gaining greater depth, and also consider what implications this has for the teaching and learning of both boys and FSM pupils in particular.

In order to successfully address identified priorities it is important to understand the context of the data. Context will provide explanation for some of the data trends, and without fully understanding the reasons for the outcomes it is difficult to devise a meaningful plan. There is a huge range of factors that impact on internal pupil progress data, staffing issues and high pupil turnover being two of the most common. It is therefore helpful to question if the data deserves further investigation. If you are not entirely sure of the reasons for the data outcomes, then you may need to investigate further using appropriate monitoring procedures.

Once you understand better the context behind the data you can then begin to consider your actions to support learning. Planning what to do next requires you to draw on your understanding of effective pedagogy and subject knowledge. The following questions illustrate what a good leader will try to discern from the school's results.

- How do I ensure that the teaching is adapted to meet the needs of the underperforming pupils?
- What pedagogy underpins effective teaching in this aspect of English?
- What good practice exists to meet the needs of this pupil group?
- How will this inform the subject leader's actions for the year?
- What should be put in place to monitor the progress of this pupil group?

Once the actions required to meet the English targets are determined they will be written into the subject leader's action plan. The document *Narrowing the Gaps: Guidance for literacy subject leaders* (DCSF, 2010) collates research information into best practice teaching of English to vulnerable pupil groups. The document provides a useful starting point for considering how to adapt English teaching.

Purposeful, meaningful monitoring

Time out of the classroom is a limited resource in all schools, so the effective subject leader will ensure any opportunity to conduct monitoring is purposeful and informative. Prior to monitoring it is important to think carefully about why monitoring is being carried out, and the subject leader will usually have clear questions in mind to investigate.

 Effective subject leaders undertake a specific monitoring activity in order to find answers to certain questions. Questions might include:

1. What is the current picture of pupil learning in English?
2. What are the pupils' views about their English learning?
3. Are teachers employing effective teaching approaches that ensure quality learning in English?
4. Are teachers implementing staff development training in their planning and teaching?
5. How are teachers using assessment to inform their planning and teaching?
6. How successful is the learning environment for English?

Each of the above questions is best matched to a certain monitoring practice. Questions 1 and 3 will be better understood through the examination of internal school assessment data and national end of key stage data. The danger in relying only on data is that it is remote from actual practice and fails to consider contexts for learning. **Data analysis** should therefore be accompanied by an examination of the children's work and this is referred to as book scrutiny. **Book scrutiny** gives the English subject leader opportunity to see the products of teaching. This enables the subject leader to understand better the quality of the learning, the skills the children are developing and the pace of their progression. It will also reveal how the teacher is marking the work and whether quality feedback is provided to pupils. Book scrutiny enriches the subject leader's statistical understanding and provides a context for the data about pupil attainment.

Question 2 will provide deeper information to support your understanding of teaching and learning. By talking to pupils about their learning experiences and observing them whilst engaged in lessons the subject leader is able to ascertain pupil attitudes and perceptions of English. **Pupil interviews** reveal how much the children enjoy their learning in English. Pupils who talk enthusiastically about their English lessons and have a positive perception of themselves as readers and writers will reinforce a view that the teaching and learning of English is good.

Questions 4 and 5 focus on planning and the use of assessment to inform and shape learning experiences in the classroom. Adaptive teaching makes use of formative assessment to determine how lessons need to change to meet pupil need. Adaptations will be evident during lesson observations (covered in detail in Chapter 10), but **planning scrutiny** can also be informative. Planning scrutiny can be particularly helpful if there has been a recent policy change or the school is trying out a new teaching approach. Looking at planning will help the subject leader to understand if teachers are making the relevant changes to planning to implement any new English practice.

Question 5 requires the subject leader to monitor the learning environment. Conducting a **learning walk** is a common way to do this and enables focused observation of English in the physical environment. Classroom organisation, display and the provision of resources are monitored during this practice. This chapter will discuss in more detail the practices of data analysis, book scrutiny, planning scrutiny, pupil interview and the learning walk.

Any one of these monitoring processes can be used to find out more about the reasons behind the current picture of English presented by summative data. Equally the monitoring processes can be used to evaluate the impact of changes implemented as a result of data analysis.

Planning scrutiny

The monitoring of planning and learning happens through processes that are complementary to lesson observation (Chapter 10 covers lesson observation guidance). Planning is often reviewed at key points in a school year. The most useful time to monitor planning is after there has been a significant change to policy, or renewed focus on a certain pedagogy or teaching approach. What you decide to scrutinise in the planning is largely dependent on what policy changes you have made and what the school development focus is.

 What do good subject leaders think when reviewing planning?

* Are objectives appropriate and do they demonstrate clear aspirations for all children?

- Does planning reflect an engaging and motivating curriculum in terms of content and delivery?
- Does the planning reflect a focus on appropriate teaching approaches?
- Does the planning include different teaching approaches and/or resources for those children who are currently underachieving?
- Is there an appropriate balance of shared work for both reading and writing?
- How does the teacher adapt the planning to address appropriate next steps in learning?
- Does the planning include explicit modelling of particular skills to support children's development?
- Are there planned opportunities for talk within lessons?

In some instances the subject leader might need to discuss plans with the teacher. It is important to allow time for teachers to discuss particular lessons where they have altered their plans. Plans that contain alterations are good because it will indicate that the teacher has recognised misconceptions that need to be addressed or has acknowledged that learning needs to progress faster than envisaged. It is good practice to devote some staff-meeting time to discuss how new approaches to planning are working.

Evaluating the learning

Monitoring the learning progress of pupils throughout the year is important to ensure that time is given to reflect on progress towards English targets. Monitoring through formative assessment processes has the potential to affect pupil outcomes in English far more than summative assessment processes (Richmond, 2016). Ongoing monitoring ensures the opportunity to identify progress and provide additional support to both pupils and staff when required. Monitoring internal assessment data and other procedures such as book scrutiny is key to continual evaluation of learning.

Analysing internal school tracking data

Formative tracking data will reveal children's achievements in English as they journey through the school. School progress data enables the subject leader to consider pupil progress in individual classes, year groups or phases. It also enables tracking of particular vulnerable groups. Exactly what tracking data is presented, and how, will vary widely depending on the individual school approach to assessment. Whilst the appearance of the tracking data may vary, the general principals behind formative assessment are similar, with schools judging whether pupils are *working towards, working above* or *working below expected standard* in reading, writing and GPS.

- Are all year groups showing the same rate of progress in reading and writing?
- Which year groups/classes are making expected progress?
- Which year groups/classes are not making expected progress?
- What factors might explain these differences in progress? How do I know?
- If I don't know, how could I find out?
- Is there a need for specific support and training for staff?
- Is there a need for intervention and support for pupils?
- How can I present this analysis to the staff?

Consider the data in Table 11.2 and ask the same questions that good subject leaders use to scrutinise the class tracker information.

Table 11.2 Extract from Year 2 tracking data

Year 2	Expected or above	Greater depth
Reading (R)	85%	19%
Writing (W)	86%	6%
Mathematics (M)	89%	18%
GPS	86%	17%
W, R and M combined	85%	5%

Attainment data for Year 2 Autumn term

The issue with the current Year 2 data is attainment in writing. The percentage of pupils working at *greater depth* in writing is lower than for all other aspects of English and mathematics. Writing might therefore become a target for this year group as they progress towards the end of Key Stage 1.

Monitoring class or year group assessment tracker information can help the subject leader to work with the class teacher to move children's learning on. Firstly, the subject leader needs to support the class teachers to understand who needs help and with what. To do this the subject leader needs to examine the teacher's class assessment tracking data. The class tracker information in Table 11.3 displays the assessment information for

Table 11.3 Extract from the class writing tracker

Year 2 class Mrs Browne	Spelling	Handwriting	Composition	Vocabulary, grammar and punctuation
Child A	W	W	W+	S
Child B	B+	B+	W	S
Child C	W	W	W+	W+
Child D	B+	B+	W+	W+
Child E	W	W+	S	S

B – working below age-related expectations
W – working within age-related expectations
S – working securely within age-related expectations

the pupils in one class in Year 2. The terms B, W and S indicate how well the pupil is meeting the required age-related expectations for English: B, below age-related progress; W, working at age-related progress; and S, securely working at age-related progress.

The English subject leader and the class teacher need to analyse the class assessment information to look for trends. At first sight it appears that the pupils are doing well in composition and vocabulary, grammar and punctuation. Child D and child B are making expected progress in these two areas, but they are not doing as well with spelling and handwriting. It is for the class teacher and the subject leader to see if this is the same for any other pupils in the class. If it were the case that other pupils were falling behind in handwriting and spelling, then specific teaching support or intervention work would need to happen for the identified pupils.

There is currently a wide range of assessment tracking tools, and schools vary in their approach to recording pupil progress. However, the principles of how the English subject leader should analyse the data remain the same.

 The subject leader supports staff in identifying **who** in the class needs support.

- Are there known underachieving groups?
- What is engagement like for these children? Are they confident in the classroom? Do they participate well?

The subject leader supports staff to identify **how** they can support the identified pupils.

- What aspects of English learning do pupils in the class need to develop in order to achieve age-related expectations?
- What approaches have you used for underachieving groups? What might better support pupil learning?

- What methods of working support the children? Do they work better during group tasks or independent work?
- What scaffolded support and resources can better meet their needs?

Book scrutiny

Looking at a representative sample of books from across the school is a helpful way to monitor English. The children's work is their response to the learning (the outcome of planning and teaching) and book scrutiny enables the subject leader to reflect on the standard of work. When reading the work, the subject leader will think about how it relates to the tracking data for the year group or class.

 When conducting book scrutiny the subject leader will consider the following:

- Is there evidence of writing in a range of forms?
- Is there evidence of response to reading a range of text types and genres?
- Is the marking policy used? Are there targets for each child?
- Is feedback useful and relevant, and linked to the learning outcomes?

Pupil interviews

Pupil voice is widely considered to be important when considering school improvement (Rudduck and McKintyre, 2007). Government guidance and Ofsted both endorse pupil voice as good practice to support the evaluation of teaching and learning. Other agencies and organisations advocate the practice because it empowers and values young people's opinions. Consultation with pupils is now regular practice in most schools and pupil interview is one approach. During pupil interview children are invited to talk about their learning experiences. The subject leader can ask questions to discover what the pupils find interesting and challenging about their learning. Pupils are very perceptive, and can provide the subject leader with new insights that will help to identify any concerns or issues affecting the pupils and consider ways forward to support them.

When talking to children it is obvious that they need to be encouraged to speak openly, but be mindful that they are unlikely to say anything that they think might displease you. It may be that they hint at things without actually explicitly saying what they mean. You may well need to investigate any hints further. Group interviews are preferable, as pupils will feed from each other's points and will generally feel more comfortable giving responses in a group situation.

It is important to put the children at ease. Say something along the lines of, 'I hear that you are doing great things in English. I want to hear all about your learning in English and I have a few questions I would like to ask you. I will be writing while you talk to make sure I capture all the important things you tell me, but it is not a test. I want to learn from you...'

The following questions are just a guide:

- Can you tell me about an English lesson you have enjoyed this year?
- What made it good?
- How does the teacher help you to do well? In a particular task/or with reading/or with writing?
- Do you think you are a good reader? How do you know? What do good readers do?
- Do you think you are a good writer? How do you know? What do good writers do?

Go with the flow of the conversation and remember to thank them at the end.

The learning environment

The school environment provides significant impact on how English is viewed by pupils, teachers and parents. Consider how the school environment encourages the children to learn about English. Consider if the school utilises a wide range of materials that are culturally rich and age appropriate. Is there an opportunity for pupils to contribute to display? Do resources represent their choice, views and cultural identity? Observe how the classroom environment helps the children with their learning through either display or scaffolds to support reading and writing. All these factors will support children's engagement with English and thus their progress.

- Are there examples of children's writing celebrated in public places?
- Are these different types of writing or is there a focus on narrative?

- Are the children encouraged to write in meaningful contexts around the school environment?
- Can they contribute to signage or interactive message boards around the school?
- How is reading celebrated in the school? Are writing and reading celebrated in school assembly?
- Are there displays that encourage pupils to recommend and share their reading material?
- Do classrooms have engaging and exciting book corners?
- Is the school library regularly used? Is it well stocked, organised and inviting to the pupils?
- Does the library host reading clubs or communities of readers?
- Do classrooms have working walls, displays and language banks to support the current reading and writing focus?
- Is there evidence that the children make use of the layout and displays within the classroom to support their learning?

Learning walk

The use of learning walks has become a common way for schools to ascertain a snapshot understanding of teaching and learning. As the name suggests, it involves walking around the school, observing the whole building (displays and resources as well as teaching and learning) and going into classrooms. During a learning walk the subject leader will walk into lessons and observe (and possibly discuss) the lesson with the teacher. It may also be possible to talk to pupils about the learning and look at their work.

- Listen to pupil-led and teacher-led discussion about the task
- Observe the teacher modelling, questioning and explaining
- Observe the pupils' engagement with the learning
- Read/listen to pupils' responses to the activity
- Talk to the pupils about the current text/activity in general

The learning walk enables the subject leader to look at English learning across the school, and have a glimpse of the types of teaching approaches used, the resources provided, the learning environment, the grouping of children, the level of pupil engagement and the level of teacher confidence in delivering English learning. In a sense, the learning walk covers all monitoring procedures from book scrutiny to pupil interview to lesson observation, albeit in far less depth.

The impact of new approaches

As each school year comes to an end the cycle of school improvement completes. Ongoing analysis of tracking data will hopefully ensure your success in meeting the desired goals in English. The analysis of year-end, summative key stage data helps us understand the extent to which the subject leader's action plan has met the desired goals. This stage both completes the annual cycle of school improvement and begins it anew. Whilst data hopefully provides evidence of the successes of any initiatives in English teaching it will also raise new or ongoing concerns, and the identification of new English foci begins.

References

Department for Children, Skills and Family (DCSF) (2010) *Narrowing the Gaps: Guidance for literacy subject leaders.* Nottingham: DCSF.

National College of Teaching and Leadership (NCTL) (2015) 'Resources for teaching and learning:

A collection of materials from the National College.' Available at: www.nationalcol lege.org.uk/?q=node/611 [accessed 31 March 2018].

Page, D. (2016) 'Conceptualising the surveillance of teachers.' *British Journal of Sociology of Education*, 38 (7), 991–1006.

Richmond, J. (2016) 'Curriculum and assessment in English 3 to 19: A better plan.' Available at: https://ukla.org/downloads/Assessment_and_Examinations_3_to_19. pdf [accessed 2 March 2018].

Rudduck, J. and McKintyre, D. (2007) *Improving Learning through Consulting Pupils.* Oxon: Routledge.

Standards and Testing Agency (STA) (2015) 'Scaled scores at Key Stage 1.' London: Standards and Testing Agency. Available at: www.gov.uk/guidance/scaled-scores [accessed 2 March 2018].

Waters, M. and Martin, T. (1999) *Coordinating English at Key Stage 2: The subject leader's handbook.* London: Falmer Press.

Working with families to support literacy development

Mary Scanlan

This chapter opens with a brief historical overview of home–school partnership, focusing on the role of the family in literacy learning. It illustrates, through three case studies, practical ways in which English subject leaders might develop effective relationships with families to support pupils' learning and progression. These case studies focus in turn on reading, writing, and speaking and listening. It examines why this is an important area for subject leaders to consider and concludes by suggesting that drawing on everyday at-home practices might be the most effective way to support literacy learning in the school.

What does the English subject leader need to know about home–school partnership?

The need for schools and families to work together to support children's learning has long been acknowledged. The Plowden Report (Central Advisory Council for Education, 1967) emphasised the key role that parents[1] play in their child's learning. This important part of a teacher's skill set is recognised in documentation such as the Teachers' Standards (DfE, 2011) and within the early years curriculum (DfE, 2017). In addition, as this area is linked directly to school improvement, the effectiveness of engagement with parents and carers is judged by Ofsted (2018). Best practice focuses on whole-school approaches which embrace the individual community in terms of social, ethnic and language difference.

Pugh and De'Ath (1989) studied 130 settings and developed a continuum of parental involvement which ranged from *non-participation* to *control*. *Non-participation* might be active (e.g. parents making a conscious decision not to be involved) or passive (e.g. lacking the confidence to engage). In this model the next levels were termed *supporters, participants* and *partners*. Where parents made decisions and determined practice, this was theorised as *control*. In the United States, Epstein (1995) identified six areas within home–school partnership where opportunities exist for collaboration. These were *parenting, communicating, volunteering, learning at home, decision making* and *collaborating with the community*. Epstein additionally identified challenges in each area; for example, in the area of *communication* these might include considering the needs of parents who do not speak English, reviewing the quality of communications and establishing two-way communication. In their review of parental engagement for children aged 5–19, Goodall and Vorhaus (2010) identified three categories in this area: home–school links, support and training for parents, and family and community-based interventions. This chapter will focus on the first category, home–school links.

In a wide-ranging review of the literature on the effect of parental involvement on children's achievement, Desforges and Abouchaar (2003) found that what they termed *at-home good parenting* had a significant positive effect on attainment at school across all social classes and ethnic groups. This good parenting was defined as providing a settled environment in which learning was stimulated through talk and activities, where positive views of education were held and in which parents had high aspirations for their children. This Home Learning Environment (HLE) has been shown to have an impact on learning throughout the primary school years and beyond (Taggart *et al.*, 2015). However, it is important not to reinforce unhelpful stereotypes. Klett-Davies (2010) suggested that what is seen as good parenting appears to be synonymous with middle-class values and practices, and families who appear not to share these values can be further marginalised with the resulting disadvantage entrenched. Indeed, as can be seen from the discussion below, much research has uncovered rich literacy practices across all families and social groupings.

However, practice in this area is not always straightforward. Docking (1990) highlighted that some practitioners have concerns about their work with parents. She identified these might be *ideological*, such as issues regarding professional boundaries, *psychological*, e.g. feeling threatened by having one's practice scrutinised, *professional*, such as perceived lack of training and *practical*, e.g. a lack of time. The issue of how well teachers are prepared to work with families, in both their initial and continuing training, continues to raise concern. As Goodall and Vorhaus (2010) comment, 'To engage effectively with parents, staff require training and coaching, particularly when working with parents whose backgrounds are very different to their own' (Goodall and Vorhaus, 2010: 5). This last point regarding diversity is important. Just as all children and their families are unique, so are practitioners, and there is a need to be aware of one's own, perhaps implicit, values. It is suggested that good practice in this area should start with schools and practitioners explicitly interrogating their own values and beliefs (Wheeler and Connor, 2006).

Literacy and home–school partnership

The content of a literacy curriculum for primary schools can be contentious. In the UK there have been several iterations of English within National Curriculum documentation (DES, 1990; DfE, 2013; DfEE, 1999). The presence of the traditional subjects of reading and writing seems to be a constant, with a more recent acknowledgement of the importance of speaking and listening (sometimes termed *oracy*). As discussed above, after the publication of the Plowden Report parents were asked to be generally supportive of the aims of the school. In terms of literacy, this support was focused on schools aiming to promote school-type literacy practices in the home, largely in response to research which demonstrated the positive impact of parents supporting children's reading at home (Topping and Lindsay, 1991). This parental teaching role was enshrined in the legislation through the mandatory Home–School Agreement published by the DfEE (1998). In this document, parental responsibility was spelt out in detail; for example, in Key Stage 1, parents were asked to read with their child for twenty minutes per day. As McNamara *et al.* (2000) commented, this legislation positioned parents as active partners in the production of educated children. This document was made optional in 2016.

Research also began to look at how parents might support children's writing development. Weinberger (1996), working with a sample of children aged 3 to 7, found that support was diverse and widespread, but focused on transcription, with, for example, parents supplying words children could not spell and scribing for children to copy. There was, however, far less support with the compositional aspects of writing. Weinberger's research raised the issue that perhaps a teacher-like way of supporting children's writing did not come naturally to most parents and that there might be more accessible methods of involvement.

The positioning of speaking and listening, within a literacy curriculum, has also been interesting. In the original programmes of study for the National Curriculum in 1990, speaking, listening, reading and writing were seen as interconnected components of literacy teaching and learning, and a programme of study entitled 'Speaking and Listening' was introduced alongside those for 'Reading' and 'Writing'. This framework provided a continuum, which moved from exploratory, tentative talk to a more polished product. Currently, requirements for speaking and listening in the National Curriculum consist of a list of twelve brief undifferentiated statements for Key Stages 1 and 2 (Richmond, 2017). Research had also evidenced the interconnectedness of speaking and writing; for example, Bearne (2005a, 2005b) defined four different types of talk, which, she claimed, paralleled types of writing. These were *formative, informative, performative* and *evaluative*. She defined *informative* talk as an opportunity to explain ideas, knowledge and opinions, and *formative* talk as helping to capture, shape and develop ideas in the beginning part of a planning and teaching sequence. *Performative* talk allowed learners to talk at some length about a story, process or argument, and *evaluative* talk supported reflection and self-evaluation. She highlighted that teachers played an important role in modelling these ways of talking. Additionally, she highlighted the impact that parents might have in supporting writing through talk in the home: 'Homes and families are more significant to developing writers than might have been thought, particularly in providing experience in a range of spoken forms of language which are the bedrock for writing' (Bearne, 2002: 10).

In the late 1990s the research framework concerning how home–school partnership might support children's literacy development shifted. Researchers became more interested in literacy as a practice, which was grounded in social, historical, cultural and political contexts of use. Influenced by the work of Gee (1990) and Street (1984), researchers began to explore discrepancies or discontinuities between home and school. Heath (1983) highlighted that for some children there was a disjuncture between home and school literacy practices, which meant that accessing school literacy was problematic. Others focused on so-called *local literacies*, the complex web of activities that families engage in. Rather than looking at school literacy practices and seeing whether they were present in the home they focused on documenting the full range of home literacy practices (Barton and Hamilton, 1998). Others started to explore different communities' specific out-of-school literacy learning. Gregory and Williams (2000) considered the home literacy practices of Bangladeshi families in London, in particular the important role played by siblings in supporting literacy development, and Kenner (2004) explored the range of texts and writing within the home.

More recent research in the area has continued with this sociocultural focus. Feiler *et al.* (2007) explored whether the home literacy interests of pupils were known about and reflected in the curriculum practices of schools. The following discussion is underpinned by research undertaken by the author as part of the Home–School Knowledge Exchange[2] (HSKE) project. The project used a 'funds of knowledge' framework, which highlighted the wealth of knowledge families draw on, but which is not always recognised within the official school curricula (Moll and Greenberg, 1992). Part of the project explored the different understandings parents and teachers had of children's literacy learning and devised ways in which this might be shared and built on to support pupil progress, both at home and in the school.

It must be acknowledged that, despite this body of research and evidence of excellent practice in schools (Goodall and Vorhaus, 2010), there is currently no direct mention of parental support for literacy learning in the statutory framework for Key Stages 1 and 2 (DfE, 2013). This, it might be argued, is an unfortunate omission. In contrast, the statutory curriculum for younger children (DfE, 2017) highlights parental partnership as a key tenet of good practice. Subject leaders can therefore draw on their experience of these two differing curricula when considering the role of families in supporting children's literacy learning.

- We understand that working in partnership with families raises attainment.
- We recognise that all families want to, and can, support their children's literacy development.
- We know that families can support all areas of literacy development: reading, writing, speaking and listening.

Case study: Using technology to support parent engagement in reading

One of the starting points of the HSKE project was finding out what information parents and teachers wanted to share in terms of the children's literacy learning (Feiler et al., 2007). In one school, through a questionnaire given to parents, and looking at the School Development Plan, literacy and in particular reading were identified as a joint concern. Therefore, the class teacher created a DVD which focused on this area. This included a whole-class sharing of a Big Book, group work, a guided reading session and a child receiving individual support. Additionally, every DVD was accompanied by a booklet, which gave parents information on strategies to support and extend their children's reading in the home. Suggestions were included such as, 'When your child brings home a new reading book, talk about the pictures together before he/she reads it for the first time'.

Personalised DVDs or video clips on a school website can have many advantages. They can be an opportunity for parents who, for a variety of reasons, cannot visit during the school day to see everyday classroom life. They allow schools to share classroom practice, and schools might target parents who cannot attend setting-based events such as curriculum evenings. The content needs to be carefully planned by the teacher, for example, by ensuring that every child appears. Practical issues need to be addressed, such as who will do the filming, and use might be made of adult help in the classroom or older children in the school. Another issue is informed consent. Permission needs to be gained from all participants and parents need to be informed about plans for the finished DVD or video. It is also useful to provide an opportunity for parents and teachers to watch the finished version together. Schools might arrange screenings at different times in order that parents who work might attend, and refreshments can be offered to help create a welcoming atmosphere.

The responses to the project DVDs were positive. Parents commented that they felt more able to support their child's learning in the home; for example, after watching one which focused on reading, a parent commented: 'I learnt a lot from that, because I'd just open the book and start to read it, but if you look through the pictures and you explain the story, by the time you get to read it then you're more into it, aren't you?' Another common parental response was appreciation of having a record of their child's time in the classroom, and this was especially true for parents who for various reasons did not go into school: 'It's always good to see how it works in the classroom, because that's not an opportunity you'd normally have.'

Recent developments in ICT have created huge opportunities in this area. For example, the use of tools such as online learning journals means there can be a real-time sharing of teaching and learning in classrooms, using written observations, photographs and video clips. Parents are able to view these and add contributions from the home. Schools are increasingly using blogs, tweets and text messaging to communicate with parents and many now ensure Web pages are translated into a range of languages. However, more can be done; as Goodall and Vorhaus note: '...the evidence suggests that levels of parental engagement could be improved if more schools made use of the potential of technology to support at-home learning' (Goodall and Vorhaus, 2010: 43).

- Does your school development plan identify where you might want to work with parents?
- Are there areas where technology might support literacy learning, e.g. short explanatory video clips for parents?
- Do you ask parents what activities they would like the school to provide so they can support children's literacy learning?

Case study: Engaging home support for writing in school

Writing can quite often be supported by a stimulus of some kind, such as a visit, an artefact or a story. Photographs provide immediacy and a level of detail which young children might find hard to record in other ways and are an excellent means of conveying the intimacy of the home in the school setting. Therefore, children in the project were given a disposable camera and were asked to use it over a school holiday, as it was felt that this might give them more opportunities to use the camera than a normal school week. The activity supported the curriculum, as children were asked to take photographs that linked to forthcoming school topics, e.g. *The Local Area* and *Living*

Things, as well as things/places/people that were important to them. When the photographs were developed, parents and children were given an opportunity to remove any that they did not wish to be in the public domain.

They were then used in a variety of ways to promote writing. One school sent the photographs home together with brightly coloured card, and parents and children were asked to write about what was happening in the photographs. These were then used to make an eye-catching display in the school corridor. A second activity involved inviting parents into the classroom to take part in a writing workshop using the photographs to make books with their child. This activity was designed to allow parents (who held most information about the photographs) to feel that they, not the teacher, could most fully support their child's learning, even though the activity was carried out in the context of the school. Children responded positively to the presence of their parents in the classroom, with one child noting his father's support had been '...fun, he helped me. He reminded me what I could write and what things were and when they were'. Teachers noted the enthusiastic response by the children, who had particularly enjoyed having their own cameras and had been excited to get their photographs back. A teacher who had linked the activity to a topic on *Living Things* commented that it was a wonderful way to start a project. Similarly, the school which had focused on *The Local Area* was amazed by the depth of knowledge displayed by the parents.

When asking children to reveal their out-of-school lives in this manner, practitioners need to be sensitive in ensuring that the information brought in is respected. They also need to accept that some families will choose not to participate. Also, it is important to recognise that some parents might feel a sense of unease at being invited into the classroom to help with writing, and alternative activities might be more successful, for example those based on other curriculum areas such as art (e.g. making photograph frames).

- What opportunities do you provide for children's out-of-school writing to be shared in the school setting?
- What opportunities do you offer for parents to come into the classroom to support literacy learning?
- Do you offer opportunities for parents to share information about home literacy practices with the school?

- How do we share the school English curriculum with parents?
- How do we find out about the wide range of literacy practices children and families engage in?
- How do we find out what support and/or activities families might like the school to provide?

Case study: Drawing on oracy in the home to support writing in school

It might be argued that one of the best ways that parents can support children's literacy learning is through everyday speaking and listening in the home (Bearne, 2002). Building on the activity in which photographs from the home were used to support writing, a further activity was then devised in which artefacts from the home, collected in a shoebox, were used to promote creative writing in the classroom.

The activity started with a letter written jointly by the class teacher and the children to explain the purpose of the activity:

> We are interested in finding out more about what motivates children to write, and also to produce high-quality written pieces...The idea of the shoebox is for each child to be able to use it to collect items they think would be a good and motivational stimulus for writing.

The importance of parental oracy as a key part of the activity was also evident at this early stage: 'It would be helpful if you could discuss with them what they wish to include.'

When the shoeboxes were returned to the school, every child presented their contents to the class and discussed how they were going to use them in their writing. This opportunity for oral rehearsal links clearly to Bearne's formative and performative talk for writing (2005a, 2005b). After the activity had been completed the teacher and children again jointly composed a letter to go home explaining how the boxes had been used. The children described the kinds of stories they had written: 'Some of them were serials. Some stories were very long and interesting', and 'Some of us used other people's boxes to write about and it could be fun.' They also explained why they had found the process helpful: 'Some of us found it better because we didn't waste as much time thinking up ideas.'

This case study focuses on one child, Christopher (and his father), to explore how speaking and listening in the home can support writing in the school and the impact on both pupil and parent. However, before we look at the support given in the home it is interesting to explore how writing was perceived by both Christopher and his father. Christopher was viewed by the school as a high-attaining pupil. When he was asked whether he thought he was good at writing, his response acknowledged the aspects of both composition and transcription: 'I think I'm a bit messy. I think my ideas are good, but I think what I might actually write in my book, it's a bit messy.' This evaluation was shared by his father: '...so my main preoccupation with his writing isn't so much what he's writing but how neatly he's writing.'

Christopher's box contents:

- *A small reindeer (put in by Mum and Dad)*
- *Red and blue jumping beans*
- *A silver spoon*
- *A dice (for 'jumping on')*
- *Two acorns (put in by Mum)*
- *A green pen (magic)*
- *A disc from a shooting robot*

When it came to choosing artefacts, it was very clear that Christopher's father had understood the purpose of the activity, which was to support creative writing: '...With the reindeer, I might have said something like, "What happens to the reindeer, what does he do?".' Christopher also understood the reason for choosing particular artefacts: '...They [the artefacts] did have some quite good ... stories.' An interesting point was that even when help had been offered by his father in terms of creative ideas, e.g. what the reindeer might do, Christopher chose not to act upon this input.

Interviewer: 'What sort of idea did they [the parents] have about a story?' 'They could go on an adventure or something ... but I didn't use that.' Christopher's father confirmed that his advice had not been acted upon: 'There was a small sort of reindeer thing which I thought was more obvious ... I don't think that featured much in the story at all!' Instead, Christopher had chosen some jumping beans to write his story about. His father commented: 'Well, I must say I didn't imagine that they would become particularly inspiring...'

> While the blue jumping bean was still eating, the red jumping bean sneaked the basket and ate all the sweets. The blue jumping bean was full so he said he would eat his sweets when he got back to earth. They jumped down to England and the blue jumping bean opened the basket and his sweets were all gone! Greedy lump said the blue one to the red one.

Figure 12.1 Extract from Christopher's story

After the activity had been carried out in the classroom the teacher assessed the children's writing and stated that in her judgement, several children had what she termed a 'literacy breakthrough'. These breakthroughs included children being motivated to write and also producing more extended and better structured pieces of writing. In Christopher's case, the breakthrough was in terms of inspiration and composition:

> It worked well for Christopher; definitely, I mean he came up with a really good piece. There was only one thing that he really wanted to write about and it was these jumping beans ... and he is one that would sometimes sit in a session and say, 'I just can't think what I'm going to write.'

Christopher also articulated how the artefacts had provided support: 'Because it kind of gives you a character and some things that could be in it, like involved in the story.'

Another interesting finding was that this breakthrough was sustained. The author returned to the school several months later and the class teacher commented of Christopher:

> Now he <u>has</u> sustained that, he now really likes writing. He only wrote about jumping beans for weeks and weeks and weeks and weeks. But his mum came in and said he was writing them and reading them for a bedtime story to his little sister, and he was still doing them at the time we were doing SATs, he did a jumping bean story even then! In terms of composition that breakthrough was sustained.

Parents also felt that the activity had been successful. Christopher's father highlighted the fact that the artefacts from home had contributed to the activity's success: 'The fact that the objects came from home and were personal to him made the whole thing more special ... I don't know quite why it works but it does work.'

- How could you provide opportunities for children to write about subjects that are meaningful to them, in particular their out-of-school lives?
- How could you provide opportunities for children to talk through story ideas before they are asked to write?
- How could you plan for collaborative writing opportunities?

- Communicate with families, sharing knowledge and expertise.
- Communicate in a range of ways which include written information, video clips on the school website, use of Internet platforms and text messages.
- Offer a range of support to parents, e.g. workshops, to support phonics teaching, and resources that can be borrowed to support reading such as Story Sacks.

Case study learning points

As subject leader:

✓ **Ensure** that all teachers in your school offer numerous opportunities to share relevant aspects of the literacy curriculum, so parents can support children in the home. This is important for all year groups.

✓ **Be innovative** in how you communicate with parents; try a range of methods such as letters, text messages, through the website, etc.

✓ **Ensure** that your literacy resources reflect the culture and experience of the families you teach; for example, try to display written materials which represent a range of scripts.

✓ **Offer numerous opportunities** to involve families and be inclusive, e.g. being mindful of parents who work, those who have a child with SEND, parents who have EAL, etc.

✓ **Find out about** the different literacy practices of families in your school.

✓ **Build on the home literacy practices** of the children in your school, e.g. displaying materials from home.

Notes

1   The use of the word 'parents' in this chapter includes all natural parents and any person or carer who has parental responsibility for a child.
2   The Home School Knowledge Exchange (HSKE) project was funded by the ESRC (reference number L139 25 1078).

References

Barton, D. and Hamilton, M. (1998) *Local Literacies: Reading and writing in one community*. London: Routledge.

Bearne, E. (2002) *Making Progress in Writing*. London: RoutledgeFalmer.

Bearne, E. (2005a) 'Finding the written voice (1).' *The Primary English Magazine*. April, 30–2.

Bearne, E. (2005b) 'Finding the written voice (2).' *The Primary English Magazine*. June, 29–32.

Central Advisory Council for Education (1967) *The Plowden Report: Children and their primary schools*. London: HMSO.

Department for Education (DfE) (2013) 'The National Curriculum in England: Key Stages 1 and 2 framework document.' Available at: www.gov.uk/government/publications/national-curriculum-in-england-primary-curriculum [accessed 21 February 2018].

Department for Education (DfE) (2011) 'Teachers' Standards Guidance for school leaders, school staff and governing bodies.' Available at: https://assets.publishing.service.gov.uk/government/uploads/system/uploads/attachment_data/file/665520/Teachers__Standards.pdf [accessed 6 July 2018].

Department for Education (DfE) (2017) 'Statutory framework for the early years foundation stage.' Available at: www.gov.uk/government/uploads/system/uploads/attachment_data/file/596629/EYFS_STATUTORY_FRAMEWORK_2017.pdf [accessed 21 February 2018].

Department for Education and Employment (DfEE) (1998) *Home–School Agreements: What every parent should know*. London: HMSO.

Department for Education and Employment (DfEE) (1999) 'The National Curriculum.' London: DfEE/QCA. Available at: www.educationengland.org.uk/documents/pdfs/1999-nc-primary-handbook.pdf [accessed 21 February 2018].

Department of Education and Science (DES) (1990) *English in the National Curriculum (No.2)*. London: Her Majesty's Stationery Office.

Desforges, C. and Abouchaar, A. (2003) *The Impact of Parental Involvement, Parental Support and Family Education on Pupil Achievement and Adjustment; A Literature Review*. Nottingham: Department for Education and Skills.

Docking, J. (1990) *Primary Schools and Parents*. London: Hodder and Stoughton.

Epstein, J. (1995) 'School, family, community partnerships: Caring for the children we share.' *Phi Delta Kappan*, 76, 710–12.

Feiler, A., Andrews, J., Greenhough, P., Hughes, M., Johnson, D., Scanlan, M. and Yee, W. C. (2007) *Linking Home and School Learning: Primary literacy*. London: RoutledgeFalmer.

Gee, J. P. (1990) *Social Linguistics and Literacies: Ideology in discourses*. London: Falmer.

Goodall, J. and Vorhaus, J. (2010) *Review of Best Practice in Parental Engagement*. London: DfE.

Gregory, E. and Williams, A. (2000) 'Work or play? Unofficial literacies in the lives of two East London communities.' In: Martin-Jones, M. and Jones, K. (eds), *Multilingual Literacies: Reading and writing different worlds*. Amsterdam: John Benjamins.

Heath, S. B. (1983) *Ways with Words: Language life and work in communities and classrooms*. Cambridge: Cambridge University Press.

Kenner, C. (2004) *Becoming Biliterate: Young children learning different writing systems*. Stoke-on-Trent: Trentham Books.

Klett-Davies, M. (2010) *Is Parenting a Class Issue?* London: Family and Parenting Institute.

McNamara, O., Hustler, D., Stronach, I. and Rodrigo, M., with Beresford, E. and Botcherby, S. (2000) 'Room to manoeuvre: Mobilising the "active partner" in home–school relations'. *British Educational Research Journal*, 26 (4), 473–89.

Moll, L. and Greenberg, J. (1992) 'Creating zones of possibilities: Combining social contexts for instruction.' In: Moll, L. (ed.), *Vygotsky and Education*. Cambridge: Cambridge University Press.

Office for Standards in Education (Ofsted) (2018) *School Inspection Handbook*. London: Ofsted Publications. Available at: https://assets.publishing.service.gov.uk/government/uploads/system/uploads/attachment_data/file/699810/School_inspection_handbook_section_5.pdf [accessed 6 July 2018].

Pugh, G. and De'Ath, E. (1989) *Working Towards Partnership in the Early Years*. London: National Children's Bureau.

Richmond, J., with Burn, A., Dougill, P., Raleigh, M. and Traves, P. (2017) *Curriculum and Assessment in English 3 to 11: A better plan* and *Curriculum and Assessment in English 11 to 19: A better plan*. London: Routledge.

Street, B. (1984) *Literacy in Theory and Practice*. Cambridge: Cambridge University Press.

Taggart, B., Sylva, K., Melhuish, E., Sammons, P. and Siraj, I. (2015) 'Effective pre-school, primary and secondary education project (EPPSE 3–16+): How pre-school influences children and young people's attainment and developmental outcomes over time.' DfE Research Brief. Available at: http://dera.ioe.ac.uk/23344/1/RB455_Effective_pre-school_primary_and_secondary_education_project.pdf [accessed 21 February 2018].

Topping, K. and Lindsay, G. A. (1991) 'The structure and development of the paired reading technique.' *Journal of Research in Reading*, 15 (2), 120–36.

Weinberger, J. (1996) *Literacy Goes to School*. London: Paul Chapman Publishing.

Wheeler, H. and Connor, J. (2006) *Parents, Early Years and Learning Activities*. London: National Children's Bureau.

13 Hot topics
Grammar and writing

Lisa Baldwin

This final chapter will explore how key issues in the teaching of English are subject to constant change and how important it is for the subject leader to be clear about their own pedagogy. Focusing on one aspect of English, we will explore how different media outlets report on English education and consider why government reports and guidance require scrutiny. The chapter will discuss the importance of managing changes in English education through a pragmatic approach. Finally, we consider how the effective English subject leader considers the needs of their school within the broader context of government policy and guidance. Consideration will be given to how the recent focus on grammar has affected teaching approaches and pedagogy. Finally, the chapter will reflect on how this current 'hot topic' serves to illustrate how the English subject leader must navigate their school through significant externally driven change.

Current debate: Old controversy

Since the introduction of the new National Curriculum (DfE, 2013) in September 2014, grammar has become a 'hot topic' for education. The previous 'hot topic' debate around phonics instruction and reading approaches (known as the 'reading wars') was replaced by 'grammar wars' (Locke, 2009; Myhill *et al.*, 2013), forcing reading to take a back seat while media attention focused on grammar.

Past perspectives on grammar teaching reveal that there is little 'new' in the current discussion. In a review of the literature on grammar over the last fifty years, Myhill and Watson (2014) discuss how educational argument revolves around differing beliefs about the acquisition of grammar knowledge. Advocates of *explicit* grammar teaching argue that metalinguistic understanding has an important role to play in the English curriculum, impacting on Standard English language skills. Proponents of *implicit* grammar knowledge support the view that an understanding of grammar is acquired through experience with language in meaningful contexts.

If we consider the statement below from the National Curriculum (DfE, 2013) it is clear that it is the explicit approach to grammar teaching that is advocated:

> Once pupils are familiar with a grammatical concept [for example 'modal verb'], they should be encouraged to apply and explore this concept in the grammar of their own speech and writing and to note where it is used by others.
>
> *(DfE, 2013: 64)*

The National Curriculum states that grammar teaching should begin with technical understanding before pupil learning moves on to application of the technique in written and spoken form, or exploration of the technique by other writers. Myhill and Watson (2014) assert that there is no research that underpins this teaching approach. Research evidence indicates that whilst some studies showed increased understanding of technical terms in decontextualised tasks, there was no change to writing quality (Andrews *et al.*, 2016; Commons Education Select Committee Report, 2017).

Grammar, morals and standards

When Michael Gove took up government office in the education department, the media reported him for his fastidious attitude to grammar and writing style. The content of the email he sent to civil servants in the education department became public, and one man took the limelight as a result of the communication. In his email Michael Gove directed civil servants to the book *Gwynne's Grammar* by Nevile Martin Gwynne. The result was resurgence in interest for Gwynne's book and for his teaching techniques.

Thrust into media focus, the author took the opportunity to communicate his view that grammar had been missing from education for some while. One newspaper report described Gwynne as 'apoplectic at the erosion of standards', asserting that teachers were 'not allowed to say [the child is] wrong in case it damages their self-esteem' (Grice, 2013; Gwynne, 2013). Similar views are expressed in his book. Such outrage at the perceived lack of explicit grammar teaching is a common theme in discourse about grammar. Past rhetoric has often made links between grammar, morals and standards (Cameron, 1995). Indeed Gwynne's book articulates the view that grammar is inherently linked to wider morality because 'grammar is the science of using words rightly, leading to thinking rightly, leading to deciding rightly, without which – common sense and experience show – happiness is impossible. Therefore: happiness depends at least partly on good grammar' (Gwynne, 2013: 6). Gwynne's champion, the Education

Secretary, held similar views about declining standards in English and voiced his concerns during a speech at Brighton College in 2014. He introduced the new National Curriculum (DfE, 2013), stating it was the means to redress neglected standards in English (Gove, 2014).

Curriculum change

The most significant change in the new National Curriculum (DfE, 2013) was the emphasis on spelling, punctuation and grammar, embodied in detailed appendices. Appendix 1 of the National Curriculum document contains twenty-five pages of statutory spelling content (DfE, 2013, 49–73). Appendix 2, the less weighty appendix, contains statutory content for the teaching of vocabulary, grammar and punctuation across the primary age-range (DfE, 2013, 74–9). The importance of these two statutory curriculum elements was enforced through the introduction of a new national test: the Spelling, Punctuation and Grammar (SPaG) test, now called the Grammar, Punctuation and Spelling (GPS) test.

The SPaG test was devised in response to Lord Bew's recommendations, arising from his report on testing at Key Stage 2 (Bew, 2011). In his report Bew advocated externally marked pupil testing on elements of writing, '(in particular spelling, punc-tuation, grammar and vocabulary) where there are clear "right" or "wrong" answers' (Bew, 2011: 9). When the test was introduced it was hailed as the means to ensure that children would be 'taught the skills they [need] to understand . . . language, and to use it properly, creatively and effectively' (Truss, 2013).

Previous National Literacy Strategy guidance on grammar and writing focused on the contextual teaching of grammar, and assessment processes featured no explicit testing of the metalanguage associated with grammar. The introduction of the new National Curriculum and the SpaG test (now GPS) left schools struggling to address a significant knowledge gap.

Resultant pedagogy

Research illustrates how assessment influences the focus of teachers' time and the strategies they adopt in the classroom (Moss, 2017). National tests are adminis-tered, marked and reported as data. The data are then used to report schools' success in teaching English and mathematics. Head teachers' jobs can depend on good yearly outcomes and a school's reputation for quality teaching can be either won or lost. Today there is also greater risk of poor performance resulting in 'external intervention' and forced takeover of school governance (Moss, 2017: 62). Such high-stakes accountability placed significant performance pressures on school leaders and teachers, and resulted in the decontextualised approach to the teaching of grammar (Commons Education Select Committee Report, 2017; Illing-worth and Hall, 2016).

Schools had to make up substantial ground to prepare the first cohort of pupils for the SPaG test. The result was a disproportionate focus on teaching the required grammar skills. The need for teachers to prepare pupils for the SPaG test not only dominated teaching time, it also narrowed the English curriculum in readiness for the test. Time usually allocated to writing during English lessons was squeezed to accommodate a focus on explicit grammatical language skills (Centre for Research in Writing at the University of Exeter, 2016).

Media reporting: The flawed test

The introduction of the SPaG test sparked controversy and was widely reported in the media. Firstly, concern was voiced about the test promoting the simplistic notion that language is fixed and that grammar is uncomplicated. In a newspaper article entitled 'Dear Ms Morgan: In grammar there isn't always one right answer', Michael Rosen challenged Lord Bew's 'evidence-free assumption' that spelling, punctuation and grammar questions have 'right and wrong answers' (Bew, 2011: 9; Rosen, 2015). Rosen raised the point that any one word in the English lexicon could be accurately identified using multiple grammatical terms, depending upon the context within which it was used. He cited examples from SATs test papers where the words 'my', 'your', 'her', 'his' and 'their' were referred to as determiners but also, in the same SATs paper, as possessive pronouns. Rosen (2015) went on to challenge the government's assumption that there is an undisputable place to correctly punctuate writing. The positioning of some punctuation, he stated, can relate to writing style: something that writers make differing authorial choices over.

In May 2017, during SATs week, *The Guardian* newspaper reported teachers' concerns about GPS (previously SPaG) testing arrangements. Teachers' opinion of the test was endorsed by Richard Hudson, an academic member of the team who had advised government on grammar when the 2014 curriculum was devised. He was quoted as saying the National Curriculum approach was 'not based on good research evidence' (Mansell, 2017). Hudson was the final advisory panel member to add a voice of dissent to the government's approach to grammar.

Media reporting: The impact on writing

The grammar debate does not just focus on concerns over inaccuracies and incon-sistencies within the SPaG (now GPS) test papers. It also raises concern over the detrimental impact the focus on grammar has on writing. David Crystal echoed Rosen in his criticism of the curriculum's approach to grammar, describing it as having 'too much emphasis on linguistic labeling as an end in itself ... rather than ... as the starting point in discussions of effective writing' (Crystal, 2013). Michael Morpurgo agreed (Ward, 2017), voicing concern that the emphasis on technical aspects of writing inhibited children's use of imagination. It was his view that writing had become the means to demonstrate a repertoire of grammatical techniques.

The government's press release announcing the introduction of the SPaG test stated, 'It will mean that primary schools will once again place a strong focus on the teaching of key writing techniques and ensure that children leave primary school confident in these skills' (Truss, 2013). Counter debate acknowledged the need for children to understand how to improve their writing but cautioned that an undue focus on grammatical or transcriptional elements could have a profoundly negative effect on children's confidence and writing development (Richmond et al., 2017).

Michael Gove's reported email to civil servants advised them to consult 'the great writers to improve your own prose – George Orwell and Evelyn Waugh, Jane Austen and George Eliot, Matthew Parris and Christopher Hitchens' (Leftly, 2015). Rather ironically, many of these (and other) 'great writers' would not have met the end of Key Stage 2 criteria for expected level writing. Charles Dickens' love of short, simple sentences would not have met the requirement for complex sentences. Similarly, Jane Austen's frequent use of the comma in sentences and Hilary Mantel's love of the semi-colon would inhibit these acclaimed writers from achieving success in an end of Key Stage 2 writing assessment.

Grammar and writing: Where are we now?

So, what does the current national assessment picture reveal about grammar and writing? Has the increased focused on grammar defied research and led to improvement in children's writing and a rise in standards? To answer these questions we need to look at pupil attainment under the new curriculum. At the time of writing, the DfE interim report on National Curriculum assessments at Key Stage 2 in England, 2017 states the following:

- Attainment in grammar, punctuation and spelling (GPS) is the highest of all test subjects (reading, writing, GPS and mathematics).
- The proportion reaching the expected standard in the writing teacher assessment is 76 per cent compared to 74 per cent in 2016.
- Attainment at the expected standard in reading is 71 per cent compared to 66 per cent in 2016.
- Nationally pupils are attaining the highest achievements in GPS, then writing and then reading.

(DfE, 2017: 1–2)

The good English subject leader is critical of data and should always consider the reason why class, school and national data present a certain picture. Reasons for the current trend in pupil attainment could be due to:

- lack of uniformity between the assessment methods for each aspect of English. The range of test approaches might make it easier to achieve success in one aspect over another (assessment tools include multiple-choice questions, teacher assessment and written question papers);
- lack of teacher confidence to make writing judgements using the new assessment regulations. The abolishment of levels and lack of government clarity on assessment might have led to lower, safer assessments of pupils' achievement in writing;
- increased focus on GPS in the taught timetable meant that pupils were better prepared for this particular SATs assessment.

Consider each of the reasons for the about-turn in pupil attainment. Based on your own experience in schools, what do you think underpins the national attainment data?

The interim report on National Assessment data at Key Stage 2 shows pupils are attaining higher standards in writing than in reading, and highest of all in GPS. The current results are in direct contrast to previous attainment results until 2011/12. Earlier SATs assessment generally demonstrated the highest pupil attainment being achieved in reading, rather than writing. If we reflect on developmental knowledge about language learning we would expect children to first acquire an understanding of the spoken word before learning to read the written word. The final developmental stage is the ability to write, and indeed writing is the most cognitively complex skill of all literacy learning. We would therefore expect pupil outcomes to follow this continuum, with reading outcomes higher than writing. The national test results reported in 2016 and 2017 demonstrate a different developmental continuum, with pupils doing better in writing than reading, and best of all in GPS.

Expert challenge: What does the evidence say?

The Myhill *et al.* study in 2012 found that teaching grammar through exploration of how authors make language decisions made a strong impact on the students' writing. Whilst this study focused on secondary school teaching it is important to consider how this learning can impact on primary school teaching of grammar and writing. In October 2016 Myhill submitted written evidence to the Parliamentary Select Committee (Centre for Research in Writing at the University of Exeter, 2016). In her submission she stated the GPS test lacked clarity and was flawed. She criticised the way that the curriculum and the test ignored research that grammar, when taught in meaningful contexts, supported writing development. It was her opinion that the current approach to the teaching of grammar for the tests ran 'counter to the goal of improving writing' (Centre for Research in Writing at the University of Exeter, 2016).

In 2017 Professor Dominic Wyse gave evidence to the House of Commons Education Select Committee inquiry into assessment. He stressed that there was 'undue separation of the composition of writing from the transcription elements of grammar, spelling and punctuation' and 'an undue emphasis on decontextualised grammatical knowledge' (House of Commons Education Committee Oral Evidence: Primary Assessment, HC 682, 2017b).

The outcome of expert challenge is evident in the Commons Education Select Committee published inquiry into primary assessment (2017a). The report raises concerns that the emphasis on 'technical aspects of writing' diminished the focus on creativity and had not led to improvement in pupil writing (House of Commons Education Committee, 2017a). The recommendations resulting from the inquiry was for the spelling, grammar and punctuation tests to be made non-statutory at Key Stage 2, replaced by internal teacher assessment (House of Commons Education Committee, 2017a).

Government changes

It is significant to note that government writing exemplars, designed to support teacher judgements on writing at the end of Key Stage 2, have recently changed. In 2014–16 the writing exemplars judgement criteria are dominated by the list of grammatical techniques (see Table 13.1).

Writing was predominately judged by assessment of the pupils' repertoire of grammar skills. Whether the grammatical technique is used effectively was not mentioned, and composition is outweighed by the range and number of grammatical techniques the child needed to employ in their writing in order to achieve age-related expectations. In 2018 the new guidance looks very different (see Table 13.2).

The shift in emphasis provides greater balance between grammatical features and compositional skill in writing. Whilst it is clear the prominence of grammar in writing assessment has changed, it is difficult to say that this is directly due to challenge from media, academia or the teaching profession. The shift indicates a moderation of government view and it will hopefully result in a pedagogic shift in the teaching of writing and a renewed focus on composition. The assessment change makes it difficult to track whole-school and national trends in pupil achievement or make comparisons between yearly data. Further change also presents new challenge for teachers, requiring further adaptation of teaching and continued uncertainty when making judgements about children's writing.

Table 13.1 End of Key Stage 2 writing exemplars for working at the expected standard 2016

The pupil can write for a range of purposes and audiences (including writing a short story)

creating atmosphere, and integrating dialogue to convey character and advance the action

selecting vocabulary and grammatical structures that reflect the level of formality required mostly correctly

using a range of cohesive devices, including adverbials, within and across sentences and paragraphs

using passive and modal verbs mostly appropriately

using a wide range of clause structures, sometimes varying their position within the sentence

using adverbs, preposition phrases and expanded noun phrases effectively to add detail, qualification and precision

using mostly correctly	*inverted commas*
	commas for clarity
	punctuation for parenthesis
making some correct use of	*semi-colons*
	dashes
	colons
	hyphens

spelling some words correctly (Years 5 and 6)

maintaining legibility, fluency and speed in handwriting through choosing whether or not to join specific letters

(Adapted from STA, 2016)

Table 13.2 End of Key Stage 2 writing exemplars for working at the expected standard 2018

The pupil can:

write effectively for a range of purposes and audiences, selecting language that shows good awareness of the reader (e.g. the use of the first person in a diary; direct address in instructions and persuasive writing)

in narratives, describe settings, characters and atmosphere

integrate dialogue in narratives to convey character and advance the action

select vocabulary and grammatical structures that reflect what the writing requires, doing this mostly appropriately (e.g. using contracted forms in dialogues in narrative; using passive verbs to affect how information is presented; using modal verbs to suggest degrees of possibility)

use a range of devices to build cohesion (e.g. conjunctions, adverbials of time and place, pronouns and synonyms) within and across paragraphs

use verb tenses consistently and correctly throughout their writing

use the range of punctuation taught at Key Stage 2 mostly accurately (e.g. inverted commas and other punctuation to indicate direct speech)

spell correctly most words from the Year 5/Year 6 spelling list, and use a dictionary to check the spelling of uncommon or more ambitious vocabulary

maintain legibility in handwriting when writing at speed

(Adapted from STA, 2018)

Evidence-informed practice

The intention was that the new National Curriculum (DfE, 2013) would give freedom to teachers after a period of significant prescription. Unfortunately, the assessment regime has not helped schools to realise these newfound 'freedoms' and this is a tension felt by schools across the country. Faced with new curriculum policy and accountability measures the issue for the English subject leader is deciding what to do for the best. The need to meet government standards, measured by testing (however flawed), will be important for your school.

This 'hot topic' illustrates how government requirements, in particular assessment arrangements, require a balanced, pragmatic approach to implementation. Grammar, punctuation and spelling are undoubtedly important elements of English education. A lack of understanding of how to use grammar and punctuation will lead to ineffective written and spoken communication. The issue for grammar within the new curriculum is that it is presented as a body of rules to be learnt and tested in isolation from reading and writing experiences. It is difficult to see how the government's SPaG test is well matched to its aim of raising standards in writing. In order to affect the quality of writing it is more important that children are able to demonstrate they can employ grammatical techniques purposefully, rather than be able to articulate the metalinguistic learning underpinning the SPaG test (Myhill *et al.*, 2013). Pedagogy that supports children's understanding of how grammar affects writing through meaningful contexts is the more appropriate way to improve writing standards. Application of appropriate grammatical techniques to writing in certain genres or text types, exploration of grammar use in quality texts through shared reading and use of grammatical terminology in meaningful discussion will support pupils' writing development (Myhill *et al.*, 2012; Myhill *et al.*, 2013; Waugh *et al.*, 2016).

Policymakers often perceive teachers to be 'interchangeable cogs in a delivery system' (Goodman *et al.*, 2014: 31), but a good English subject leader is more than just a cog. They are the engines that drive teachers to deliver high-quality learning experiences that enable children to become competent and confident writers and users of language. As the English subject leader you can decide either to react to government policy by narrowing your curriculum to focus on test success, or to hold onto the principle of delivering meaningful reading and writing experiences. All of the case studies in this book are from schools that successfully meet the challenge of today's primary English education through the delivery of a rich and creative English curriculum. It is vitally important that as the subject leader of English you understand that the best way to prepare children for doing well in assessment tests is to teach a broad and balanced curriculum.

- Read research and keep up to date with best practice to ensure that evidence-based practice underpins teaching approaches;
- Ensure the delivery of a broad and balanced English curriculum;
- Accept that sometimes teaching has to react to meet government policy and assessment change, but ensure that any focus on newer aspects of English policy is short term, especially if it is detrimental to other areas of literacy learning;
- Think critically about new requirements and ensure they are pragmatic in their response.

And finally...

It might be helpful to conclude this chapter by drawing an analogy between the current 'hot topic' debate on grammar and the journey that the 'reading wars' has taken since the introduction of the government's phonics 'first and fast' approach (DfE, 2010: 2). The introduction of phonics teaching brought about a similar significant pedagogic shift in the teaching of reading. Statutory requirements for schools to teach systematic, synthetic phonics and the accompanying phonics test resulted in significant changes to the teaching of early reading as teachers tried to ensure children were able to pass the Phonics Screening Check.

The government offered financial incentives to schools to aid the purchase of approved phonics schemes and resources. This meant that many schools made a significant financial commitment to the resourcing of phonics teaching, putting reading schemes and accompanying reading material at the centre of early reading. Reading pedagogy focused on phonic instruction and the teaching of alien words, often to the detriment of the use of real books in the classroom. Teaching focused on reading words in decontextualised contexts and for many children, reading became an activity devoid of meaning.

Experts in the field Henrietta Dombey (2010) and Teresa Cremin (2011) collated a range of research on impactful teaching approaches proven to support early reading. Drawing on evidence from sources that included the then recent PIRLS study (Twist *et al.*, 2007) and OECD data (OECD, 2002; OECD, 2009) they illustrated the importance of young people's attitudes to reading in relation to attainment. Both Dombey (2010) and Cremin (2011) articulated concern over the dominant pedagogy of a phonics 'first and fast' approach to reading, emphasising links between pupils' perceptions of themselves as readers, pupil attitude to reading, reading for meaning and reading attainment.

Research evidence preceded the introduction of a 'reading for pleasure' agenda in the new National Curriculum (DfE, 2013). Eventually, policy acknowledged the crucial link between enjoyment of reading and learning outcomes. The focus on systematic, synthetic phonics still remains and recently the government has been quick to claim improved performance in the current PIRLS report (McGrane *et al.*, 2017) as proof that their singular approach to early reading works (Parvin, 2018). However, schools have been able to redress the singular focus on reading, providing a more balanced approach to early reading. At the present time the government's assertion that the SPaG test would result in better writing outcomes has been challenged and disproved by their own testing arrangements. The government has responded and taken some steps to shift undue emphasis on grammar within writing assessment. Hopefully, the recent change to the assessment writing framework will lead to a shift in the approaches schools adopt when teaching grammar and writing. This should provide the opportunity for research-led approaches to dominate the teaching of grammar. We might even dare to dream that one day, writing for pleasure will be embedded within statutory curriculum guidance.

References

Andrews, R., Torgerson, C. J., Beverton, S., Freeman, A., Locke, T., Low, G., Robinson, A. and Zhu, D. (2006) 'The effect of grammar teaching on writing development.' In: *British Educational Research Journal*, 32 (1), 39–55.

Bew, P. (2011) 'Independent Review of Key Stage 2 testing, assessment and accountability: Final report.' DfE publications. Available at: www.gov.uk/government/uploads/system/uploads/attachment_data/file/176180/Review-KS2-Testing_final-report.pdf [accessed 21 February 2018].

Cameron, D. (1995) *Verbal Hygiene*. London: Routledge.

Centre for Research in Writing at the University of Exeter (2016) 'Written evidence submitted by the Centre for Research in Writing at the University of Exeter.' Available at: http://data.parliament.uk/writtenevidence/committeeevidence.svc/evidencedocument/education-committee/primary-assessment/written/40810.html [accessed 22 November 2017].

Cremin, T. (2011) 'Reading for pleasure and wider reading.' *UKLA*. Available at: https://ukla.org/downloads/November_11_Resource_TC_Reading_for_Pleasure.pdf [accessed 20 February 2018].

Crystal, D. (2013) 'On a testing time.' *DCBlog*. May 2013. Available at: http://david-crystal.blogspot.co.uk/2013/05/on-testing-time.html [accessed 22 November 2017].

Department for Education (DfE) (2010) 'Phonics teaching materials: Core criteria and the self-assessment process.' Available at: https://assets.publishing.service.gov.uk/government/uploads/system/uploads/attachment_data/file/298420/phonics_core_criteria_and_the_self-assessment_process.pdf [accessed 10 July 2018].

Department for Education (DfE) (2013) 'English programmes of study: Key Stages 1 and 2 National Curriculum in England.' Available at: https://assets.publishing.service.gov.uk/government/uploads/system/uploads/attachment_data/file/335186/PRIMARY_national_curriculum_-_English_220714.pdf [accessed 3 July 2018].

Department for Education (DfE) (2017) 'National Curriculum assessment at Key Stage 2 in English, 2017 (interim).' Available at: www.gov.uk/government/uploads/system/uploads/attachment_data/file/624576/SFR30_2017_Text.pdf [accessed 31 March 2018].

Dombey, H. (2010) *Teaching Reading: What the evidence says*. Leicester: UKLA.

Goodman, K. S., Calfee, R. C. and Goodman, Y. M. (2013) *Whose Knowledge Counts in Government Literacy Policies?: Why expertise matters*. London: Routledge.

Gove, M. (2014) 'Education Secretary Michael Gove's speech to Brighton College.' Available at: www.gov.uk/government/speeches/education-secretary-michael-goves-speech-to-brighton-college [accessed 10 February 2015].

Grice, E. (2013) 'The glamour of grammar: an object lesson.' Available at: www.telegraph.co.uk/education/9987974/The-glamour-ofgrammar-an-object-lesson.html [accessed 10 July 2018].

Gwynne, N. M. (2013) *Gwynne's Grammar: The ultimate introduction to grammar and the writing of good English*. London: Ebury Press.

House of Commons Education Committee (2017a) 'Primary assessment eleventh report of session 2016–17, HC 682.' Available at: https://publications.parliament.uk/pa/cm201617/cmselect/cmeduc/682/682.pdf [accessed 22 November 2017].

House of Commons Education Committee (2017b) 'Oral evidence: Primary assessment, HC 682.' Available at: http://data.parliament.uk/writtenevidence/committeeevidence.svc/evidencedocument/education-committee/primary-assessment/oral/45729.html [accessed 22 November 2017].

Illingworth, M. and Hall, N. (2016) *Creative Approaches to Teaching Grammar*. Oxon: Routledge.

Leftly, M. (2015) 'Michael Gove is instructing his civil servants on grammar.' Available at: www.independent.co.uk/news/uk/politics/michael-gove-instructing-his-civil-servants-on-grammar-10334298.html [accessed 22 February 2018].

Locke, T. (2009). 'Grammar and writing – the international debate.' In: Beard, R., Myhill, D., Riley, J. and Nystrand, M. (eds), *The Sage Handbook of Writing Development*. London: Sage, 182–93.

Mansell, W. (2017) 'Battle on the adverbials front: Grammar advisers raise worries about SATs tests and teaching.' *The Guardian*. Available at: www.theguardian.com/education/2017/may/09/fronted-adverbials-sats-grammar-test-primary [accessed 22 November 2017].

McGrane, J., Stiff, J., Baird, J. A., Lenkeit, J. and Hopfenbeck, T. (2017) *Progress in International Reading Literacy Study (PIRLS): National Report for England*. Oxford: OUCEA, Department of Education, University of Oxford.

Moss, G. (2017) 'Assessment, accountability and the literacy curriculum: Reimagining the future in the light of the past.' *Literacy*, 51 (2), 56–64.

Myhill, D., Jones, S., Lines, H. and Watson, A. (2012) 'Re-thinking grammar: The impact of embedded grammar teaching on students' writing and students' meta-linguistic understanding.' *Research Papers in Education*, 27 (2), 139–66.

Myhill, D., Jones, S., Lines, H., and Watson, A. (2013) 'Playful explicitness with grammar: A pedagogy for writing.' *Literacy*, 47 (2), 103–11.

Myhill, D. and Watson, A. M. (2014) 'The role of grammar in the writing curriculum: A review of the literature.' *Child Language Teaching and Therapy*, 30 (1), 41–62.

OECD (2002) *Reading for Change: Performance and engagement across countries. Results from PISA 2000*. New York: Organisation for Economic Cooperation and Development.

OECD (2009) 'What students know and can do: Results from PISA 2009.' Available at: www.oecd.org/pisa/pisaproducts/48852548.pdf [accessed 10 July 2018].

Parvin, T. (2018) 'The President's message – Tracey Parvin.' *UKLA News: Spring 2018*.

Richmond, J., Burn, A., Dougill, P., Raleigh, M. and Traves, P. (2017) *Curriculum and Assessment in English 3 to 11: A better plan*. Leicester: UKLA.

Rosen, M. (2015) 'Dear Ms Morgan: In grammar there isn't always one right answer.' *The Guardian*. Available at: www.theguardian.com/education/2015/nov/03/morgan-grammar-test-right-answer-spag-english-spelling-punctuation-grammar [accessed 22 November 2017].

Standards and Testing Agency (STA) (2016) '2016 teacher assessment exemplification: End of Key Stage 2, English writing.' Government publications. Available at: www.gov.uk/government/uploads/system/uploads/attachment_data/file/510832/STA-Ex2016-KS2-EW-MorganAnn_PDFA.pdf [accessed 20 February 2018].

Standards and Testing Agency (STA) (2018) '2018 teacher assessment exemplification: End of Key Stage 2, English writing.' Government publications. Available at: www.gov.uk/government/publications/2018-teacher-assessment-exemplification-ks2-english-writing [accessed 20 February 2018].

Truss, E. (2013) 'Press release: New grammar, punctuation and spelling test will raise children's literacy standards.' Available at: www.gov.uk/government/news/new-grammar-punctuation-and-spelling-test-will-raise-childrens-literacy-standards [accessed 22 February 2018].

Twist, L., Schagen, I. and Hodgson, C. (2007) *Readers and Reading: The national report for England PIRLS*. Slough: NfER.

Ward, H. (2017) 'Morpurgo: "Dark spider" of SATs is bringing fear to classrooms.' *TES*. Available at: www.tes.com/news/school-news/breaking-news/morpurgo-dark-spider-sats-bringing-fear-classrooms [accessed 22 November 2017].

Waugh, D., Warner, C. and Waugh, R. (2016) *Teaching Grammar, Punctuation and Spelling in Primary Schools*. London: Sage.

Appendix 1
Audit of subject knowledge

Knowledge and understanding of spoken language and Standard English	Secure and confident	Area for development
Do you understand how this is different to dialect and accent? Do you understand theories of language acquisition? Do you know how this relates to the development of early language and communication? Do you understand the importance of sound discernment and phonological development? Do you understand the importance of oral storytelling? Do you understand what is meant by the term Standard English? Do you know how to define a sentence? Can you define the different types of sentences there are? (Exclamations, simple and complex, commands, statements) Do you understand terms such as clause, phrase, subject, object and predicate? Can you define terms such as pronouns, determiners, adjectives, verbs, adverbs, conjunctions and prepositions?		

Knowledge and understanding of reading and spelling	Secure and confident	Area for development
Can you explain the difficulties of representing the (approximately) forty-four phonemes of English with only twenty-six letters of the alphabet? Do you understand technical terms associated with phonics such as grapheme, decode, encode and phoneme? Can you segment words by phoneme? Do you know the difference between a digraph and a blend? Do you understand the structure of English words (morphology)? Do you understand terminology such as morpheme (bound and unbound), root, suffix and prefix? Do you understand how inflectional suffixes affect the grammatical formation of words? Do you know how derivational suffixes change the function of a word in a sentence or form new words?		

(Continued)

Knowledge and understanding of grammar	Secure and confident	Area for development

Do you know the eight main word classes?

Can you define a sentence?

Can you explain the difference between a simple, compound and complex sentence?

Can you identify components of sentences – phrases, clauses – and define a main clause, subordinate clause and an adverbial phrase?

Do you know what a compound word is?

Can you explain the difference between an active and a passive sentence?

Can you describe the differences between writing in the first, second and third person? Do you know how to write in the first, second and third person?

Do you know the different types of verbs and how verbs change according to tense? (Finite and non-finite verbs, verb tense, present and past participles)

Knowledge and understanding of punctuation	Secure and confident	Area for development

Can you identify common errors such as the comma splice and suggest alternatives?

Do you know when you can use a semi-colon?

Do you know when you can use a comma?

Can you explain how to use an apostrophe to show possession and omission?

Can you explain and use a range of punctuation marks?

Are you aware of the conventions of punctuating dialogue as direct and indirect speech?

Knowledge and understanding of texts	Secure and confident	Area for development

Do you know how to identify a high-quality text? Do you know how to evaluate texts critically?

Do you understand story structure and narrative plot?

Do you know the text structure and key language features of a range of genres, which might include fairy stories, fables, non-fiction text, science fiction and adventure?

Are you knowledgeable of other, newer literacies such as electronic texts, multimodal texts and hybrid texts?

Do you have a working knowledge of texts suitable for use in the classroom?

Do you have knowledge of non-fiction texts? Do you understand their structure and language features, e.g. recounts, reports, explanations, instructions, persuasion and discussion?

Do you understand the qualities of poetry?

Do you understand the features of poetry such as onomatopoeia, assonance, alliteration, personification, metaphor, simile and rhythm?

Do you understand the different forms of poetry such as Haiku, shape poetry and riddles?

(Continued)

Knowledge and understanding of reading comprehension	*Secure and confident*	*Area for development*

Do you understand the Simple View of Reading?

Do you understand theories of reading development and the process of reading?

Do you know how attitudes to reading affect attainment?

Do you have a knowledge of books that you could recommend to pupils and staff alike? Do you understand how to explore the potential of texts?

Are you able to identify devices used by authors in their texts to create desired effects/convey meaning/influence the reader, etc.?

Do you understand strategies for teaching comprehension such as prediction, questioning, clarifying, summarising, thinking aloud and visualising?

Do you understand what higher-level comprehension skills are?

Do you understand the importance of dialogic talk in developing reading comprehension? Do you know how to scaffold talk and ask quality questions?

Knowledge and understanding of writing	Secure and confident	Area for development

Do you understand the distinction between transcription and composition?

Do you understand how to form cursive script? Are you a good model of handwriting for pupils?

Do you understand the writing process? Do you appreciate the cognitive demands made of children by the writing process? Do you understand the role of reading and talk in relation to the writing process?

Do you understand how the writing process links to the writing teaching sequence?

Do you understand how drama supports the provision of meaningful contexts for writing?

Are you confident at modelling shared writing in the classroom?

Appendix 2
Checklist prompts for lesson observation

The characteristics of an effective phonics lesson

Planning and teaching

- The teacher ensures that children practise previously taught phonemes;
- The new phoneme (or phonic learning) is clearly introduced;
- The teacher articulates the phonemes correctly;
- All children are encouraged to participate and have the opportunity to practise saying the phoneme;
- The children are taught the name of the grapheme as well as the phoneme it is associated with;
- The children are clearly shown how to say, read and write the grapheme and are given opportunities to practise writing the letter;
- The children are taught how to blend and/or segment through effective teacher modelling;
- All children are encouraged to participate and have the opportunity to practise saying the phoneme, read the corresponding graphemes, blend phonemes to read words and segment words into phonemes/graphemes for spelling;
- Children have opportunities to apply their phonic knowledge and skills in purposeful reading and writing activities.

Delivery

- The lesson is lively and fast-paced throughout;
- The lesson is fun and interactive, short and focused;
- Visual aids, resources and objects are used effectively to support the teaching.

Learning and progress

- The teacher observes and questions learning throughout the lesson to assess individual children's progress;
- Pupil misconceptions are identified and addressed;
- Pupils have acquired secure knowledge of letters and sounds at a level appropriate to age-related expectations;
- The lesson is appropriately challenging for all the pupils;
- Pupil progress is **at least good** for different groups of children and **exemplary** for some children.

(Continued)

The characteristics of an effective reading comprehension lesson

Planning and teaching

- The planning and teaching provides activities that support lower- and higher-order reading comprehension skills;
- The planning is clear about the purpose of teacher-led/child-led discussion of the text;
- The teacher plans appropriate questions and prompts that support the children in communicating and extending their responses to the text;
- Planned activities provide opportunities for the children to explicitly learn specific reading comprehension skills through scaffolded discussion and teacher modelling;
- The teacher enables exploratory talk through the use of effective, open questioning to pursue children's line of thought;
- There are opportunities for children to respond to each other;
- The teacher uses their subject knowledge of texts, and the technical features of language, to extend and deepen pupils' understanding;
- The teacher explains why a strategy is useful and supports the pupils in understanding how to apply it to the text.

Delivery

- Texts are engaging and appropriate for the pupils;
- The text is available and visible to all pupils;
- Children's ideas are captured for future reference;
- The classroom environment is respectful of children's ideas and response to the text;
- Shared reading is a lively and animated process.

Learning and progress

- Children's understanding is checked through effective questioning;
- Teacher-led talk develops the child's comprehension skills;
- A range of scaffolded support and challenge enables all the learners to make good progress;
- Pupils demonstrate reading comprehension skills at a level appropriate to age-related expectations;
- Pupil progress is **at least good** for different groups of children and **exemplary** for some children.

The characteristics of an effective writing lesson

Planning and teaching

- The aims of the writing task are clear, with a focus on compositional and transcriptional aspects of writing;
- The teacher discusses the features of language through shared reading, highlighting features relevant to the writing task;
- The lesson incorporates appropriate pedagogical opportunities that support the children with writing composition. This includes the teacher scribing, shared reading, and opportunities for talk and drama;
- The teacher demonstrates to the children what successful writing looks like, through shared or modelled writing;

(Continued)

(Cont).

The characteristics of an effective writing lesson

- Pupils are given the opportunity to plan and compose writing that enables them to practise using the taught features appropriate to the style and genre of the writing task;
- Pupils are given opportunity to apply taught grammar and technical language features appropriate to the writing task;
- There is planned opportunity for pupils to edit and improve (both elements of composition and transcription) through either peer review or self-review processes.

Delivery

- The teacher selects an appropriate stimulus or quality text to support the writing;
- There is a clear context and audience for the writing;
- Appropriate resources are provided to scaffold and support pupils' writing;
- Pupils are provided with good-quality models for writing in required style, form or genre;
- Working walls and vocabulary banks display a record of the children's writing journey and provide a useful resource bank for them to draw from when writing.

Learning and progress

- Pupils are provided with specific teaching support as identified by assessment for learning processes;
- All pupils make good progress and demonstrate writing skills in line with age-related expectations;
- Pupils understand language features and grammatical terms relevant to the writing and can use them in their writing to good effect;
- Pupil progress is **at least good** for different groups of children and **exemplary** for some children.

Index

Locators in **bold** refer to tables and those in *italics* to figures.

Printed in Great Britain
by Amazon

65884836R00131